Religion
and Social Class

The Scottish Series

General editor: Alexander Scott

The Scottish Series will include in its range books on every aspect of Scottish literature and social history from the earliest times to the present, including anthologies (both poetry and prose), new editions of Scottish classics, scholarly studies, critical surveys, and collections of essays. These volumes will be designed for the general reader and the serious student alike, and the editors of the various volumes will be recognised authorities in their different fields.

The following volumes have already been published:

The Hugh MacDiarmid Anthology, edited by Michael Grieve (Mac-Diarmid's son) and Alexander Scott. Issued in honour of the poet's eightieth birthday, this constitutes the most representative selection of his work published to date, illustrating the full scope of Scotland's greatest living writer.

A Scottish Ballad Book, edited by David Buchan, Senior Lecturer in English Studies, University of Stirling.

The following volumes are planned for publication:

Burns: Critical Essays: edited by Donald A. Low, Lecturer in English Studies, University of Stirling.

The 18th Century Scottish Lyric, edited by Thomas Crawford, Senior Lecturer in English, University of Aberdeen.

The general editor of the series, Alexander Scott—the poet, dramatist, critic and biographer—is Head of the Department of Scottish Literature in the University of Glasgow.

The Scottish Series

Religion
and Social Class

THE DISRUPTION
YEARS IN ABERDEEN

A. Allan MacLaren
Department of Sociology
University of Strathclyde

Routledge & Kegan Paul
London and Boston

First published in 1974
by Routledge & Kegan Paul Ltd
Broadway House, 68–74 Carter Lane,
London EC4V 5EL and
9 Park Street,
Boston, Mass. 02108, U.S.A.

Printed in Great Britain by
T. & A. Constable Ltd
Hopetoun Street, Edinburgh
© A. Allan MacLaren 1974

ISBN 0 7100 7789 0
Library of Congress Catalog Card No. 73–91034
Published with the support of the Scottish Arts Council

For William McLaren
In memory of my father who died on 3 January 1963,
aged 66 years

Contents

Contents

Contents

Acknowledgments

I should like to thank my friend and colleague, Malcolm Gray, who over a number of years has provided thoughtful assistance and fruitful discussion. Both he and Christopher Smout read and made useful comments on the original draft of this work. Needless to say neither is in any way responsible for the views expressed therein.

Other colleagues require mention as having aided, in many different ways, the cross-fertilisation of elements from history and sociology: Michael Flinn, John Hargreaves, Raymond Illsley, James Kincaid, Stuart McCalman, Peter Musgrave, Marc Nott, Andrew Sykes and Donald Withrington. Marc Nott has also given inestimable assistance throughout—from the preparation of the manuscript to the finished work.

I should also like to thank Cecile Fleming of the Department of Sociology for assistance in the preparation of the index.

The Directors of The Company of Scottish History Limited have kindly granted permission for the inclusion of a short section of my article 'Presbyterianism and the working class in a mid-nineteenth century city' published in the *Scottish Historical Review*, vol. 46, 2, no. 142, October 1967.

Abbreviations

Charl. U.P. Man. Min.	*Charlotte Street United Presbyterian Church: Managers' Minutes*
Est. Gen. Sess.	*Register of the General Session of St Nicholas*
Est. Greyf. Sess.	*Greyfriars Parish Kirk Session Minutes*
Est. Presb.	*Records of the Presbytery of Aberdeen*
Est. South Sess.	*South Parish Kirk Session Minutes*
Est. South Assoc.	*South Parish Parochial Association Minutes*
Est. Trin. Sess.★	*Trinity Parish Session Book*
Est. West Sess.★	*Session Register of the West Parish*
Free Greyf. Deac.	*Minute Book of the Deacons' Court of Free Greyfriars*
Free Presb.	*Minute Book of the Free Presbytery of Aberdeen*
Free South Sess.	*South Free Church Session Minutes*
Free Trin. Deac.★	*Trinity Free Church Deacons' Court Minutes*
Free Trin. Sess.★	*Trinity Free Church Session Minutes*
Free Trin. Teach.★	*Trinity Sabbath School Teachers: Minutes of the Quarterly Meeting*
Free West Deac.★	*Free West Deacons' Court Minute Book*
Free West Sess.★	*Free West Church Kirk Session Minute Book*
N.S.A.	*New Statistical Account*
U.P. Presb.	*Minutes of Aberdeen United Presbyterian Presbytery*

★ At the time of writing these records were still held by the appropriate kirk sessions in Aberdeen. All of the remainder were lodged at the Scottish Record Office, Edinburgh.

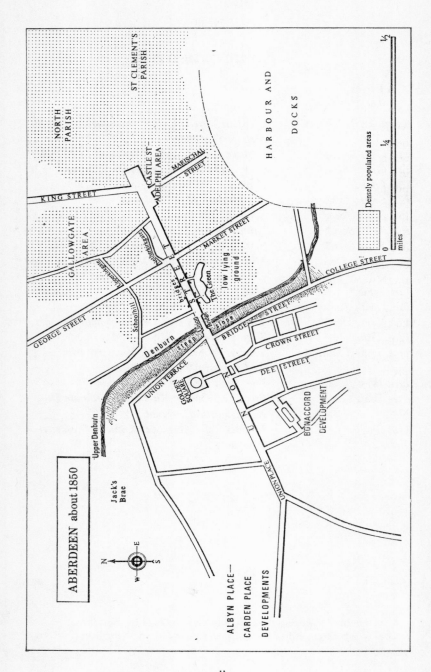

ABERDEEN about 1850

N E
W   S

Jack's
Brae

Upper Denburn

ALBYN PLACE—
CARDEN PLACE
DEVELOPMENTS

NORTH
PARISH

ST CLEMENT'S
PARISH

KING STREET

GALLOWGATE
AREA

CASTLE ST—
ADELPHI AREA

MARISCHAL
STREET

GEORGE STREET

Schoolhill

Denburn

Upper Denburn

UNION TERRACE

steep slope

GOLDEN
SQUARE

UNION PLACE

Bridge Street

Bridge Street

MARKET STREET

The Green
low lying
ground

slope

COLLEGE STREET

BRIDGE STREET

CROWN STREET

DEE STREET

BONACCORD
DEVELOPMENT

HARBOUR AND

DOCKS

Densely populated areas

0   ¼   ½
miles

Chapter 1

The Social and Economic Background

A Frankenstein to rend off their limbs of privilege and leadership.*

More than any other urban centre in Scotland Aberdeen provided the best example of a true regional capital supported by and serving the needs of a large agricultural hinterland. Until the arrival of the railway in 1850 the seaport provided virtually the only outlet for the surplus produce of the surrounding counties. Communications by road were poor and, like the roads, the sea passage to Edinburgh—150 miles to the south—was subjected to all the vagaries of the north-east climate. This relative isolation undoubtedly was an important factor in the development of Aberdeen as an important seaport serving the needs of the region and undertaking extensive trade with the Baltic, Poland, and the Netherlands. At first the exports were the natural products of the area—skins, furs, wool, and especially salmon, and the imports were manufactured goods of finer quality and kind than could be produced locally. Later, however, with the help and expertise of foreign artisans induced to settle in the area, the city developed in the seventeenth and eighteenth centuries as a major exporter of woollen goods and hosiery produced in the north east and it was claimed that 'Aberdeen brought more money into Scotland than all the other towns'.[1]

The Growth of Industry in the City

It is clear that the great expansion in manufacturing industry which took place in the latter part of the eighteenth and the early nineteenth centuries was based on the profits of earlier trading and commercial enterprises conducted by several well-known local families. Before industrialisation itself took place:[2]

the foundations had been laid of the industrial fabric of Aberdeen and the surrounding counties. Landed gentry and burghal merchants vied with one another in their commercial and mercantile efforts. There was not a seaport on the Baltic, not a city

* T. C. Smout, 'Scottish landowners and economic growth, 1650-1850', *Scottish Journal of Political Economy*, vol. 11 (1964), p. 234.

in Germany or the Low Countries or Scandinavia but Aberdonians were to be found in it as traders on their own account or as agents for Aberdeen firms. The Forbeses of Craigievar and the Skenes of Rubislaw owed their affluence to some member of the family who had amassed a fortune by foreign trade. Robert Gordon, belonging to a cadet branch of the Gordon stock, bequeathed the wealth he had acquired as a merchant in Danzig to found the school which is still known as Robert Gordon's College.

Not all the merchants who ploughed back into industrial enterprise what they had won by trade were successful. Fortunes were won and lost. Alexander Livingston lost all that he had acquired as a merchant trader in Holland in an attempt to pioneer the linen industry in Aberdeen. Nevertheless towards the end of the eighteenth century there were twenty-two textile-exporting firms in the city.[3]

Textile manufacturing was undoubtedly the most important single industry and involved the production of linen, wool, and cotton. Near each other, on opposite sides of the River Don, stood the largest linen factory and perhaps the biggest cotton factory in the United Kingdom. In the town itself and for eight miles along the River Don there were other textile factories of substantial size. One firm, Gordon, Barron & Co., with factories at Woodside and Schoolhill employed 3,000 hands in 1820 and were said to have been 'the only firm in Scotland that imported the raw cotton and carried it through the several processes of spinning, weaving, bleaching, printing, and finishing as cloth'.[4] Both this firm, and another linen manufacturer, Leys, Masson & Co., established their own iron foundries in 1797 and 1804 for the supply and renewal of their machinery, and to furnish castings extensively for millwrights throughout the north east.[5] Foundries and engineering works independent of the textile industry emerged and developed rapidly in the same period, and by 1836 about a third of all woollen manufacturing in the north east was centred in Aberdeen, the largest firm being Alexander Hadden & Sons who produced hosiery, worsted, and carpets at their factory in the Green.[6] By 1845, prior to a major crisis from which textile industry never recovered, 12,300 people were employed in flax, cotton, and woollen manufacturing.[7]

Engineering and ship-building also played an important part in the local economy. In 1801 the output from the Aberdeen shipyards—forty-two vessels totalling 3,461 tons—was the largest in Scotland and despite heavy losses during the Napoleonic Wars the tonnage registered at the port was greater than that of any other Scottish seaport.[8] The annual rate of building between 1830 and 1840 increased twelvefold in the number of ships and twenty times in the amount of tonnage, and by 1839 Alexander Hall & Co. had launched the first of their Clipper ships which were to bring them international fame.[9] Rapid development had also taken place in the use of iron in shipbuilding. Only five years after the launching of Aberdeen's first iron ship by John Vernon & Sons it was claimed that the world's largest iron ship was under construction in an Aberdeen yard.[10] Hall's, Vernon's, Duthie's and several smaller shipyards, along with the eight foundries in the town, employed more than 1,000 men in 1845.[11] There were also more than eight ropeworks—three of which were 'chiefly employed in the manufacture of cordage for the ships'—providing work for more than two hundred men and boys.[12]

Four firms were engaged in paper manufacturing in or near the city and employed directly between three and four hundred workers. Comb-making, first established in 1788, underwent rapid expansion in the 1830s 'on a larger scale than has been done in any other part of Scotland'. By the application of steam-power more than 40,000 combs were manufactured weekly providing employment for 245 workmen.[13]

All of these industries, textile manufacturing, ship-building and engineering, ropemaking, paper, and comb manufacturing, established themselves in the last quarter of the eighteenth century in what has been described as 'probably the most prosperous period in the history of the city'.[14] The rapid development of these industries in the early nineteenth century coincided with the application of important innovations in other fields of entrepreneurship. Although whale-fishing was in decline, and early attempts to promote herring-fishing had failed, the export of salmon had greatly increased following the introduction of ice as a preservative and it was reckoned that in an average season in the 1840s 20,000 salmon of around ten pounds each, and 40,000 grilses of about four pounds each, were shipped from Aberdeen to the London market.[15] Likewise from 1822 the city had established itself as a meat-preserving centre as a result of experiments in curing. Eight thousand head of cattle were exported by sea in 1836 and the city found itself the market, supply centre, and clearing-house for an agricultural hinterland which itself had undergone an economic transformation.[16] Important technical innovations in the process of treating and manufacturing granite had led to a drastic reduction in costs and by the 1830s an average of 20,000 tons found its way south especially to the London market.[17]

Urban Development: the Construction Industry

Essential to the successful development of all the aforementioned industries was the improvement and reconstruction of the harbour area. As early as 1770 this need was recognised by the city magistrates who two years previously had constructed Marischal Street as a means of improving access to the harbour itself. In 1773 authorisation was given to the city council to borrow money to carry out improvements and in 1780 these were completed at a cost of £18,000. Pressure on harbour facilities soon made further improvement necessary and between 1810 and 1832 more than £80,000 was spent on vast schemes of reconstruction which included not only the construction of break-waters, and wharves, but the diversion of the River Dee to a different course. A lighthouse was constructed in 1833, but the harbour was not converted finally to a wet dock as opposed to a tidal basin until 1850.[18] A second and more convenient approach road was constructed as a speculative venture by the Aberdeen Market Company which involved the demolition of a large area of slum property and the construction of Market Street, Hadden Street, Exchange Street, and the New Market.[19] This work was finally completed in 1842 and cost around £42,000.[20]

In line with the construction of improved harbour facilities vast and ambitious schemes were begun in 1801 to improve access to the city itself. Union Street was constructed on a series of arches traversing the Denburn valley and other low-lying areas; the whole scheme involving extensive demolition and the erection of large retaining walls. The construction of King Street and George Street were much simpler operations involving far less engineering skill but requiring vast amounts of manual labour.[21] The construction of the Aberdeen-Inverurie canal between the years 1801 and 1807 at a cost of £40,000 and with seventeen locks over its eighteen miles must also have absorbed large amounts of labour.[22] It was not, however, until the completion of the new bridge over the River Don in 1830 and the opening up of the country by turnpike and other roads linking these access roads that the great advantages to the trade of the city accrued.[23] The immediate stimulus to the local economy in the expenditure of such vast sums of money, in the provision of continuous employment, and migration to the city, must have been considerable.

The building of the Union Bridge over the Denburn valley had also very important long-term effects on the urban development of the city.

The bridge and the newly constructed line of Union Street opened up the areas west of the city for residential development. Prior to its construction the Denburn had marked the western edge of the city—those few houses lying beyond were in open country and generally used only for summer residence.[24]

> Professional men and merchants lived, as a rule, on the premises where they conducted their business, and the wealthiest families had been well content to reside in such aristocratic streets as the Gallowgate, the Guestrow, or the Shiprow.

Although the lines of the new streets had been drawn and the access roads constructed house building tended to remain centred east of the bridge in Union Street, the south end of King Street, and St Nicholas Street. The development of the areas west of the Denburn did not really get under way until thirty years after the erection of the Union bridge. When the development of the new areas across the Denburn and south of Union Street did take place the houses tended to be occupied by men who not only rejected but were rejected by the older wealthy families who lived in the aristocratic streets east of the Union bridge.[25]

Population, Migration, and the Changing Balance

A clear indication of the rapid economic development of the city can be obtained from its remarkable rate of population growth particularly in the first three decades of the nineteenth century. In 1750 the population stood at around 12,000. By 1850 it had increased by nearly six-fold to close on 72,000. The rate of growth was not even and was undoubtedly closely related to the demand for labour within the local economy. In the fifty years after 1750 the population more than doubled and stood at around 26,000 at the turn of the century. Thereafter the rate of growth reached phenomenal proportions and in the three decades down to 1831 there was a decennial increase of 29·6, 25·7, and 29·5 respectively.[26] Whilst it is clear that a portion of this increase must be put down to natural increase—the population of Scotland had an average decennial increase of about 13·5 per cent in these three decades —much of the gains were made from a relative decline in the population of the rural hinterland. If Aberdeen city is excluded from the Aberdeenshire figures the decennial increase in the county was only

5·3, 12·1, and 9·0 per cent respectively in these decades. The figures from the counties of Kincardine and Banff substantiate the migratory pattern from the countryside to the city. In Kincardine the decennial increase was 4·0, 7·4, and 6·7 per cent, and in Banffshire the increase was 2·7, 16·8, 9·1 per cent respectively. The movement from the countryside to the towns was, of course, a national and not just a regional phenomenon. Nevertheless, regional factors were important in determining the pattern and extent of the movement, a particularly important aspect being job availability. Whilst Glasgow maintained a uniformly high decennial increase throughout the first six decades, Aberdeen and Dundee (starting with approximately the same population in 1801) varied considerably in their rate of population growth. The collapse of the textile industries in Aberdeen in the 1840s resulted in the decennial increase for 1851-61 dropping to 5·5 per cent which was marginally less than the increase for the remainder of the county. Dundee, on the other hand, lagging behind Aberdeen in the first three decades, rapidly overtook it in the second three decades, largely one might expect on the expanding prosperity of the jute industry.[27]

Aberdeen, however, differed radically from Dundee and other developing urban centres in at least one other important aspect. The population of the city was far more homogeneous than any of the other developing urban centres of comparable size. The 1851 census shows that out of a population of about 72,000 fewer than 20,000 were derived from outside the city or the county, and the relative isolation of the region together with the falling-off in job availability which coincided with the high-point in Irish immigration, meant that few Irishmen had actually settled in the city. The 1,270 Irish natives were slightly outnumbered by resident English and even this number may well have been inflated by the presence of railway navvies engaged on the construction of the line which reached the city in 1850.[28]

It is customary to analyse migration in terms of what are called 'push' and 'pull' factors. Although the concept of 'push and pull' is not in itself an adequate sociological explanation of the factors dictating migratory patterns it remains a useful means of distinguishing to some extent the interplay of the various forces at work. The 'pull' factors, expressed in economic terms, were the growth of industry and consequent availability of employment in the city. The effects of industrialisation were felt beyond the bounds of the city, however, and were not confined simply to increasing employment opportunities. The growth of industrial capitalism not only radically altered the socio-economic structure of the city by creating an urban proletariat, it also reshaped the structure and forms of production of the rural hinterland. Directly, and indirectly, it was industrial capitalism which created both 'push' and 'pull' factors and created a new urban-rural dichotomy.

Perhaps the most notable example of the coincidence of 'push' and 'pull' factors is to be seen in the growth of the textile manufacturing industry in the city. Over a few decades Aberdeen changed from being an entrepôt for the export of hosiery and textile goods produced in the rural hinterland to an urban centre whose economy was largely based on the manufacture of textiles on a factory system. The rise of the city as a textile manufacturing centre saw the rapid decline of the rural north east as an area supplementing its income in large part by domestic manufacture. The importance of this supplementary income was immense. As early as 1723 it had been recognised by the gentlemen of Aberdeenshire that their rents were 'for the most part paid by the produce of their manufactures' and that these manufactures—spinning and knitting of hosiery—ought to be improved in order to increase the prosperity of the county.[29] The supplementation of income was particularly crucial in the poorer areas of the county where agricultural productivity was low owing to a variety of reasons. From Kincardine O'Neil to Strathdon women were employed in large numbers in spinning and the knitting of woollen stockings. In the parish of Rayne 'all the women, some of the boys, and old men even' were employed in knitting and by their combined efforts earned about £400 per annum without which 'the rents of the crofts could not be paid'.[30] The same was true of Glenmuick where the parish minister claimed that it was the 'industry and diligence' of the women which supported the families of the indolent crofters.[31] Likewise in the poorer coastal districts of north Kincardineshire 'being within a few miles of Aberdeen, the females have constant employment in knitting stockings to manufacturers. By their unremitting labour . . . they earn money to pay their rents.'[32] The domestic hosiery industry reached its height between 1750 and 1790 when between £110,000 and £120,000 was earned annually by the Aberdeen merchant houses, and 'Aberdeen stockings were the talk of Europe and the despair of competitors'.[33] After 1790 it declined steadily in importance because of the loss of continental markets during the Napoleonic War, and the inroads of the stocking-frames of Nottingham and Hawick.[34] By the 1840s hosiery knitting had ceased to be of any importance as a supplementary income for the payment of rents. Even those women subsisting on the meagre comfort of parochial relief could not 'by their utmost exertions earn more than 9d. . . . while the same class would formerly have had no difficulty in realising at the same occupation the sum of 3s. 6d. per week'.[35]

The mechanisation of spinning had also led to a similar rapid contraction in the geographical distribution of the industry. As Hamilton aptly describes it: 'the work of spinning was speedily passing from the fireside to the factory'.[36] Throughout the north east ministers lamented the decay of the industry, regarding its decline as one of the chief causes of pauperism. 'The state of the country, especially as it affects infirm or aged females, is altered much for the worse, by the introduction and extensive use of machinery for spinning flax, and knitting stockings. . . . It requires no small interest to find even occasionally something to do in that line, and the allowance is scarcely a third of what it then was', wrote the minister of Old Deer Parish[37] and his complaint was no isolated one. By the 1840s it is clear that flax-spinning, like knitting, had ceased to be of any importance in supplementing agricultural incomes. The decline of flax-spinning, of course, was not determined simply by increased mechanisation and geographical centralisation. Linen was being replaced by cotton which was produced in the city and its immediate vicinity. The decline was marked by a shrinking in flax production in Aberdeenshire—by 1810 the area under cultivation was only a fifth of what it had been some thirty years earlier.[38] This shrinking in the area under flax, combined with the general decline of the supplementation of agricultural incomes by domestic industry, was both cause and effect of other factors leading to movement of population into the city. These factors must now be considered briefly.

Agricultural Improvements and Their Social Effects

Whilst it is clear that domestic industry inhibited movement from the land by providing additional income for crofters and other small tenants who otherwise would have been unable to meet their commitments, it is also the case that by providing this additional income domestic industry acted against any general movement towards agricultural improvements such as had taken place in the Lothians. Although some outstanding improvements had been undertaken by certain landlords these 'were like oases in the desert' and even as late as the turn of the century a large part of Aberdeenshire was still cultivated in the old ways.[39] Hamilton sees the disastrous harvest of 1782 as a factor serving to arouse farmers from their apathy and to push them into improvements which by 1811 had led them into new forms of cultivation and new implements of agriculture which brought 'about the decay of handicraft or home industry'.[40] The failure of the harvest in 1782 was a serious affair—so serious that the commissioners of supply for the county recommended that the magistrates see to it that all dogs, other than working animals, ought to be destroyed.[41] It is far more credible, however, that the *decline* in domestic industry, combined with the high grain prices of these years, provided the long-delayed incentive to improve, rather than that the agrarian changes themselves had any substantial effect on domestic industry. Whatever the factors involved it is clear from Dr Keith's survey of Aberdeenshire in 1811 that extensive changes had occurred involving the introduction of threshing-machines, a more efficient plough, and the new system of turnip husbandry. The effects of the latter were that Aberdeenshire changed from a cattle importing county to become one of the most important cattle producing areas in the country.[42] When Lord Cockburn visited the north east in 1838 he remarked upon the changes in his *Journal*: 'I know of no part of Scotland so much, and so visibly, improved within thirty years as Aberdeenshire. At that time the country between Keith and Stonehaven was little else than a hopeless region of stone and moss.'[43]

However startling the overall change might have appeared, there was considerable diversity in the pattern, pace, and social effects, within the county itself. In some parishes the old ways tended to linger on. In others the pace of change was speedy but the improvements led to an actual increase in the number of smallholdings when what had formerly been waste land was brought under cultivation for the first time. Thus in Old Deer crofters were settled on 'spots which used to be waste' and the parish population increased from 3,267 in 1788 to 4,428 in 1836.[44] On Donside in the parish of Alford, which was wholly agricultural, the introduction of 'beneficial improvements' had converted the 'rude and unproductive husbandry' and 'without any removal of the natives'.[45] A few miles further north in Rayne, although the rents were high and the competition great, it was still possible for an industrious farm-servant to get a lease on a smallholding 'proportioned to the amount of his savings'.[46] In other parishes, however, improvements forced migration. In Pitsligo 'in the landward part of the parish, the population . . . decreased, in consequence of many crofts and small farms, on which large families often resided, having been thrown into more extensive ones'.[47] Engrossing of small farms also occurred in Fintray parish,[48] and in Strathdon a sharp decline in population followed the enlargement of farms—the number of inhabited houses declining in eight years from 344 to 290.[49] In neighbouring Aboyne and Glentanner a similar steep decline in population was attributed to 'the increased size of farms and a diminution of the cottar system'.[50] Further north in Clatt improvements and reclaiming of waste land had also been accompanied by enlargement and evictions and consequent decline in population: 'Where clusters of cottages at one time flourished, there scarcely now remain any vestiges to point to their former site'.[51] Similarly in the parish of Daviot the diminished population resulted from improvements and a prohibition on subletting by the proprietors.[52]

It would seem therefore that agricultural improvements as such did not lead to a decline in rural population. The important factors were whether or not these improvements involved the absorption of existing smallholdings into larger units, or the reclamation of waste land and its redistribution into smallholdings. Overall, although there was a net increase in the number of smallholdings as a result of improvements by reclamation, this increase was insufficient to meet the needs of the rising population. Although some parishes—such as New Deer—were able to absorb as much as a 10 per cent decennial increase in population[53] these were exceptions rather than the rule. Most parishes were unable to provide for anything like this figure and there was a decline in the rate of increase in population as a result of migration. Notwithstanding this, it was also true that in those parishes where improvements by reclamation were impossible owing to the nature of the land, or the lack of interest of the landlords, or the 'slothful and indolent' tenantry, the population remained static or underwent absolute decline.[54] This decline in the county population, whether relative in the sense of a falling-off in the rate of increase, or absolute when an actual reduction occurred in certain parish populations, coincided as we have seen with the rapid rise in urban population.

The New Urban Labour Force

Whilst it is not possible to ascribe any precise motivation concerning the movement of rural population into the city it is clear that certain general factors influenced migration. Nevertheless, given the complex pattern of changes taking place in the Aberdeenshire parishes, it is equally clear that generalisations such as 'push' and 'pull' factors have considerable limitations. Expressed in economic terms the 'push' and 'pull' concept is misleading as it tends to imply that twin processes were at work in initiating migration when both were derived from changes taking place in industrial capitalism in the wider society and economy. None the less one might maintain that it is a useful concept as it distinguishes between those compelled to leave the rural environment and seek urban employment, and those who left on their own accord presumably because of social and economic aspirations. From the viewpoint of the industrial employer there would appear to be a *qualitative* difference between the two types, the latter being more likely to adapt quickly to the new urban environment. Such a hypothesis would be difficult, if not impossible to prove, as it assumes a distinction between two processes which are essentially the same, and by over-emphasising the differences it loses touch with the wider largely non-economic factors.

In many ways it is more constructive to analyse early nineteenth-century migration along lines suggested in recent sociological research into contemporary migration into the city of Aberdeen whereby migration is explained by countervailing 'pull' factors: 'the pulling power of the new place of residence and the strength of ties with the old'.[55] Viewed in this way what occurred in the first three decades of the nineteenth century was the destruction of the old eighteenth-century rural society and the values which had governed it. The result was an increasing disenchantment of large sections of rural community with the form of the new society which took the place of the old, and which laid new and specific demands upon its members. The new agricultural technology dictated the life styles and work rhythms of both the peasant farmer and labourer, forcing tenants to adopt differing crop rotations and requiring knowledge of the mechanical operation of new agricultural machinery, and the specialist techniques of stock rearing. Even those in the forefront of the improvers had occasional doubts concerning the new society. Arthur Harvey, Secretary of the Royal Northern Agricultural Society, recalled when 'there was in farming life . . . much that is awanting now. Plenty of good fellowship and friendship, and plenty of leisure time to cultivate this social spirit.'[56]

The sweeping changes occurring in agricultural technology were reflected in the need for a more specialist labour force. Whilst Harvey could permit himself to become sentimental concerning the fellowship and friendship of the old way of life, he came down to hard facts on the problems of recruiting labourers knowledgeable in the new methods:[57]

all practical farmers are fully aware of the difficulty of getting almost any qualification but that of a good ploughman—few being able to build stacks—fewer to feed the threshing machine, or efficiently dress grain by proper adjustment of the fan; and fewer still as good stock-keepers.

Whatever the immediate effects of improvements on agricultural employment it seems clear that the longer-term effects of enclosure for cattle-breeding, and labour-saving devices such as the new plough, threshing machine, and winnowing machine, led to a fall in demand for labour at a time when the supply must have been increasing as a result of the rising population. Concurrent with this decline in demand, farmers increasingly sought a qualitative change in the labour force in that they required agricultural workers who were skilled in the new techniques. For those reared in the old ways, and mindful of the old values, the emergent rural society must have appeared perhaps just as alien as the industrial society of the city which offered alternative and certainly more lucrative employment. As the ties with the old place of residence weakened with the disappearance of former life styles, and as the knowledge of the city grew with the reports of those who had already left, so the pull to migrate grew stronger and the pull to remain in an uprooted rural environment declined. The balance between the countervailing 'pulls' differed from parish to parish depending on the pace of change and the social consequences of the change; as well as affecting specific sections of the social structure to varying degrees. Those most immediately affected would presumably be those most fully committed to domestic manufacturing—the choice being to seek agricultural employment or to move into the town. In other parishes, as we have seen, improvements could bring increased opportunities for landless labourers who aspired to become tenants of smallholdings which had been reclaimed, although it seems likely that in most parishes the increase in smallholdings was insufficient to meet the pressures of a rising population. Where farms became larger at the expense of the smallholdings the choice was simply one of seeking employment as a farm servant or moving in search of opportunities elsewhere—and this usually meant in the city. Some, however, remained intransigent, refusing to leave the countryside, and eked out a precarious existence by begging and stealing. Certainly those moving into the city to become the new industrial proletariat were a mixed body of agriculturists whose common problem would seem to be adaptation to the new urban environment. As migrants they fell into three main (although often overlapping) types of worker. There was the agricultural labourer displaced by the new machinery and unwilling or unable to adapt to the new technology. There was a smaller group of former smallholders, and crofters from the more remote highland parishes of the north east. Finally there was the full-time domestic worker whose craft or skill had become redundant as a result of the new industrial technology centred on the city. Although one must recognise that these are essentially 'ideal types' in that any one migrant may have had experience of all three activities, it is useful for analytical purposes to consider them separately. Each of these groups will now be considered.

The Displaced Agricultural Labourer

Some thirty years before Lord Cockburn found Aberdeenshire 'a hopeless region of stone and moss' (see p. 9) another observer, visiting in an official capacity, was more favourably impressed by the peasantry:[58]

> This county is populous, and is turning more so daily. The people are sober and industrious, at the same time sufficiently docile. Wages for men servants are moderate; for women they are much higher than in the Lothians, owing to the extensive manufacture of stockings . . . which has taught them all to knit; and so industrious they are, that, in travelling the high road, they knit as busily as at home.

A sober, industrious, docile labour force prepared to work for relatively low returns would at first appear to be just the raw material required by the urban employer for conversion to the new industrial proletariat. However, if the north-eastern agriculturist was all of these things, and the ministers' views in the *Statistical Accounts* generally support such an opinion, he was a worker reared in a society where weather, seasons, tradition, and to a considerable extent inclination, dictated the work rhythms. Until the end of the eighteenth century clocks and watches were rarely used: 'the proper time to get up and thresh was a matter of guesswork'.[59] Even when work had begun the pace tended to be varied. The flailman (who would soon be replaced by a mechanical thresher) 'was paid by the boll; and when *in the humour* for a regular set-to, would thrash out the almost incredible quantity of six bolls in a day'.[60] Hard and unremitting toil was the exception and never the rule; the rural north east before the coming of agricultural improvements was a slow-moving society steeped in old customs, traditions and superstitions:[61]

the labour imposed was not very continuous or systematic. In summer, with no green crops, such as turnips, to care for, and nothing in the shape of improvement to carry out, once the 'fauld dyke' had been erected . . . there was little to do except to see to the drying and carrying home of the peats and turves for winter fuel; . . . when shearing came, of course, all were busy enough, and really hard work it was. The period of harvest was much more protracted then than now, and it was no unusual thing for the shearing to extend over six weeks or so. As was right and proper they made harvest a time of cheerfulness and mirth.

Celebration of the harvest was only one occasion among many for the interruption of normal work. 'All great domestic events were accompanied by roystering and drinking—at a christening there was much, at a funeral there was more, at a wedding there was most.'[62] Despite the actions of presbyteries and kirk sessions, superstition prevailed and pre-Christian pagan ceremonies and festivals were still surreptitiously observed, and there remained fairly open belief in the powers of witches and witchcraft.[63] As 'there was no formal religious service of a public sort' in presbyterian rural society there was abundant time for recreation. At Fastern's Eve (Shrovetide) and at Yule 'three entire days were abstracted from the routine of daily labour' for the purpose of cock-fighting, wrestling, and other such pastimes.[64]

As we have seen, domestic industry provided an essential supplement to the income of the peasantry without which they eventually could not subsist. It was a form of production peculiarly suited to the work patterns of the rural workers, many of whom also found smuggling a convenient and useful source of additional income in the latter part of the eighteenth and the beginning of the nineteenth centuries.[65] These additional sources of income had stabilised the rural economy; their decline, as we have seen, was accompanied by widespread improvements in methods of cultivation and in agricultural productivity which ultimately were to alter the whole life style of most sections of rural society. The improved agricultural technology produced not only a new orderliness in the fields; it sought and required a new technical and moral discipline from the agricultural labour force. However, although 'in their everyday life rude roystering, drunken-quarrelling, and fighting' had been the 'too frequent recreations of the common people',[66] the new society brought new social stresses and tensions which even those who applauded the economic changes did not find entirely to their liking. The old rural life had had:[67]

its own features of attraction, as contrasted with the life that followed it. There was a sense of quiet leisureliness about the manner in which each man held his position and transacted the business of his daily life; an absence of hurry and headlong competition, and a feeling of neighbourliness and hospitality amongst the constituent membership of each small community that did much to make life not merely tolerable, but rationally enjoyable. The changes which have occurred in these respects, we may warrantably say; have not all been in the nature of an unqualified social gain.

Parish ministers although applauding 'a great and favourable alteration' in the practice of agriculture were dismayed at the resultant effects on the relationship between master and servant. Agricultural labourers no longer attached themselves to the same master 'till they married and got possessions' and thus felt a close bond between themselves and the farmer and an interest in everything about the farm.[68] It was a constant lament that farm servants were forever on the move, seldom remaining in the same employment for longer than six months which was the normal feeing contract. The old feeling of community had vanished and there was a growing distinction between employer and worker: 'Some households exhibit the unseemly aspect of two distinct communities living under the same roof, and having no religious intercourse with each other—a wall of entire separation being reared between the master and his servant.'[69] Gone forever were the days when a farmer would employ a piper to play to the labourers 'all the time of the harvest'.[70]

It was also a feature of the new agricultural society that not only were the agricultural labourers constantly on the move, never settling permanently with one employer, but that bands of 'sturdy beggars' roamed the countryside terrorising the inhabitants and compelling them 'to give the best *vivres* their houses afford. They likewise pick up poultry, apparel, and what they can lay hold off.'[71] The problem was extensive. The same minister who complained of the 'two distinct communities' appealed for the 'employment of a sufficient number of constables to perambulate the parish . . . to put down the evil' caused by the invasions of such men.[72] Before the end of the eighteenth century the problem was becoming serious. It was claimed that:[73]

> there is no place sends forth such legions of these itinerants as Aberdeen, meaning the county as well as the town of that name. . . . It would be both creditable and recommendable in them to

take measures . . . to provide for their own poor at home, rather than send them off, like a flight of locusts, to prey upon their neighbours, who are under no obligation to receive or relieve them.

The fact that the beggars were organising themselves to intimidate farmers was a further cause for concern: 'these persons are ready for prey of all kinds; everything that can supply them with provisions or bring them money is their spoil, if it can be obtained with any appearance of safety. They file off in small parties, and have their places of rendezvous, where they choose to billet themselves . . . the farmer is afraid to refuse their demands, or to complain of the oppression.'[74] Even as late as the 1840s, despite the economic attractions of the city and the activity of the Aberdeenshire magistrates, the problem was unsolved and 'thousands of vagrants wandered the country and plundered the inhabitants'.[75] For many it is clear that the 'pull' to remain in the countryside, even under these conditions, was greater than the 'pull' of industrial employment in the city of Aberdeen.

The Crofter and Smallholder

There was little economic distinction between the small farmers of certain rural parishes of the north east and the crofter of a highland parish. Both were being pressed by economic circumstances of the same type to vacate smallholdings which were no longer economically viable. 'Small farms . . . cannot afford profits, after payment of rents, sufficient to maintain the occupiers and their families. It is truly wonderful how any of them can continue on their present footing.'[76] The difference between the small farmer of Lonmay and that of Crathie was social and cultural rather than economic. The highlander was perhaps even less suited than the peasant to the rigours of industrial employment in the city. Further removed from the city and less affected by the changes taking place in agriculture, the highland peasantry existed in a state of privileged destitution. Although most were able to converse in English, the Gaelic language remained the language spoken in the highland parishes and traditional associations and attitudes still prevailed as late as the 1840s. The absence of itinerant vagrants in the highland parishes of Aberdeenshire was both symptomatic of the general destitution of the inhabitants and the continuing survival of a spirit of community. Nevertheless, despite the highlanders' tenacious attachment to the soil of their fathers, most highland parishes showed both a relative and an absolute decline in population in the first half of the nineteenth century.[77] Some of those who left made up the stream of overseas emigrants although most almost certainly found their way into the city in search of employment in the textile industry, granite quarrying and public works.[78]

Whether those who left were of a different calibre from those who remained is impossible to establish. Certainly highlanders were portrayed as a section of society 'torpid with idleness and most wretched . . . till the famine pinches they will not bestir themselves'.[79] Although one might defend the highlander on the grounds that he held to a code of values which were not understood by the emerging bourgeois society it is equally clear that such a code had little place in the new urban environment. The highlanders were 'a people who are all gentlemen, only because they will not work'.[80]

The Redundant Craftsman

The third general type from which the urban labour force was created was the redundant craftsman or full-time domestic worker. These men were never a homogeneous group simply because industrialisation, and mechanical innovation, proceeded at different rates affecting and displacing craftsmen to varying degrees and extent. As a general type he would appear to stand nearer industrial society than either the agriculturist who was a part-time linen weaver 'paid by the piece' and 'not obliged to labour any precise number of hours a day',[81] or the highlander who was too much of a 'gentleman' to work at all. Nevertheless it could be argued that the redundant craftsman trained to the pre-industrial way of life was no more amenable raw material than either of the others. The rise and fall of the craft of hand-loom weaving is generally used to demonstrate the dire effects of mechanical innovations on certain sections of the community in the early industrialisation period. Over a period of about forty years the hand-loom weaver experienced greater prosperity and deeper destitution than perhaps any other worker. Just as the crofter clung to his land long after it had ceased to be economically viable in the changed circumstances, so did the weaver tend to cling to his craft. Like the crofter his work rhythms were just as erratic:[82]

Four days did the weaver work, for then four days was a week, as far as working went, and such a week to a skilful weaver brought forty shillings. Sunday, Monday and Tuesday were of course jubilee, lawn frills gorged freely from under the wrists of his fine blue, gilt-buttoned coat. He dusted his head with white flour on Sunday, smirked and wore a cane. Walked in clean slippers on Monday, Tuesday heard him talk war bravado, quote Volney and get drunk. Weaving commenced gradually on Wednesday.

Whilst the introduction of factory-based weaving led to a rapid decline in the fortunes of the hand-loom weaver other crafts were equally, if less dramatically, affected by the process of industrialisation. Many continued or attempted to coexist alongside the new processes by becoming itinerant craftsmen offering their services in the more remote rural areas of the north east. Blacksmiths accustomed to using peat rather than coal offered farmers the convenience of immediate on-the-spot service by seeking out work, as did the wright who found iron replacing wood. Horners, skilled in the working of bone, and 'tinklers', in the repair of kettles and other utensils, survived despite a declining demand for their services. Local millers and tailors who made a living from working home-spun cloth found themselves redundant as new materials and technology replaced their cruder pre-industrial skills and methods. Such men eked out a precarious existence and ultimately were either forced into the city in search of alternative employment or entered the ranks of the sturdy vagabonds.[83]

Those who chose the latter course and resisted the 'pull' of industrial employment in the city were a declining number. Whilst more than 2,500 vagrants were reported in the county in 1841, by 1871 less than a hundred could be found. The institution of a rural police force with powers under the Trespass Act to prevent encampments or lighting of fires 'near any private road, cultivated ground, or plantation' ended the era of the 'masterful beggar' in Aberdeenshire, and drove the most reluctant into the city, no doubt to swell the numbers of the urban poor.[84] The great recruitment of the new urban labour force, however, took place in the first three decades of the nineteenth century and required no legal sanctions in order to move the population. By 1841 economic necessity combined with an increasing disenchantment with the new rural environment ensured that the 'pull' of the city was stronger than the 'pull' to remain—certainly for the vast majority.

The new labour force whether recruited from farm labourers, former crofters and smallholders, or redundant craftsmen, was extremely raw from the urban employers' standpoint. A redundant pre-industrial craftsman was, at best, a reluctant factory workers in terms of work rhythms he was no more adapted to the pace and demands of the textile machine than were the crofter or labourer who were accustomed to the dictates of season and climate. Whilst the crofter, as a holder of land, had enjoyed a measure of economic independence albeit it amounted to little more than privileged destitution, the agricultural labourer had been both exploited and protected by the system of 'feeing' his labour on a six-monthly contract which gave him little financial reward but guaranteed that he would be fed, however inadequately. For men used to raising their own food or receiving food in lieu of wages adaptation to the weekly wage and family budgeting was no easy matter, particularly in view of the numerous counter-attractions and temptations to be found within the new industrial environment.

The Dynastic Elite and the Emergent Middle Class

As was seen earlier in this chapter the growth of Aberdeen as a centre of industrialisation was based in large part on capital accumulated by several well-known local families. The peculiar homogeneity of the north-east population may well have contributed to the close co-operation of these families which represented both landed and merchant interests. A stronger tie no doubt was their close economic inter-dependence. Whilst the country gentlemen depended on domestic manufacturing among their tenants as the most important source of income for the regular payment of rents, the wealth of the city was based on the export of these same goods. A prime example of co-operation between the two interests can be seen in the mid-eighteenth century when the city magistrates supported the setting-up of a spinning school where women were taught 'to spin with both hands' and the country gentlemen contributed prizes for those who produced the best linen yarn and brown linen cloth.[85] It was a prominent Aberdeenshire family who founded the first wool manufacturers at Gordon's mills on the River Don[86] and it is clear that the need for water power must have created additional links between local entrepreneurs and the county gentry. William McCombie, a snuff merchant in the city, owned a mill producing three hundredweight of snuff each week which was sited on the Culter burn near its junction with the River Dee. He also later bought an interest in the nearby Culter paper mills. McCombie also had estates at Skene, and later Leochel-Cushnie, in which he undertook 'extensive and tasteful improvements'.[87] Interest in agricultural improvements was not in any way confined to an easily recognisable landed gentry. Whilst landed families such as the Sinclairs, Grants, and men such as the Earl of Findlater, and Udny of Udny, are easily recognisable, many of the merchant class in the city were also associated with improvements in agriculture both in the county and the immediate suburbs of the city.[88] Some of these men must have bought out landed families to obtain their estates or obtained favourable leases at the expense of the older gentry—James Chalmers, an Aberdeen printer, was given the lease of Gordon family lands at Essilmont and Hallhead by the Duke of Cumberland in 1746.[89] Generally, however, it would seem to be a two-way process with the landed gentry interesting themselves in mercantile affairs just as much as the merchants concerned themselves with agriculture. One suspects that inter-marriage and kinship ties must have been the more important determinant and D. S. Macmillan's analysis of the sources of overseas investment from Aberdeen illustrates the importance of family ties.[90] What is clear is that the initial impetus to industrialise was based on capital accumulated by a closely knit class of merchants and country gentlemen—a dynastic élite—who did not regard industrialisation as any threat to their social power in the community.

T. C. Smout has shown in a stimulating article just how important the landed class were in the initial thrust to industrialise and his conclusion is particularly significant if applied to Aberdeen where the landed and merchant class formed a dynasty of interests:[91]

> The eighteenth century landowners strove side by side with the middle classes to develop a new kind of dynamic economy, as they believed to their mutual advantage—and when they succeeded, it became a Frankenstein to rend off their limbs of privilege and leadership.

The problem confronting this dynastic élite was the usual one of allowing industrialisation to proceed at a pace which enabled them to maintain their social power in the community. As long as there was a convergence of interest between the merchant and landed sections of these families their authority was secure. With the decline of the domestic form of production, the growth of a new attitude towards agricultural productivity, and the growth of Aberdeen as a centre of industrial factory-based manufacturing, there increasingly developed an urban-rural economic dichotomy. Mounting agitation for the repeal of the corn laws found the urban section actively promoting the launching of the *Aberdeen Herald* under the able editorship of James

Adam—a man whose own viewpoint would appear to be a reflection of the attitude of the old dynastic élite with regard to political economy, and religion. Adam was a forthright spokesman for the principle of free trade and campaigned for the repeal of the corn laws; thus emphasising the developing urban-rural differences. At the same time as the crisis developed in the Church of Scotland over the issue of patronage Adam was an energetic defender of the Establishment and ridiculed the principle of non-intrusion and those who supported it in the church courts.[92]

Whilst Adam's unrestrained advocacy of free trade must have furthered the development of the ideological contradictions in the old order it is clear that a considerable degree of co-operation continued between the county and town families. This was certainly the case with regard to overseas investment where large sums were raised in Aberdeenshire to further speculations in the U.S.A. and Australia although the actual control over the policy of these companies lay in the hands of a relatively small number of men of the old urban-based families such as Anderson, Blaikie, Jopp, Murray, Stronach, Cadenhead and others.[93] Indeed by a series of interlocking directorates control was exerted over a wide range of investment concerns such as the Scottish Australian Companies, Aberdeen Town and County Bank, the Aberdeen Banking Company, the North of Scotland Bank, Galena Investment Company, Aberdeen Fire and Life Assurance Company, and the Great North of Scotland Railway Company.[94] Given sound banking practice and a reasonable economic climate such an arrangement could have acted as a stabilising force. However it is clear from Keith's study of the North of Scotland Bank that neither of these factors were present in the 1840s. Although Keith may be correct in his claim that 'Aberdeen on the whole may be described as in a flourishing condition' in these years[95] it is certainly the case that the local economy staggered from one financial crisis to another in the 1840s, each crisis becoming more severe.

From 1837 onwards there was a series of closures of the smaller textile mills and ship-building yards which, although having little effect on the financial stability of the bank, were a precursor of what was to follow. The bursting of the railway bubble found the bank in the unfortunate position of having co-directors in the Railway Company and of general public knowledge 'that the Board of the Bank was always ready to oblige the Board of the Railway'.[96] As the directors struggled to retrieve the situation an even more serious crisis descended upon them in the total collapse of the Aberdeen textile mills of Leys,

Masson & Co., and Alexander Hadden & Sons which were heavily indebted to the bank. The stoppage of these two mills ended an era in the economic development of the city for neither were to survive. Aberdeen virtually ceased to be a textile manufacturing centre—output declining from 81,000 bales in 1845 to somewhere around 9,000 in 1855.[97] Whilst the North of Scotland Bank itself survived, the old dynastic élite was shattered by these economic crises as well as other pressures which began to make themselves felt on the social structure at about the same time. When the *Aberdeen Herald*, spokesman for the old social order, described the catastrophe of the 1848 mill closures as 'the most disastrous that has occurred for many, many years', it was a fitting epitaph.[98] And yet when Harriet Beecher Stowe visited the city only a few years later she was well impressed by what she found:[99]

> in no city which I visited in Scotland did I see such neatness, order, and thoroughness as in Aberdeen; and in none did there appear to be more gratifying evidence of prosperity and comfort among that class which one sees along the streets and thoroughfares.

The prosperity that the eminent lady observed 'along the streets and thoroughfares' belonged to a new middle class whose dynamism was derived from men whose roots were urban, and generally obscure. The gradual disintegration of the old landed-merchant class alliance left the door ajar for the arrival of Professor Smout's 'Frankenstein'—a new urban-based bourgeoisie who began to push their way upwards in the 1830s; to feel sufficiently strong to test their strength in the 1840s; and finally to coalesce with the remnants of the old dynastic élite in the 1850s to form a new middle-class establishment. The arrival of these new men, and their effects on society and the religious establishment, will be the theme of the chapters following.

Notes

1 W. Watt, 'Fifty years of progress in Aberdeen', *Transactions of the Aberdeen Philosophical Society* (April 1903), p. 100.
2 A. Keith, *The North of Scotland Bank Limited* (Aberdeen, 1936), p. 6.
3 Ibid.
4 Watt, loc. cit. Keith, op. cit., p. 10.
5 Keith, op. cit., p. 9. Watt, op. cit., p. 101.
6 Keith, op. cit., pp. 10-11. *NSA*, pp. 71-2. (Unless indicated otherwise *NSA* refers to the Aberdeen volume.)

7   *NSA*, p. 70.
8   Keith, op. cit., p. 6.
9   D. S. Macmillan, *Scotland and Australia, 1788-1850* (Oxford, 1967), pp. 328-9.
10 *NSA*, p. 71.
11 Ibid., p. 72.
12 Ibid., pp. 72-3.
13 Ibid., p. 73.
14 Keith, op. cit., p. 4.
15 *NSA*, p. 76.
16 D. Bremner, *The industries of Scotland* (Edinburgh, 1869), p. 477.
17 *NSA*, pp. 68, 71.
18 William Robbie, *Aberdeen; its traditions and history* (Aberdeen, 1893), pp. 290, 349-53.
19 Watt, op. cit., p. 103.
20 Robbie, op. cit., p. 405.
21 Ibid., pp. 332-4.
22 *NSA*, p. 68.
23 Watt, op. cit., p. 103. Robbie, op. cit., p. 334.
24 Robbie, op. cit., p. 330.
25 Ibid., p. 334. See ch. 4. See also 'Map of Aberdeen in 1822' at end of that volume.
26 These figures, and those immediately following, are derived from B. R. Mitchell and P. Deane, *Abstract of British historical statistics* (1962).
27 See Watt, op. cit., pp. 118-19.
28 Census of Population, 1851. See also J. J. Saunders, *Scottish democracy, 1815-40* (Edinburgh, 1950), p. 130.
29 Extract from a 'Memorial to the Trustees for the Improvement of Manufactures, 1728'; cited by Alexander, *Notes and sketches illustrative of northern rural life in the eighteenth century* (Edinburgh, 1877), p. 136.
30 Ibid.
31 Ibid., p. 137.
32 Ibid.
33 H. Hamilton, *The Industrial Revolution in Scotland* (Cass, 1966), p. 28. Alexander, op. cit., p. 137. Keith, op. cit., p. 8.
34 Hamilton, op. cit., p. 28.
35 *NSA* (Fyvie), p. 343.
36 Hamilton, op. cit., p. 108.
37 *NSA*, p. 159.
38 Alexander, op. cit., p. 140.
39 Hamilton, op. cit., pp. 50-1.
40 Ibid., p. 51.
41 Alexander, op. cit., p. 54.
42 G. S. Keith, D.D., *General view of the agriculture of Aberdeenshire, drawn up under the direction of the Board of Agriculture* (1811), pp. 154, 219, 228, 463, 465.
43 Cited by A. Keith, op. cit., p. 11.
44 *NSA*, p. 150.
45 Ibid., p. 507.
46 Ibid., p. 429.

47   Ibid., p. 399.
48   Ibid., p. 169.
49   Ibid., pp. 547-8.
50   Ibid., p. 1063.
51   Ibid., p. 852.
52   Ibid., p. 830.
53   Ibid., p. 178.
54   Ibid. (Glenmuick, Tullich and Glengairn), pp. 779-80.
55   R. Illsley, A. Finlayson and B. Thompson, 'The motivation and character-istics of internal migrants: a socio-medical study of young migrants in Scotland' in C. J. Jansen (ed.), *Readings in the sociology of migration* (Pergamon Press, 1970), p. 138.
56   A. Harvey, *The agricultural labourer: his present condition and means for his amelioration* (Aberdeen, 1858), p. 9.
57   Ibid., p. 46.
58   The viewpoint of Mr Andrew Wight who was appointed by the Com-missioners on the Annexed Estates to visit Aberdeenshire, Alexander, op. cit., p. 119.
59   Ibid., p. 145.
60   Ibid.
61   Ibid., pp. 142-3.
62   H. G. Graham, *Social life of Scotland in the eighteenth century* (Edinburgh, 1899), p. 186.
63   Ibid., pp. 190-5. Alexander, op. cit., pp. 192-9.
64   Ibid., pp. 173-9.
65   Ibid., pp. 182-9.
66   Ibid., p. 211.
67   Ibid., p. 214.
68   *NSA* (Kinnellar), pp. 116, 117.
69   Ibid. (St Fergus), p. 199.
70   Alexander, op. cit., p. 143.
71   *Old Statistical Account* (Peterhead), cited in Alexander, op. cit., p. 167.
72   *NSA* (St Fergus), p. 213.
73   *Old Statistical Account* (Forfarshire), cited in Alexander, loc. cit.
74   Ibid., p. 166.
75   W. Watson, *Pauperism, vagrancy, crime and industrial education in Aberdeen-shire* (Aberdeen, 1877), p. 19.
76   *NSA* (Lonmay), p. 229.
77   For example see Crathie and Braemar (*NSA*, p. 651), Birse (*NSA*, p. 793), Aboyne and Glentanner (*NSA*, p. 1063).
78   A Gaelic chapel was erected in Aberdeen, in 1795, to supply religious ordinances to these highlanders: see A. Gammie, *The churches of Aberdeen* (Aberdeen, 1909), pp. 187-8.
79   Pennant's *Tour, highlands of Scotland in 1750*, p. 7. Cited by Graham, op. cit., p. 226.
80   Alexander, op. cit., p. 63.
81   Cheap rural labour was exploited by Aberdeen firms which adapted their production on this basis; Richards & Co., at Stewartfield, and Crombie at Fintray: *NSA*, pp. 159, 171.

82 W. Thom, *Rhymes and recollections of a hand-loom weaver* (1845), p. 9.
83 Alexander, op. cit., pp. 155, 159, 157, 159-60, 146-53. Improvements in communications tended to affect local millers adversely, e.g. the opening of the Inverurie canal led to grain being conveyed to Aberdeen for milling or export: *NSA* (Rayne), p. 431.
84 The problem of rural vagrancy was solved in Aberdeenshire although it continued in other areas of Scotland. See Watson, op. cit., pp. 18-21.
85 Alexander, op. cit., pp. 138-9.
86 A. Keith, op. cit., p. 8.
87 *NSA*, pp. 110-11, 1126. It is interesting to note that other city merchants had established themselves in the parish (Leochel-Cushnie) before McCombie 'got the mains or home-farm into his possession'. Hadden's employed women on a domestic basis, and it was in this same parish that Chalmers got a lease in 1746. See below.
88 A. Keith, op. cit., p. 12. Alexander, op. cit., p. 119.
89 *NSA*, pp. 1, 124. See also Alexander Dingwall who purchased the estate of Brucklay about 1815: *NSA*, p. 268.
90 Op. cit., pp. 326-63.
91 T. C. Smout, 'Scottish landowners and economic growth, 1650-1850', *Scottish Journal of Political Economy*, vol. 11 (1964), p. 234.
92 Macmillan, op. cit., p. 335. R. M. W. Cowan, *The newspaper in Scotland* (Glasgow, 1946), pp. 148-9. See ch. 3, pp. 53-5.
93 Macmillan, op. cit., pp. 326-63.
94 Ibid., pp. 342-3. A. Keith, op. cit., pp. 49-54.
95 A. Keith, op. cit., p. 33.
96 Ibid., p. 53.
97 Ibid., p. 55.
98 Cited by A. Keith, op. cit., p. 55.
99 *Sunny memories of foreign lands* (London, 1854), vol. 1, p. 122. I am indebted to Dr C. Duncan Rice who provided me with this reference.

Chapter 2

The Superiority of the Free Church
by 1851

Our numbers were not perceptibly diminished during the months of Mr Leslie's indisposition.*

The Disruption of the Church of Scotland which took place in May 1843 was not the first secession from the Establishment although it was by far the most serious. Two important secessions had taken place prior to the Disruption—both in the eighteenth century. The first secession occurred in 1733 when the General Assembly expelled four ministers who had formed the most implacable opposition to the Patronage Act of 1712. These ministers withdrew and with others formed what was called the Associate Presbytery. In the course of the eighteenth century the new body was itself torn by schism and by 1799 had broken up into four groups—the Old Licht Burghers, the New Licht Burghers, the Old Licht Anti-Burghers, and the New Licht Anti-Burghers. The differences among the four groups were based on the interpretation of the doctrine of predestination, as well as the problem of whether the covenants made the taking of oaths to civil authorities illegal. In 1820 the New Licht sections found common ground and formed the United Secession Church. The Old Licht sections, however, continued their separate ways—the Burghers finding their way back into the Church of Scotland in 1839, and the Anti-Burghers continuing a separate existence as the Original Secession Church (later the United Original Secession Church) until the mid-nineteenth century.[1]

The second secession from the Establishment took place in 1752 and led to formation of the Relief Church. Although this body was also opposed to patronage in the Church it had little in common with the first secession being much more liberal in attitude and closer to English non-conformity. (In 1847 the Relief Church and sections of the United Secession Church merged to form the United Presbyterian Church.) Prior to the Disruption therefore, there was a substantial body of dissenting presbyterians in the form of the United Secession Church, the Original Secession Church, and the Relief Church, as well as another body, the Reformed Presbyterian Church which had originated from the Cameronian sect of 1690. Support for all of these dissenting

* W. Robbie, *Bonaccord Free Church; a retrospect* (Aberdeen, 1887), pp. 71-2.

presbyterian denominations was derived from sections of the lower middle class, notably shopkeepers, and tradesmen, and from the artisans and peasantry. Although their total numbers were substantial the fact that they remained separate denominations resulted in their relative isolation. Their existence outwith the Church of Scotland had important qualitative effects in that their absence from the General Assembly slowed up the development of a coherent Evangelical party within the national Church and thus strengthened the Moderates. Not only this, when the Evangelicals did emerge as a potent force within the Establishment their actions were to no small extent governed by the fear that if secession took place they might share the same fate of becoming a 'puny Scotch sect' and be regarded in the same light as 'pestilent fanatics'.[2] Indeed the general 'feelings of contempt and aversion with which Seceders were regarded' could lead to active social discrimination. One Aberdeenshire landlord included among the various offences by which tenants were held to have forfeited their lease 'knowingly or wilfully taking into their service, or harbour, or set ground to any Seceders or thieves, vagabonds or beggars . . . or to such as are suspected to harbour any of the above-mentioned'. In the city itself the first secession minister found it unsafe to appear on the streets 'unless accompanied by some of his members of good standing'.[3] It was easy, long after the Disruption itself, to rationalise the earlier secessions in terms of being 'the first skirmishes' before the battle[4] but in 1843 the fear of loss of social respectability as a result of secession was to be an important force contributing to the dynamism of the new Church.[5]

The 'Ten Years' Conflict' and the Disruption: an Outline

As we have seen, the origins of the Disruption can be traced to earlier secessions in the eighteenth century. However, although one might argue that it was the issue of patronage in the Church which precipitated the Original Secession and the formation of the Relief Presbytery, and finally the Disruption itself, the whole question of patronage tended to polarise and provide a demarcation between two distinct sections existing within the Church of Scotland. These sections differed on more than the patronage issue. The struggle between the Moderate and Evangelical parties was institutionalised into a debate over the rights of patrons to appoint ministers, but the differences between the parties ran much deeper than this. 'It was a cleavage between two incompatible philosophies of life.'[6] The Moderates, as their name suggests, were more tolerant and permissive in their attitude towards society and certainly less puritanical regarding their own behaviour. Culturally and socially they were more akin to the country lairds to whom many in fact owed their appointment; theologically they stressed 'mere morality', rejecting the fervent 'enthusiasm' and emphasis on predestination and hellfire of their Evangelical counterparts. More at home in polite society than the pulpit, their sermons tended to become elegant addresses read to their congregations, and whilst under their leadership the Church became a more tolerant and enlightened body closely associated with great cultural developments, such changes lost the Church a quarter of its membership to dissenting bodies by the end of the eighteenth century.[7]

The Evangelicals, hardline Calvinists in their attitude towards Salvation and the need to regulate society on Calvinist principles, remained powerful in the Church in the first half of the eighteenth century although there were visible signs of puritanism losing its impetus by the 1730s. The real change in the balance of power took place in the third quarter of the century. Although still strong enough in 1757 to have a minister suspended for attending a theatre, by 1784 the Moderate-dominated General Assembly deliberately altered its timetable to allow its clerical delegates the opportunity of attending a matinée performance at an Edinburgh theatre.[8]

The revival of the Evangelical party coincides with the period of rapid industrialisation, urbanisation, population growth and migration of the late eighteenth and the early decades of the nineteenth century. Social and economic change brought new problems for the Church of Scotland particularly regarding parochial organisation, poor relief, and education. Once again patronage in the Church emerged as the demarcation line between the Moderates and the Evangelicals who held by non-intrusion. It was not until 1833 that this Evangelical section won control over the General Assembly under the notable leadership of men such as Thomas Chalmers, Thomas Guthrie, and Robert Candlish. The following year the Assembly passed two Acts which began the 'ten years' conflict' leading to the Disruption. The Veto Act made it the right of a congregation to refuse, without giving reasons, a patron's nominee; and the Chapel Act admitted to membership of the church courts, ministers of *quoad sacra* parishes and chapels-of-ease (their incumbencies having been created as a solution to the overpopulation of certain parishes) who, prior to the Act, had no real status before the law or the Church. A long struggle ensued over the issue of the legality of the Veto Act notably at Auchterarder and Marnock and in each case the House of Lords found in favour of the patron and against the veto. The issue became a struggle between the State and the majority of the General Assembly who claimed the right of the Church to modify its own statutory constitution. The non-intrusionists pushed the matter to the point of secession by issuing the Claim of Right in 1842 which reaffirmed the position of the Church with regard to the State. The government refused to intervene in the matter and the following year at the General Assembly in May 1843 and in the weeks thereafter about a third of the ministers seceded from the Church of Scotland and formed the Free Church.[9]

The ministerial support for the Free Church was drawn from two distinct socially and geographically diverse sources. The first of these sources is the more easily identified because of its geographical regionalism. Support was by far the strongest in the north, in the Synod of Ross, and in the Synod of Sutherland and Caithness, where secession ran as high as 75 and 65 per cent respectively.[10] In no other synod did the Free Church gain a majority and in the southern synods of Merse and Teviotdale, Galloway, and Dumfries, secession was as low as 25, 22, and 19 per cent respectively. The real significance of this regional variation between north and south can only be disclosed by more detailed research in these areas, but nevertheless certain interesting features do emerge. The traditional regions of dissent against Erastianism—the covenanting areas of the south west and the borders—provided fewer seceders than anywhere else on the Scottish mainland. One can only speculate as to the outstandingly different response in the northern highlands. Certainly the vast majority of the population in the synods of Ross, and Sutherland and Caithness lived in total destitution by subsistence agriculture and without tenurial security. These synods had also been the scene of the clearances and evictions of the previous generation and it seems clear that the Church of Scotland had become closely associated in many minds with the interests of the landlords.[11] No less than thirty-nine of the forty-one seceding clergymen in the two northern synods were ministers of endowed churches. Support for the ministers was high—secession no doubt afforded an excellent opportunity for a depressed peasantry to express its spiritual and moral superiority without fear of eviction or legal retribution.

The second main source of support for the Free Church is not apparent if analysis is confined to the synodal percentages. For example although only 41 per cent of the ministers seceded in the Synod of Glasgow and Ayr, the majority seceded in the predominantly urban presbyteries of Greenock (12 out of 16), and Glasgow (31 out of 58). Likewise in the Synod of Lothian and Tweeddale the seceders had a majority in the presbyteries of Edinburgh (34 out of 55), and Haddington (11 out of 20), and in the Synod of Angus and Mearns the seceders were in a majority in the Presbytery of Dundee (15 out of 28). The same is true of the Synod of Aberdeen—'like a lump of ice in the heart' of the Evangelical north[12]—where the seceders did gain a majority in the Presbytery of Aberdeen. The pattern emerges in an even clearer form when one takes into account the fact that the presbyteries were not coterminate with the burgh boundaries. If one eliminates the rural parishes within these presbyteries and restricts the count to that of the urban parishes approximately coterminous with the development of each city, the dominance of the Free Church is evident: in Glasgow 25 out of 34 seceded; in Edinburgh 24 from 35; in Dundee 9 from 14; in Aberdeen all 15 ministers left the Establishment.

The seceders therefore originated from two main sources. First from the highland clergy of the northern synods—representing an economically depressed and often illiterate peasantry; and second from the city ministers who represented a class not only prosperous enough to provide their stipends but also by their financial contributions to support the greater part of the highland clergy. As we shall see in the case of Aberdeen, despite the prosperity of this class, the task of providing churches, manses, schools, and above all stipends, for the highland Free Church, was to prove a heavy burden and was to influence the course of development of the Free Church to no small extent.[13]

The Census of Religious Worship, 1851

Although presbyterians were not the only denominational groups in mid-nineteenth-century Aberdeen, they were the most influential and by far the most important numerically. The census of religious worship which was conducted throughout Britain on 30 March 1851 provides the best source for assessing the strength of the various denominations in the city, but unfortunately owing to certain shortcomings in its conduct, structure, and compilation, difficulties do emerge in interpreting the figures. Before looking at the figures it is necessary therefore to consider some of these difficulties.

1 The Conduct of the Census

The most immediate difficulty which emerges is that the census itself was carried out on a purely voluntary basis—no church or individual was compelled to make any return, either in whole or in part. Horace Mann, the statistician to the Registrar-General, who compiled the report claimed that the voluntary aspect of the census 'was much more awkward in Scotland than in England; the enumerators were less careful . . . to deliver forms, and parties were less willing to supply information'.[14] Although no real explanation is offered by the report as to why parties were less willing to provide the necessary information it must have been obvious when the report was published in 1854 just what this meant. Mann was not impolitic enough to hint that denominational competition was an important factor although it was quite clear that in 1851 a considerable number of Established congregations had failed to make up the serious numerical losses suffered at the Disruption. The Free Church was at its peak and although soon to go into a long decline its strength in 1851 was an acute embarrassment to Established Church congregations which were 'thin on the ground'. Throughout Scotland it was the Established Church which provided by far the greatest number of non-returns.[15]

In Aberdeen the report claimed twelve non-returns although it actually lists thirteen. These were: Establishment 2, United Presbyterian 1, Free Church 1, Episcopal 1, Congregationalists 2, Baptists 3, isolated congregations 2, and Society of Friends 1. It seems clear in fact that there were two, not three non-returning Baptist churches—this being one of several errors in compilation, concerning the Aberdeen figures.[16] Because the original census schedules are not available[17] there is no means of identifying the actual churches which failed to make returns. Nevertheless as it has a bearing on the estimation of the Aberdeen figures it is necessary to speculate as to which churches these might have been.

There would appear to be two distinct possibilities concerning the failure of these twelve churches to make returns. First the churches did not receive the actual schedules, i.e. 'the enumerators were less careful' and overlooked certain congregations because they were unaware of their existence or because they regarded them as numerically and perhaps socially insignificant. And second, the churches were well enough known and received schedules but for some reason (the most obvious being the thinness of the congregation) did not return them.

In the carefully chosen language of the report they 'were less willing to supply information'.

The two 'isolated congregations' could almost certainly be assigned to the first category. It would seem likely that these two churches were the Church of Christ and the Christadelphians, both of whom had congregations of somewhere between thirty and forty members at that time but were not thought worthy of being listed in the *Post Office Directory*.[18] The problem of defining what exactly comprised 'a place of worship' may well have resulted in the two Congregational, and the one Free Church, not receiving schedules. It seems highly likely that these were the mission churches run by the Congregationalists at Albion Street and Woodside; and the Northfield mission which was associated with the Free Church.[19] None of these 'ragged churches' were thought worthy of inclusion in the *Directory* although their existence was well known. Each congregation probably numbered between fifty and eighty. The Society of Friends was listed in the *Directory* but may have been disregarded because of the smallness of the congregation—it had declined to twenty-eight members by the middle of the century.[20] On the other hand, being the only Quaker congregation in the city, they may well have decided not to reveal their numerical weakness, and so could be included in either the first or the second category.

Although there were three Baptist churches in the city—John Street, Correction Wynd, and South Silver Street—only one made a return on census Sunday. The Baptists were divided into 'Scotch' and 'English' sections—John Street being English and the other two Scotch. Although a fairly recent history of the Baptists in Scotland states that 'there was neither a national nor doctrinal significance' between the two sections, the difference being simply one of whether the minister was supported by the congregation (English) or continued to carry out his secular pursuits whilst acting as a minister (Scotch),[21] it seems clear that the Scotch congregations in Aberdeen regarded themselves as 'strict' Baptists unlike their English counterparts. There was no inter-communion between the two sections and when the John Street Church fell into serious financial and numerical difficulties and suggested a merger with the South Silver Street congregation the Scotch Baptists rejected the idea.[22] The Baptists, whether Scotch or English, were numerically weak in 1851, and neither John Street nor Correction Wynd had ministers at that time. John Street had for years before suffered a dwindling membership and Correction Wynd, in fact, may have been defunct.[23] Certainly neither of these congregations could have mustered a congregation of seventy-eight in 1851, so it seems likely that the returning congregation was the relatively more prosperous South Silver Street Church. However, like the Quakers, the Baptists might be considered to be in either the first or second category of non-returning congregations.

The non-returning United Presbyterian congregation is something of a mystery. The United Presbyterians as a denomination were a fusion of Burgher, Anti-Burgher, and Relief churches, and the tendency towards congregational schism was not eliminated by the fusion. Conjunctions and disjunctions of relatively minute sections of congregations continued and in 1851 it is not clear whether, in fact, there were five or six U.P. churches in the city. The *Post Office Directory* confuses the issue by listing the minister of Charlotte Street Church—Rev. J. B. Ritchie—as being the minister of John Street Church although no trace of this church can now be found. Charlotte Street Church had undergone congregational schisms in the 1840s and had itself resulted from an earlier disjunction from Belmont Street Church. An attempt by the minister of the church to carry sections of the congregation over into the Free Church in 1844[24] complicates the matter still further and as John Street and Charlotte Street are adjacent the problem of editorial confusion concerning the entry in the *Directory* cannot be ignored. With no positive evidence to the contrary one must accept that there were six U.P. churches and that one of these churches failed to make a return. Given the sectarian nature of these churches and their tendency to 'hive-off' it is quite possible that this non-return could be placed in the first category and the existence of the congregation was simply overlooked.

None of the three remaining non-returns could be placed in the first category as all three—two Established and one Episcopal—must have been well known. It would seem to be these churches which the *Herald* meant when shortly after the census it praised the extent to which the schedules had 'been very generally and very faithfully filled up' but also lamented that there should be a single exception:[25]

> We should hope that the three or four returns that are awanting will yet be forthcoming. If the parties that refuse to furnish them think that they are saving their own feelings, or serving any sectarian object, by concealing . . . the nakedness of the land, they may depend upon it they are much mistaken.

There were nine Established churches in 1851 at least half of whom might have been embarrassed by the thinness of the attendance. Of the three Episcopal churches—St Andrew's, St John's, and St Paul's—the first two were Scottish Episcopal, and the last, English Episcopal. All three churches had their origins in the early eighteenth century. St Paul's was called the 'English chapel' because the form of worship practised was that of the Church of England unlike the other Episcopal churches which were nearer the Presbyterian form. Traditionally the stronghold of Episcopalianism—even as late as 1830-7 all six bishops of the Scottish Church belonged to the Aberdeen district—it is clear that Episcopalianism was steadily losing ground in the second quarter of the nineteenth century.[26] The church most affected by the decline was St Paul's which was torn by internal dissension. The church had two incumbents and it was reported that 'it is well known to their hearers that their hearts are full of malice, hatred and ill-will to one another'.[27] Externally St Paul's also had its troubles as the Bishop of Aberdeen struggled to exert his jurisdiction over the church whose senior incumbent refused to recognise his authority and as a result was finally excommunicated by the bishop. The strife became so serious, in fact, that a considerable portion of the remaining congregation seceded to found a new church in the west end.[28]

To conclude regarding the non-returns: it would seem that if one accepts Mann's own projection that in the conduct of the census there was a laxity in the delivering of schedules and an unwillingness to provide information on the part of certain churches it would follow that the unifying feature of all these non-returning congregations was their numerical weakness. As many as six of these congregations probably would not have mustered fifty attendants and some of these six certainly would have had difficulty finding much more than half that figure. It follows therefore that whilst about a fifth of the churches in Aberdeen made no return this fifth came nowhere near to representing a fifth of the church-going population. It was generally believed at the time that the schedules had been faithfully filled up and that there had 'been a laudable desire evinced on the part of almost every person of influence to facilitate the acquisition of trustworthy returns', and independent estimates of attendance tend to confirm this view.[29] Although certain of the returns are suspiciously well rounded in the case of churches who were the sole representative of a particular denomination in the city (for example Roman Catholics and the United Christians), and therefore could not hide behind a denominational cloak of anonymity as multi-church denominations could, provision was made in the census for rounding-up of average attendances over the previous year and presumably these churches resorted to this practice. It would seem reasonable to assume that the conduct of the census itself does not detract from its accuracy as a source of comparing the numerical strength of the various denominations.

2 The Structure of the Schedules and the Compilation of the Report

A far greater problem than the voluntary aspect of the census is to be found in the structure of the schedules themselves. No attempt was made to ascertain how many people attended church on more than one occasion on census Sunday. Whilst the largest number chose to attend the morning services it is clear that this overall pattern cannot be applied to specific denominations. Whilst the Free Church attendance was greater in the morning than the afternoon and evening, this was not true of the Established and United Presbyterian churches, nor of the Congregationalists who favoured the afternoon. It was true, however, of the Episcopalian churches and of the Roman Catholics. The problem is also increased by the fact that certain denominations met twice, or three times, and those meeting twice occasionally did not meet in the afternoons.[30] This problem is a fairly serious one and will be left over for analysis later in this chapter.[31]

A second weakness in the structuring of the schedules was that no real effort was made to separate Sunday scholars from the adult population. In effect this may amount to an error in the compilation of the report as churches were requested to indicate separately the number of scholars attending church and figures published independently and allegedly based on the census returns suggest that churches adhered to this request.[32] As these figures give an attendance of over 6,000 at Sabbath school on census Sunday it is clear that if this number was included among the attendance figures it would materially alter the overall pattern of attendance. It would, however, be totally wrong to accept that anything like that number actually attended church. There were two basic types of Sabbath school—the congregational school catering for members, and the district school catering for children whose parents were only at best intermittent church attenders. Between them the Established and Free churches (totalling twenty-five) operated at least forty Sabbath schools, about a third of which would be district schools whose pupils would not have attended church on census Sunday. Although it would be interesting to know precisely how many children are included among the attendants it is quite legitimate to claim that these children were as much part of the regular congregation as their parents and the presence of children within the denominational figures in no way detracts from their value. Certainly had these figures been included in the report valuable information would have been available for the assessment of the relative youth and age of each denomination.

Given the difficulty of attempting to formulate a method of assessing double and triple attendances (and this difficulty may have been insuperable) within the structure of the schedule, it is clear that many of the interpretative problems arising from the figures result from errors or faulty compilation on the part of the statisticians who prepared the report. The introduction to the report tends to give the impression that it was hurriedly prepared: 'yielding to an urgent representation . . . that immediate publication is extremely desirable, you have resolved to published this volume without further delay'.[33] Certainly the mistakes and transpositions regarding the number of places of worship and the number of non-returns (Baptists and Congregationalists) in Aberdeen would be serious if carried out on a national scale, but detailed knowledge of these churches can eliminate these faults at a local level. The census has to be approached with caution as it is clear that certain of the tables provided are misleading. One table, for example, gives the percentage of attendants to sittings at the morning, afternoon, and evening services in Scotland without taking any account of the number of sittings available at each service (not all churches being open on three occasions), simply calculating the percentages on the total number of sittings.[34] Fortunately, information provided elsewhere in the report allows one to correct this misconstruction.

Despite these faults in compilation, and the failure of twelve congregations to make returns, the census remains a valuable source of assessing the numerical strength of the various denominations in the city. The more difficult problem of assessing dual and triple attendances remains to be discussed within the pattern of denominational attendance.

Church Accommodation and the Pattern of Attendance

The report 'adopting the estimate that accommodation for 58 per cent of the population is sufficient for all practical purposes' found that Scotland bore favourable comparison with England.[35] However, the

Scottish figure of 63·5 per cent sittings to population does require closer investigation. An analysis of the accommodation available in the larger cities considerably alters the picture: Glasgow with a parochial population of 340,605 had sittings for 29·5 per cent of its people; Edinburgh with a population of 188,929 had sittings for 40·2; Dundee, 81,494 with sittings for 44·8, and Aberdeen with a population of 73,227 had sittings for 47·0 per cent. Allowing for regional variations these figures seem to indicate that despite the great expansion of accommodation after 1843 when the Free Church building programme got under way, the churches generally were still far short of tackling the problem of population explosion within the traditional parochial boundaries. In Aberdeen, certainly, notwithstanding the remarkable expansion of the Free Church after 1843 the proportion of seats available to the population in 1851 was about the same as it had been in 1837.[36] Of the sittings available more than a third of the total were held by the Free Church; a little over a quarter by the Establishment; a little over a tenth each by the Congregationalists and the United Presbyterians; and of the remainder only the Episcopalians held more than one twentieth.[37] The accommodation offered by each denomination is no real criterion, by itself, of relative strength. Clearly accommodation offered must be closely linked to the attendance achieved.

A notable feature of the pattern of attendance in Aberdeen is the uniformity of the overall proportion of the seats occupied in the various churches at the three services. This is all the more surprising in the light of the differing pattern of denominational habits—most churches meeting in the morning and afternoon, some morning and evening, and some, especially the Congregationalists, continuing the tradition of having three services each Sunday. With forty-three churches open in the morning, thirty-four in the afternoon, and fifteen in the evening, the percentage of seats occupied was 53·7, 53·6 and 53·0 respectively.[38]

This remarkable uniformity in attendance—despite the great variation in the number of churches open at each service—is a mean average concealing a considerable diversity in denominational patterns. Using the morning service as a base for comparison (as all churches were open in the morning) the following order emerges: Roman Catholics 87·5 per cent of all sittings occupied, Episcopalians 70·1, Free Church 67·7, Original Secession 47·1, Methodists 43·2, Established 41·3, Congregationalists 35·7, United Presbyterians 34·0, Glasites 30·0 and Baptists 27·1.[39] These denominational figures do, however, require further clarification.

The Roman Catholic figure is strikingly high and leads one to question its authenticity. Certainly the figures are exceptionally well rounded and could scarcely be accurate but this does not mean that they did not represent an 'average' attendance. There was one Roman Catholic church in the town and its success was regarded by the Presbyterian ministers as a danger to society.[40] Much of the success was due to the personal popularity of the priest—Charles Gordon—who spoke the broad vernacular of the district and whose 'addresses contained homely utterances in this tongue, which were often not without effect'.[41] It was said of Gordon that whilst he:[42]

> does not do much in spreading the truth, he is a worthy example in distributing charity, and calling at hovels and hospitals, and helping the old and infirm at the broth kitchen, and many other good works, but particularly in visiting the sick; for whereas many . . . would not enter a sick person's room, nor even the Infirmary, but would cry over the gate at the porter how such and such a person was, Mr Gordon will go to the bedside of the sufferer and administer temporal as well as spiritual consolation.

Nevertheless, whilst Gordon obviously was an important factor in the success of this congregation, it is clear that the number itself—87·5 per cent of sittings occupied—is inflated by certain peculiarities associated with the church building and the congregation. The Roman Catholic chapel was small in relation to the congregation (a much larger building was constructed in 1860)[43] and being the only church available was filled to overflowing. Moreover the congregation, despite the pressure on seats, clearly preferred, or were expected to attend, the morning service—the afternoon figures being less than half those of the morning. It is also clear that however poor the congregation most held sittings in the church. If one relates attendance to appropriated sittings the proportion of the church occupied rises to 93·3 per cent—only fifty seats being offered gratis.

The Episcopalian congregations also filled their churches well on census Sunday morning (70·1 per cent) but their response to a hostile Presbyterian-dominated environment differed from the Roman Catholic one of carrying the Word forth to the spiritually destitute. Although missionary work was undertaken later in the century[44] by 1851 they had lost most of what support they had enjoyed from the lower orders of society and were reliant on Episcopalian families of long-standing in the community. Episcopalianism had retreated to within the safety of its church walls and little or no attempt was being made to broaden its social basis of support. Of the two returning churches it was said of one that:[45]

> salvation they believe, is not to be found without the walls of their own chapel, and they take care to keep it there, for they have no prayer meetings, nor city missionaries, nor any means of grace, but a cold dry prayer and lesson-reading, and colder sermons.

The other church was 'very little heard of . . . the congregation sit and lean on cushions, and . . . the gospel is *not* preached to the poor, the congregation being select and upish'.[46] An official historian of the Episcopal Church substantiates these Presbyterian criticisms:[47]

> As a common rule, the members of our Church are oppressed by the selfishness of congregationalism. . . . They think only of their own narrow rights and interests without considering that the harvest of souls is so great, while the labourers are so few. They grudge the additional toil and anxiety, as the layman grudges his money and his time.

The relatively high attendance figure may well be inflated by the fact that the weaker congregation—St Paul's—probably was the non-returning church.[48] But the overall stability of the Episcopalians, the continuity of the congregations, their inward orientation, and above all their resultant lack of any tendency to 'hive-off' which was a persistent feature of Presbyterianism, meant that the church accommodation consistently bore direct relation to the size of the congregation. As there were no gratis sittings the percentage attendance to accommodation available remains the same.

The fact that the Presbyterian denominations fell behind both the Roman Catholic and Episcopal Churches in terms of percentage of seats occupied is at first surprising as the Presbyterians were far more rigorous in their attitude towards non-attendance. However, this anomaly is easily explained. Presbyterianism because of its sectarian nature was subject to continual denominational schism and 'hiving-off' of congregational dissidents. It followed that churches, although perhaps custom-built for a specific congregation at their inception, tended often to be too large for the congregation: and the sections which did 'hive-off' would either occupy empty churches or would undertake over-ambitious construction of buildings in excess of their immediate requirements in the belief, often mistaken, that they would win over many new adherents. In 1851 the Established Church was only beginning to recover from the serious losses sustained at the Disruption; and the Free Church, for a variety of reasons, had by then completed a costly and ambitious programme of church-building often more tailored to competition with the Establishment than the immediate numerical requirements of the seceding congregations.[49] The schismatic nature of the United Presbyterians has already been touched upon.[50] In nearly every case their sectarian tendency was allied to ambitious church-building. In the stormy reign of one minister of Belmont Street U.P. Church no less than three crippling secessions occurred, and in each case the dissidents erected large churches often far in excess of their capacity to fill them and laboured under continual financial crises. Indeed one U.P. congregation, which was rather more cautious, erected a large barn-like church 'in such a manner as to be easily converted into shops and warehouses'.[51] A far more realistic appraisal of attendance at the Presbyterian churches—in terms of how well filled they were—is to relate attendance to appropriated sittings rather than the total sittings available. The Established Church then produces a percentage of 62·1; the Free Church 80·1; the United Presbyterians show a dramatic rise to 72·6 from 34·0—indicative of just how overcommitted they were regarding the provision of seats; and the Original Seceders, the most sectarian of all the Presbyterians, achieve a remarkable figure of 95·5 thus surpassing every other denomination in the city including the Roman Catholics.

Of the remaining denominations only the Congregationalists were of numerical importance. Considering that they were nearer theologically to the Presbyterians than the others, one would have expected a greater proportion of seats filled than 35·7 per cent and although this figure rises to 52·0 when related to appropriated sittings the number is still comparatively low. It is possible that the low percentage may be related to a distinctive pattern of church attendance. Throughout Scotland the Congregationalists had the largest proportion of churches open for three services on census Sunday. In Aberdeen the Congregational Church returns for the three services—1,545, 1,605, 1,380 for morning, afternoon, and evening respectively—are the most uniformally regular amongst all the denominations.[52] If a relatively small proportion of church-goers attended afternoon and evening services rather than attending the morning service (on which these comparisons are based) the percentage of seats filled could be considerably altered. Moreover, the Congregationalists were active and relatively successful in the mission field[53] and 'half-day hearing' would certainly be excused on the grounds of missionary endeavours elsewhere. In one Congregational church more than fifty members were engaged in such activities.[54] Like the Presbyterians the Congregationalists had a fairly strong tendency to schism and 'hiving-off'. The first Congregational church in the city was opened in George Street in 1797, and by 1822 three other congregations had been created by 'hiving off'—Frederick Street, Blackfriars Street, and Printfield.[55] At about the same time as the Church of Scotland was torn apart by the Disruption, the Congregational Union suffered a major schism ostensibly over the issue of whether Christ died for all men and not for the elect only. In 1846 the first result of the controversy was felt in Aberdeen by the erection of an Evangelical Union church which 'hived-off' members of the Congregational churches, particularly from Blackfriars Street. St Paul Street E.U. Church was in a thriving condition in 1851 despite general opposition from the other Congregational churches and from the Presbyterians. Albion Street, began as a home mission and became a Congregational Union church about 1848.[56]

Nevertheless, despite the sectarian tendency of the Congregationalists, there is no evidence of seceding minorities over-committing themselves as appeared to be the case in the United Presbyterian schisms. The explanation of the relatively low percentage of seats occupied in the Congregational churches would appear, therefore, to lie in the three services pattern and the absence of significant sections on missionary activities.

With the exception of the Baptists who, as we have seen,[57] were a dwindling force in 1851 and with a percentage of 27·1 seats occupied were the weakest denomination, all the remainder were single-church denominations rebelling against Calvinist theology. The largest group were the Methodists 'composed exclusively of the working and poorer classes, without any rich member among them'.[58] It was argued by the Aberdeen Methodist preacher that the failure of the movement to make any real progress in Scotland was its inability to break completely from Calvinist teaching.[59] The Methodists occupied a church building which had been vacated by the Episcopalians and was too large for the congregation. As all seats were free there is no means of assessing attendance on the basis of appropriated sittings occupied. If this had been possible it seems certain that the percentage would have been considerably higher than 43·2. Of the three remaining groups none had appropriated sittings, therefore there is no means of relating attendance to numbers committed to the support of the church. In the case of the Unitarians it is impossible to relate attendance to overall sittings available as they failed to make this return.[60] The Glasites were the smallest religious group included in the census in Aberdeen. Their inclusion is no doubt related to their fairly long history and to the fact that they were considered to be 'an old and respectable body'. Followers of John Glas, a minister at Tealing, near Dundee, who founded the sect in 1730, they stressed the need for Christian love and the voluntary aspects of religion. Their numbers were too small to give a realistic percentile basis for attendance. The United Christians, like the Methodists, attracted working-class support. Their success was to no small extent based on the personal popularity of their minister with whom the congregation became closely identified.[61] As their chapel was custom-built for the congregation the attendance of 42·8 per cent on census morning is a realistic enough indicator of how well-filled the church was, although the falling-off at the evening service gives a clear indication of 'half-day' hearing among a considerable section of the congregation.

The problem of assessing the extent of 'half-day' hearing is a difficult one as it is clear from the above figures that there was considerable denominational diversity regarding patterns of attendance. In England it was believed 'after gathering opinions and making enquiries' that one-half of those in attendance in the afternoon had not been at morning service.[62] As far as Presbyterian Scotland was concerned, however, this must be considered far too high a figure. The Presbyterian churches stood out against the mildest form of Sabbath desecration and no individual nor institution was safe from their censure. In 1846 the railway companies were forced to stop the running of trains between Edinburgh and Glasgow on the 'Lord's Day' by 'pressure of public opinion' and those who had travelled by these trains 'were generally regarded as shameless violators of the Divine Law'.[63] A rigid code of conduct was enforced by the kirk sessions regarding Sabbath observance:[64]

> there were several things absolutely forbidden . . . such as bathing or swimming, watering a garden, riding (unless to church) and all games and travelling. . . . It was a common practice to pull down the window blinds . . . and certainly all walking was forbidden, above all in church hours. . . . If work had to be done the usual implements must not be used, however much they facilitated the operation. . . . A button which had come off a glove to be worn at church [was] fastened on intricately with wire to obviate having to use a needle.

The Aberdeen kirk sessions were not slow to act against Sabbath desecrators and irregular attendance at church could lead to a refusal of communion.[65] Ministers condemned from the pulpit any tendency towards 'half-day hearing' and did not hesitate to tell their congregation that 'people who take a walk on a Sunday afternoon . . . are on the road to hell'.[66] As late as 1873 an elder of one church attributed the beginning of one-service attendance to the illness of the minister:[67]

> Our numbers were not perceptibly diminished during the months of Mr Leslie's indisposition, although I have often thought it was then that a tendency to half-day hearing began to manifest itself, which has not disappeared to this day [1887]. . . . Some of our own people had got into the habit of coming up in the forenoon, although there was nothing to prevent them from appearing twice in the House of God as formerly. Mr Leslie had little or no experience of this tendency . . . and it was a thing with which he had no patience. He accordingly made a very strong point of its being the duty of all who had no good reason for absence to be present at both diets; and his repeated appeals on this subject kept the evil at a minimum point; but still it was there.

There were in fact few 'good reasons' for absence other than illness and 'half-day hearing' was expected only of domestic servants, who were in some churches required to attend special instruction classes in the evening.[68] Certainly it was confidently believed at the time that:[69]

> taking into account mistresses and servants and others prevented from attending at the first service, it is probably not too much to assume that one-fourth of the afternoon attendance was made up of parties who had not been present in the forenoon.

It would appear reasonable to assume, given the pressures of the Presbyterian Sabbath, that three-quarters of the attendants at the Presbyterian churches in Aberdeen in the afternoon or evening was made up of those who had attended the morning service.

However, one would not expect the same level of double attendance at the non-Presbyterian churches where in several instances the returns show a marked difference in pattern between morning and the afternoon and evening services.[70] Ten years or more before the Presbyterian elder noted the beginning of the *tendency* to 'half-day' hearing, single service attendance had become the established custom in one Episcopal church where the Incumbent (no doubt lacking the fire of his Presbyterian colleague) addressed his flock rather peevishly and asked:[71]

> Why is the attendance in the afternoon often so very small? . . . Charity, of course, will not impute a wrong motive to those

who come to church but once. Charity will hope that such persons are piously and profitably engaged at home. . . . Often, cold or rainy weather, or a slight indisposition . . . is made the pretext for staying at home. . . . It may not be going too far to think that the minister might be thought of. . . . The minister is human, and cold weather and pouring rain are probably just as uninviting to him as to any of his flock.

Free from the critical gaze of the kirk session, pressures of the half-yearly communion, and ministerial hellfire, the pattern of attendance at the Episcopal churches would appear to be nearer that of England where 50 per cent were considered to be double attendances. The single-church returns of the Baptists, Unitarians, Methodists, Glasites, and United Christians indicate that 50 per cent might also be a more accurate figure. The three service pattern of the Congregationalists presents a problem as we have already seen. To avoid underestimating their strength it would appear more equitable to include them among the 50 per cent double attendances although generally they would appear to be closer to the Presbyterians in their attitude towards attendance. The Roman Catholics, furthest removed theologically from the Presbyterians, showed a very large drop in attendance at the afternoon service and it is possible that the 50 per cent double attendance when applied to them might marginally underestimate their overall attendance.[72]

Attendance and the Denominations

Accepting the above estimate of double attendance, and making due allowances for non-returns,[73] one can determine the relative strengths of the various denominational groups in the city. Of the 28,423 attendants (38·59 per cent of the population) more than two-thirds belonged to a Presbyterian denomination, all the other non-Presbyterian denominations and sects making up less than a third of the attendance. Out of the 386 in every thousand who attended church, 162 belonged to the Free Church; 73 to the Established; 52 were Episcopalian; 43 were Congregationalists; 27 were United Presbyterians; 12 were Roman Catholics; 7 were Methodists; and the other groups made up less than five each.

The overwhelming numerical superiority of the Free Church is sharpened still further when one compares these figures in terms of denominational percentages of the total attendance. More than 41 per cent attended a Free Church, none of the other denominations achieved even half this figure; close on 19 per cent attended Established churches, and about 13 and 11 per cent attended Episcopal and Congregational churches respectively.[74]

Moreover, the Free Church were not only overwhelmingly numerically superior, it could be argued that qualitatively they also surpassed the other denominations. As we have seen 80 per cent of Free Church appropriated sittings were occupied on census Sunday and although this was less than the figure achieved by the Original Secession and Roman Catholic churches, it must be remembered that these were single-church denominations; the Free Church figure was spread over no less than fifteen congregations. It must also be remembered that eight years earlier not one of these congregations had been in existence as independent Free churches. In these eight years the Free Church had broken from the Establishment, built and filled new church buildings, and by 1851 claimed just over 60 per cent of all the Presbyterians in the city. It was a very remarkable achievement. One is confronted by the problem of why this body was so successful and this inevitably leads to questions concerning the social origins of the indisputable dynamism of the new Church. For example: who supported the Free Church and directed its policies in these years? Who provided the finance and the administrative expertise to make the Disruption of 1843 so different from any previous secession from the Establishment? An attempt will be made to answer these questions in subsequent chapters.

Notes

1 See Appendix, Table A. For a recent account of these various groups see W. Ferguson, *Scotland, 1689 to the present* (Edinburgh, 1968).
2 Alexander, *Notes and sketches illustrative of northern rural life in the eighteenth century*, p. 4. See also ch. 5, pp. 100-2.
3 Alexander, op. cit., pp. 210-11. A. Gammie, *The churches of Aberdeen* (Aberdeen, 1909), p. 197.
4 *The celebration of the centenary of Trinity Free Church, Aberdeen* (Aberdeen, 1895), p. 27.
5 See ch. 5, *passim*.
6 R. Rait and G. S. Pryde, *Scotland* (London, 1954), p. 262.
7 Ibid., p. 263.
8 T. C. Smout, *A history of the Scottish people, 1560-1830* (London, 1969), pp. 230-8.

9   For a detailed account of these events, see R. Buchanan, *The ten years' conflict* (1852).

10 All figures in this chapter, concerning the pattern of clerical secession, are derived from J. McCosh, *The wheat and the chaff gathered into bundles* (Dundee, 1843).

11 See *Report of commissioners of enquiry . . . on condition of crofters and cotters in the highlands and islands* (1884). All the land in Sutherland (1,299,253 acres) was owned by the Duke of Sutherland with the exception of just under 123,000 acres—*Return of owners of lands and heritages*, LXXII (1874).

12 McCosh, op. cit., p. 13.

13 See ch. 5, pp. 108-13.

14 *Religious worship and education*: report and tables (preface) (HMSO London, 1854). Mann also argued that the absence of a staff of local officers within the sphere of the Registrar-General, as in England, prevented any attempt to supply by subsequent enquiries details of the returns which were not forthcoming. It could be argued that amidst the sectarian bitterness of mid-nineteenth-century Scotland, knowledge that 'estimates' would be made if returns were not forthcoming might have simply led to falsification of returns. The right not to make a return was in a sense a safeguard against such pressures.

15 The percentages of non-returns were: Established 23, Episcopal 16, Baptists 15, Congregationalists 12, Roman Catholics 11, United Presbyterians 8, Free Church 7—ibid. (derived from Census Tables A and B), p. iv.

16 See Appendix, Table B.

17 These cannot be traced at either the Public Records Office, London, or the Scottish Record Office, Edinburgh.

18 Gammie, op. cit., pp. 371-2.

19 See ch. 8, pp. 172-6, 190-3.

20 Gammie, op. cit., p. 346.

21 George Yuille (ed.), *History of the Baptists in Scotland* (Glasgow, 1926), p. 60.

22 Gammie, op. cit., p. 272.

23 The Correction Wynd Church cannot be traced after 1851 although it does appear in the *Post Office Directory* for that year. The building was still listed as a Baptist meeting-house in the 1855 Valuation Roll of the city (f. 46), but the congregation is not mentioned by Gammie. A Baptist meeting was held nearby in a George Street hall about this time so it is possible that this group may have engrossed the remnants of the Correction Wynd congregation. Certainly by 1861 George Street had replaced Correction Wynd in the ecclesiastical section of the *Directory*: Gammie, op. cit., pp. 272-3, Yuille, op. cit., p. 89.

24 Gammie, op. cit., pp. 88-9, 104-5. See also *Charl. U.P. Man. Min.*, 1844.

25 *Aberdeen Herald*, 12 April 1851.

26 W. Walker, *The last hundred years of Scottish Episcopacy, 1792-1889* (Aberdeen, n.d.), pp. 9, 11.

27 *Chameleon*, March 1853, p. 15.

28 His excommunication was the talk of the town: see M. Angus, *Sheriff Watson of Aberdeen* (Aberdeen, 1913), p. 44. The actual secession occurred in 1854: Gammie, op. cit., p. 290.

29 *Aberdeen Herald*, 19 April 1851. The anticlerical *Herald* (see ch. 3, pp. 56-8)

published its own figures for attendance on census Sunday. These were higher than the official figures which were published in 1854. *Cornwall's New Aberdeen Directory* (Aberdeen, 1853) claims the attendance on census Sunday as being about 25,000 although it does not cite the source of its information.

30   Morning and afternoon services only were held in Scotland in the following denominational percentages: U.P. 69, Established 63, Free 61, Congregationalists 49. On the other hand 32 per cent of all Congregationalists in Scottish towns continued to meet three times each Sunday: derived from *Religious worship and education* (Table D), p. 34.

31   See pp. 36-44.

32   The *Aberdeen Herald*, 3 May 1851, printed the following figures:

No. of schools	Connected with	No. of scholars, 30 *March*	
		on the books	present
13	Established Church	1419	1120
27	Free Church	3943	3051
5	United Presbyterian	647	370
6	Congregationalist	789	638
1	Baptist	28	28
3	Methodist	411	324
1	Episcopalian	60	47
1	Catholic	150	150
5	No particular sect	540	403
62		7987	6131

Cornwall's New Aberdeen Directory, 1853-4 gives similar although 'rounded' totals: 70 Sunday schools and 8,000 pupils (p. 9).

33   *Religious worship and education*, preface.

34   Ibid. (Table 1), p. x.

35   Ibid., p. ix.

36   In a survey carried out by the elders of the various parishes in 1837 the total number of sittings was found to be 30,593. The Rev. A. L. Gordon, writing in 1842, found that there had been 'no material alteration since'. In 1841 therefore the proportion of sittings to population must have been about 48 per cent: *NSA*. On Free Church expansion after 1843, i.e. church-building, see ch. 5, pp. 105-8.

37   See Appendix, Table B.

38   See Appendix, Table C(i).

39   See Appendix, Table C(ii).

40   Charles Gordon, the Roman Catholic priest, was attacked systematically in a course of sermons held in the North Church (the Roman Catholic chapel was situated in the North parish) by six Presbyterian ministers: James Riddell, *Aberdeen and its folk* (Aberdeen, 1868), p. 79. The Presbyterian ministers also acted together to prevent Gordon having a seat amongst the managers of the House of Refuge—although he certainly took a far greater

part in the activities of that institution than they did. Later the same ministers refused to accept money collected at the Roman Catholic chapel 'for the benefit of suffering labourers during the severe season of distress'—Sheriff Watson's diary, 27 September 1836 in Angus, op. cit.; James Bruce, *The Aberdeen pulpit and universities* (Aberdeen, 1844), p. 85.

41 J. Riddell, op. cit., p. 79.
42 Bruce, op. cit., pp. 143-4.
43 St Mary's Roman Catholic Cathedral: see Gammie, op. cit., pp. 12-17.
44 See ch. 8, pp. 189-90.
45 Bruce, op. cit., p. 143.
46 Ibid.
47 Rev. George Grub, *Home mission work of the Episcopal Church of Scotland* (Edinburgh, 1883), p. 8.
48 See p. 34.
49 See ch. 5, pp. 105-7.
50 See p. 33.
51 Charlotte Street Church was capable of holding 1,000 but by 1844 was in serious financial difficulties: *Charl. U.P. Man. Min.* St Paul Street erected a church capable of holding 900 in 1842 but by 1847 had a membership of about 80 and a debt of £1,200. St Nicholas erected a church in 1845 and may well have been in similar difficulties—certainly the church building was large enough to house the congregation for forty-three years. George Street Church erected the barn-like structure: see Gammie, op. cit., pp. 89, 104, 204, 198, 98.
52 See Appendix, Table B.
53 See ch. 8, pp. 190-3.
54 George King, *Brief historical sketch of the Congregational Church in George Street* (Aberdeen, 1870), p. 28. It would appear that in the case of the George Street congregation morning and evening services were the most popular. In 1853 there was an overwhelming vote in favour of discontinuing three services and substituting morning and evening services. Eight stalwarts only voted for the maintenance of three services: J. Bulloch, *Centenary memorials of the first Congregational Church in Aberdeen* (Aberdeen, 1898), p. 92.
55 Gammie, op. cit., pp. 242-3, 252-3, 257-8, 265.
56 See ch. 8, pp. 190-1.
57 See pp. 32-3.
58 D. Wilson, *Methodism in Scotland; a brief sketch of its rise, progress and present position in that country* (Aberdeen, 1850), p. 22.
59 Ibid., pp. 23-5.
60 See Appendix, Table B.
61 See ch. 8, pp. 195-6.
62 K. S. Inglis, 'Patterns of religious worship in 1851', *Journal of Ecclesiastical History*, 11 (1960), p. 74.
63 J. R. Fleming, *A history of the Church in Scotland, 1843-74* (Edinburgh, 1927), p. 5.
64 E. S. Haldane, *The Scotland of our fathers* (London, 1933), pp. 148-9.
65 See ch. 5, pp. 128-9.
66 Bruce, op. cit., p. 96.
67 W. Robbie, *Bonaccord Free Church; a retrospect* (Aberdeen, 1887), pp. 71-2.

68 See ch. 7, p. 147.
69 W. Carnie, *Reporting reminiscences* (Aberdeen, 1902), p. 33.
70 See Appendix, Table B.
71 The Incumbent of St Paul's, *Fourth Pastoral Address* (Aberdeen, 1863), pp. xix-xx.
72 On the other hand the figure calculated from the census returns (850) is remarkably close to the figure cited elsewhere as being the Roman Catholic attendance for 1878 (848). By 1891 the number had risen to 1,006: see R. Howie, *The churches and the churchless in Scotland: facts and figures* (Glasgow, 1893), p. 100.
73 See pp. 31-4, and Appendix, Table D.
74 See Appendix, Table D.

Chapter 3

The Disruption of the Establishment

It would be well if the Assembly would enact a law against appointing servants, managers, and impudent boys to offices in the church.*

We have already noted in Chapter 2 that the Free Church drew its clerical support from two main sources; namely the highland clergy representing an economically depressed and often illiterate peasantry, and the city ministers representing an urban middle class not only prosperous enough to sustain them but able by their financial contributions to support the greater part of the highland clergy and to provide them with churches. It is this urban middle class which we must now examine more closely in this and subsequent chapters. In this chapter the analysis will be confined to an explanation of the total secession of all fifteen ministers and some evaluation of the possible effects. The pattern of secession in the congregations and kirk sessions will also be examined in terms of structural differentiation between the adherents of the Establishment and the secessionists. Before looking at these differences, however, it is necessary to examine the ecclesiastical structure of the Establishment in 1843 for it was from these churches that the fifteen Free Church congregations of 1851 had drawn their support.

Ecclesiastical Structure of Established
Presbyterianism in 1843

The fifteen city churches connected with the Establishment were: West, South, East, St Clement's, North, Greyfriars, Trinity, Union, Melville, Gaelic, Mariners', John Knox, Bonaccord, Gilcomston, and Holburn. Of these all but three lay in the old city parish of St Nicholas. Bonaccord, Gilcomston, and Holburn, were sited in Oldmachar parish, parts of which had been engrossed by the urban sprawl. These fifteen churches are best differentiated by assigning them to one of two groupings determined by their constitutional and historical development—both factors which to a considerable extent were a reflection of

* James Bruce, *The Aberdeen pulpit and universities* (Aberdeen, 1844), p. 12.

the prosperity and social status of the congregations. The first grouping is of those which were erected parishes by the division of St Nicholas in 1828; the second is made up of churches which were given the right to parish status by the Act of the General Assembly in 1834.[1] For the sake of convenience these two groupings are described by their legal distinction as *quoad civilia*, and *quoad sacra* parishes.

Quoad Civilia Parish Churches

Until 1828 the old parish of St Nicholas had been a collegiate charge—three ministers sharing the burden of administering to the needs of the parish. Of the three churches in the parish—West, East, and Greyfriars—the West Church had the highest status, both in terms of its historical origins and its congregation. Founded about 1060, it was regarded as 'the mother church of Aberdeen' and was traditionally associated with the city magistracy and attended by many of the most prominent local families. A new church had been erected on the site of St Nicholas Church in 1751.[2] The East Church had also a fairly long history, going back to the fifteenth century although the church building itself was rebuilt in 1837.[3] Greyfriars was also a pre-Reformation church but having fallen into disuse was repaired and reopened in 1759 to accommodate the growing city population. The charge was generally held by the professor of divinity at Marischal College.[4]

With the division of St Nicholas parish in 1828 all three churches became recognised parish churches along with three others—South, North, and St Clement's. The South Church was formerly a Relief Church, built about 1778, and was admitted to the Establishment in 1791 as a chapel-of-ease. The old church building was demolished and re-erected about 1830.[5] St Clement's had a longer history, going back to before 1631, although when created a separate parish the building appeared to be in poor repair and a new church was erected on the site about 1828. The parish had a close association with the fishing industry.[6] As no suitable building was available in the new North parish a church was erected and opened in 1831.[7] In all six of these parishes the right of presenting the minister lay with the city magistrates and the ministerial stipends were paid out of city funds. The stipends, ranging from £250 to £300, were higher than those of the *quoad sacra* parishes, where the money was raised from congregational collections and seat rents, combined occasionally with payments from the city Common Good Fund when the money raised was insufficient.[8] The *quoad civilia* parishes also had their own kirk sessions—elders being co-opted—a right which the other churches did not possess until after 1834. However, even after 1834, it is clear that the *quoad sacra* parish churches were not generally considered of equal status. Although ministers and elders could now participate in the affairs of the higher church courts their legal position was not safely established. After the Disruption the *quoad sacra* parishes reverted to their former status as chapels-of-ease in the Establishment.[9] Their rather dubious legal position, the insecurity of many of the ministerial stipends, and the generally lower socio-economic status of the congregations, all combined to assign them to an inferior station. The fact that these former chapels had the right after 1834 to form their own kirk sessions led to sneers from the Moderate sections of the Church regarding the status of the new elders: 'It would be well if the Assembly would enact a law against appointing servants, managers, and impudent boys to offices in the church',[10] commented one observer.

These distinctions, however, were exaggerated to some extent. Within the supposedly superior *quoad civilia* churches there was a considerable social diversity regarding the congregations. Of the six, the West was clearly the most prosperous, followed by the South and the East. Using the sacramental collections as a guideline to the wealth of the congregation, St Clement's, North, and Greyfriars fell far behind the others,[11] and whilst all six parishes contained densely populated working-class areas, this problem was particularly acute in the North and Greyfriars parishes. Indeed it is clear that certain *quoad sacra* parish churches—such as Trinity—equalled the latter three *quoad civilia* parish churches both in terms of the socio-economic standing of the eldership and the general prosperity of the congregation. Certainly, as we shall see in the next chapter, there were important differences—but these were concerned with cultural attitudes and life styles, rather than social category.

Quoad Sacra Parish Churches

Before the creation of *quoad sacra* parishes in 1834 by the Act of the General Assembly, none of the other nine churches had the right to elect a kirk session, nor did the ministers have the right to attend the church courts. Nevertheless, a fair number of these congregations raised the funds for the support of their minister and owned their church buildings. Trinity provides a good example. Originating over a dispute concerning the choice of the East Church minister by the town council, a portion of the congregation withdrew and applied to the Presbytery for permission to erect a chapel-of-ease. The cost of the church and manse amounted to about £2,000 which 'was raised almost entirely without assistance'.[12] The constitution of the church ensured that the right of electing the minister was vested in communicant male seatholders. Union Church had a somewhat similar background, having been erected as a chapel-of-ease within the East Parish in 1822. It also had its own constitution.[13] Melville had originated in 1756 as the first Secession Church in the city. It had its own constitution and owned its church building. In 1839 the congregation rejoined the Establishment but apparently had not been assigned a parish area by the time of the Disruption.[14] Bonaccord Church was the result of a schism in Trinity over the appointment of a minister in 1828. The congregation had their own constitution.[15] The Mariners' and Gaelic Churches, as their names imply, catered for specific occupational and linguistic groups.[16] The Gaelic Church had been assigned a specific parish (Spring Garden) area prior to the Disruption. Both had their own constitutions. Of the remaining three congregations Gilcomston had the longest history, being formed as a chapel-of-ease in 1771.[17] Holburn originated from a 'hiving-off' from Gilcomston in 1835 over the appointment of a minister, the church being opened in 1836.[18] John Knox was opened in 1835 as a chapel within Greyfriars parish largely as a result of the activity of the minister of that parish.[19] In all three of the latter churches closer constitutional control was maintained. Gilcomston and Holburn were sited in what had been suburbs of the city in the parish of Oldmachar. 'Small communities of working people were settled here and there in the locality, as they had found rents and taxes lower than in the city.'[20] These were largely settlements of shoemakers and hand-loom weavers. Constitutionally these two churches remained more closely tied to the parish of Oldmachar as did John Knox—sited in a heavily populated slum area—remain linked to Greyfriars. These links were forged by the occasional need for financial assistance to provide for the ministerial stipend and other requirements in the running of the churches. Whilst the other *quoad sacra* parish churches had emerged from schisms from Established churches these three had been sited to serve the needs of working-class areas. Although well enough attended their finances were never altogether secure.

In conclusion the ecclesiastical structure of the Establishment was made up of the following: at the top a group of six parish churches (*quoad civilia*) under the patronage of the town council which provided a ministerial stipend superior to that of the other nine churches. Within these six churches the élite congregation was the West Church, followed by South and East Churches. The other three congregations were less well-off. St Clement's catered for a fishing and sea-faring community, and North and Greyfriars had particularly large areas of working-class slums within their bounds. Beneath these six churches there were nine churches of mixed historical and social origins, all but three of which— Gilcomston, Holburn, and John Knox—were virtually constitutionally and financially autonomous. The next section will consider the Disruption of the Establishment and will undertake an initial analysis of the secession patterns within some of these churches.

The Disruption of the Establishment

1 The Ministerial Secession

It has already been noted that all fifteen ministers left the Established and went over to the new Free Church in 1843. This was a serious blow to the Established Church in Aberdeen and as late as 1844 it was recognised as the principal reason for the almost total desertion of many of their charges.[21] One can detect no similarity or dissimilarity in the backgrounds of the fifteen which might give a hint as to why the response in the city was unanimous. Their social origins were typical. They were derived from families whose breadwinners were ministers, farmers, merchants, schoolteachers. They were not 'angry young men' but mature middle-aged men born in the last two decades of the eighteenth and the first decade of the nineteenth century.[22] Neither can one detect any leadership pattern by which one or two convinced seceders led the remainder into secession. All to varying degrees favoured non-intrusion but not all were Evangelical and on certain social issues there was open disagreement within the group.[23] There was an almost overpowering feeling that secession from the Establishment was not altogether respectable and solace was taken in the fact that secession was unanimous. The Rev. J. Foote of the East Church found that 'One pleasing circumstance attending to our change of position here was that all the ministers . . . were of one mind, and all adhered to the Free Church.'[24] The great fear was that secession might bring loss of social respectability. The same minister on his return from the disrupted General Assembly in Edinburgh wrote with undisguised relief that 'my friends received me very kindly . . . I was not ashamed to appear on the streets'.[25]

The general reluctance of the fifteen to regard themselves as 'seceders' is reflected in the manner by which they described themselves and the Established Church. The minister of the West Church declared prior to the Disruption that the next communion he dispensed would be the last in the Establishment, 'not the last he would dispense in the Church of Scotland'.[26] Following the Disruption the line hardened and the Banner, organ of the Free Church in Aberdeen, thereafter referred to the Church of Scotland as the 'Residuary Establishment'.[27] The more extreme went further and described the Established Church as the 'residual Church'—'The Free Church is God's Establishment'.[28] At first the seceders described themselves as the 'Presbytery of Aberdeen' and demanded the return of the Presbytery records from the residuary. Clearly there was a general attempt to differentiate between themselves and earlier seceders whilst at the same time to malign those who had remained.[29] The new Church presented itself, not as a schismatic body, but as the *new* Establishment.[30] The simple explanation for the unanimity of secession of the Aberdeen clergymen might therefore be that by a chance coincidence all fifteen were men who held principle highly and were forced to secede because they could no longer remain in an Erastian Establishment. The fact that they did so only after a great deal of anxiety as to the possible social consequences of such an action would, in a sense, only make the action itself more laudable. The very simplicity of such an explanation has a certain appeal, nevertheless, whilst one cannot disregard the importance of principle in shaping their decision, certain other factors must also be considered as important elements which undoubtedly stiffened their resolution to secede.

First one must be careful not to equate fear of loss of social respectability with a dread of consequent economic insecurity. On the contrary the evidence suggests that far from sacrificing an assured stipend and the safety of the manse the seceding clergy suffered no immediate or long-term financial disadvantage as a result of the Disruption. There would appear to have been no evictions and financial preparations were begun long before May 1843. Indeed before October 1842 there was a considerable falling-off in communion collections—to such an extent that no new applicants for poor relief could be admitted to the roll.[31] It is clear that money which normally found its way into the funds of the Establishment was being diverted for other purposes by those intent on secession. Greyfriars session ceased submitting the sacramental collections to the Town Clerk towards the end of 1842 despite continual requests to do so, and for several years had neglected to record the actual amounts collected at the church door.[32] Realising also that the Establishment could lay claim to bequests and endowments left to congregations before 1843, Trinity session hurriedly distributed money which might have been utilised later by the Establishment.[33] In the same way Greyfriars session transferred the congregational library from the church to a safer place.[34] In the case of both of these sessions such manœuvres were made easier simply because almost all the elders were to secede, but the overall falling-off in collections supporting the Establishment suggests that the trend was general.

Certainly it is clear that elders and leading members of the congregations intent on secession were making active financial preparations for such an event in some cases at least seven months before May 1843. The speed at which sites were found and churches erected after May signifies a high state of preparedness.[35] The same preparedness can be seen in the arrangements made with regard to the provision of stipends for the seceding clergy. In the East Church in October 1842, probably at the half-yearly communion, 'it was ascertained what proportion of the male heads of families . . . were intending to adhere' and later the minister recorded that 'the liberality of the congregation has been exemplary'.[36] Likewise the minister of Bonaccord Church found 'new evidence of the supreme love to God' in the benevolence of the congregation revealed in a public meeting and as a result '1842 has had with me a pleasant termination'. Later the same minister wrote prior to the Disruption that many were astonished at the large sum which had been raised by the congregational 'collectors'.[37] Even in the West parish—where the Free Church initially made the least headway—support was sufficient to ensure that in the event the minister would not be called upon to sacrifice his 'snuff and other articles of luxury of which he is fond'.[38] The clergy, in fact, were being urged on by activist members of their congregations. These men were economically powerful enough to make secession on a guaranteed stipend possible and thus they eliminated one important deterrent to withdrawing from the Establishment—fear of economic insecurity.

Another important factor in determining the decision of the clergy to secede, emanated rather paradoxically, from a source violently antipathetic towards the principles of the non-intrusionists. It has been said of the *Aberdeen Herald*, edited by James Adam and a vehicle for his prejudices, that 'no other Scottish newspaper allowed less honour to the seceders'[39] and certainly the virulence of the *Herald*'s attacks on the Aberdeen clergy would appear to more than substantiate this claim. Adam's dispute with the non-intrusionist clergy was a longstanding one. In 1839 he had been attacked from the pulpit of the Union Church and described as 'an infidel villain, a blasphemous villain, a hired agent for attacking the clergy, and a satanic agent'.[40] Adam sued Allan, the minister of Union Church, and was awarded £1,000 damages. Thereafter Adam continually and increasingly attacked the principles of the non-intrusionists and the character of its clerical supporters. Their meetings were described as 'swindle conventicles'—'the sensible people pity them, the giddy laugh at them, and the weak and the weak only, are gulled by them'. The clergy were reported as 'reverend law-breakers', 'mock martyrs', 'show martyrs'. They had become involved in the agitation simply out of a desire to obtain power for themselves.[41]

Whilst this sort of approach would have infuriated the more ardent 'nons' it is also the case that the more timid might well have been deterred from secession. Adam, however, was not content to leave such ministers alone and as the General Assembly drew nearer so did the venom of his attacks increase on specific ministers. Davidson of the West parish 'does not seem to have any exalted notion of religious communion—he makes money the climax of its perfection'.[42] By 1 April Adam was arguing that secession daily became more doubtful:[43]

How far such men as . . . our own Mr Murray, and others similarly situated, may be disposed to go in precluding themselves from any chance of being secure in their livings, is difficult to say.

A week later Adam turned the screw ever tighter on the more timid by declaring in his leader article:[44]

Day after day, first in one quarter and then in another—increasing too as the crisis approaches—symptoms are exhibited of a strong disposition to backslide. . . . When the General Assembly meets . . . there will, doubtless, be many more weak brethren who will discover strong reasons, for obeying at once the dictates of prudence, and the commands of their ecclesiastical superiors.

The more moderate non-intrusionist clergy such as Murray, or Foote, or to some extent Davidson, must increasingly have been faced by a new fear just as potent as the consequent loss of social respectability after secession—fear of the total loss of social respect if they remained in the Establishment, a fear no doubt heightened by the realisation how Adam would depict those who did remain. As if finally to convince those who were not fully committed, Adam, in his leader article immediately before the Disruption, was at his most deadly. In a lengthy article headed 'Why don't they go?' Adam hammered home the simple answer:[45]

> They don't go simply *because* they would rather stay. They *pretend* that it would be sinful to remain; but they *know* and *feel* that it must be disagreeable to depart. And the certain discomfort weighs more heavily than the supposed wickedness. They won't go, if they can help it.

Adam was, of course, proved totally wrong in his estimations of the clergy, as all fifteen seceded. It is somewhat paradoxical that the *Aberdeen Herald* which was so violently opposed to the principle of non-intrusion—'We have no sympathy for the clerical schismatics who entered the Church knowing that patronage was part of the constitution'[46]—should unwittingly play such an active part in making the secession complete. Adam, however, totally underestimated the extent of support for secession among the laity. Prior to the Disruption he had declared that 'the number of seceders will be nicely proportioned to the size of the realizable fund'.[47] It was only after the event that he was to comprehend his mistake and to write bitterly that the seceders were still seeking sympathy when in fact they were enjoying stipends equal to that of the Establishment.[48]

In conclusion, although it would be extremely foolish to deny the importance of respect for principle in determining the total secession of the Aberdeen clergy, it is an oversimplification to see the event solely in these terms. For those intent on secession over the patronage issue the internal pressures from powerful economic groups in the congregations, and the external pressures from James Adam and the *Aberdeen Herald*, mattered less. For the other clergymen—whom Adam termed the 'timid schismatics'—such pressures must have been of paramount importance in stiffening wavering resolution. As the pressures mounted and more of the clergy committed themselves to secession it became easier in some ways to secede than it was to remain. Foote was relieved to find that his friends received him kindly after the Disruption. Had he remained in the Establishment he might well have *been ashamed* 'to appear on the streets'—condemned as a 'stipendary' by his colleagues, and hounded by Adam as a backslider who obeyed the dictates of prudence and abandoned the principle of non-intrusion. Such was the fate of men like Principal Dewar of Marischal College who, at the last moment, withheld his support.[49]

2 The Congregational Secession

It is obvious that the secession of the minister and the larger proportion of the church elders must have been an important factor in determining the extent of congregational secession. It has already been noted that the Established Presbytery regarded the departure of the ministers as being the most important cause of the almost total secession of many congregations. If post-Disruption survival is taken as a criterion of the extent of congregational secession it is clear that secession was greatest in the second group of churches (*quoad sacra*) outwith the patronage of the town council, especially in the six of this group which possessed their own kirk session and rights of ministerial election, namely Melville, Union, Bonaccord, Mariners', Gaelic, and Trinity. In all six congregations secession was so heavy that the Establishment was obliged to abandon the charges. The Established Church had no claim at all on Melville which was owned by the seceding managers. Union, and Bonaccord, possessed fairly substantial debts which the weakened Establishment was loath to accept along with the churches. Whilst their position was being considered the seceders took the initiative, put the church buildings up for sale, and purchased them on behalf of their respective congregations. In the case of the Gaelic and Mariners' churches the situation was different. Both churches attracted small congregations and their continuance was later to prove a financial burden to the Free Church.[50] In view of the accommodation available in St Clement's Church it would have been financially inexpedient to attempt to maintain rival congregations when secession was heavy although in the case of the Gaelic congregation it does not appear to have been total. One of the reasons upholding the translation of a minister from the Presbytery of Inverness to Aberdeen in August 1843 was that 'it was necessary to have someone who can dispense the Gaelic Ordinances'.[51] In fact in only one of these six churches did the Establishment make any effort to carry on and it could be argued that had their efforts been more vigorous Trinity might have been successfully held for the Establishment. The seceding congregation, 'finding that they could not procure a site within the parish or its immediate vicinity, resolved upon the one in Crown Street'.[52] The transition from a slum district in the harbour area to one of the most coveted west-end residential streets seems to have been effected easily by the seceders, many of whom lived in that area where others of the congregation were soon to follow. The Free Presbytery were in grave doubts regarding

Trinity's choice of site especially as it was in the immediate vicinity of another Free Church being built for the seceding Greyfriars congregation who had also deserted the slums of Greyfriars parish for the select west end. Free Trinity and Free Greyfriars, when built, stood about fifty yards apart and although Trinity prospered, Greyfriars congregation was insolvent within ten years and the building had to be sold.[53] In the case of Trinity, however, the Establishment failed to benefit from the removal to Crown Street. Two of the elders and three of the managers remained in the Establishment after 1843, but none of these men appears to have taken any further part in the running of the church which thereafter was controlled largely by a group of West Church elders.[54] No minister was settled in the church until July 1844 and the settlement was only carried out with reluctance by a large number of the Presbytery. It would be reasonable to assume that by July 1844 most of the congregation which had remained in May 1843 had become dispersed. Certainly by January 1846 the weekly collection had shrunk to around 4s. 6d. and even this may have been an exaggeration.[55] The church was abandoned and later the building was sold.

With regard to the three remaining churches within this second group—Gilcomston, Holburn, and John Knox—the Establishment pursued a more vigorous and successful policy partly as a consequence of the closer constitutional and financial links these churches had with the parish because of their socio-historical origins. The Free Church, nevertheless, disputed possession of all three buildings. In Holburn Church the Establishment acted quickly and obtained an interdict to prevent it being sold by the seceders. They did not, however, gain access to the building until the middle of 1844 and it was not until September of that year that a minister was finally ordained to the church.[56] In Gilcomston and John Knox access was gained with less difficulty. Outstanding debts were relatively small—only £12 in the case of John Knox—and ministers were ordained to both churches by the end of 1843.[57] In Gilcomston an attempt was made to make the election of the minister more democratic, the managers waiving their rights in favour of the male heads of families connected with the church. In both Gilcomston and Holburn the congregations were summoned three times at the church door to offer objections to the call, but later events tend to confirm these concessions as being made in the face of grave financial weakness. The Disruption left the Establishment in severe financial difficulties and these difficulties were particularly serious for Gilcomston, Holburn, and John Knox, which had congregations of relatively low economic status and whose ministerial stipends were not endowed by the town council. In Gilcomston where the stipend had formerly been fixed at £230 it was found that there was 'no prospect of being able to pay so large a sum'.[58] By February 1844 the situation had deteriorated and a committee appointed to enquire into the financial position of these churches put out a desperate appeal for aid.[59] Two of the elders of the West Church undertook responsibility for the debt on Holburn, but by May 1844 the presbytery were unable to pay the stipend of the minister of John Knox although it had been fixed as low as £75.[60] A steady stream of petitions poured into the presbytery from these congregations urging special collections to be made or requesting grants towards their funds.[61] Nevertheless, however serious were these financial problems, all three churches did survive. Despite Free Church claims of 'large and vigorous' secessions in these churches it would appear that the Disruption created financial rather than numerical problems for these congregations. Those who seceded tended to be those who had formerly carried a large part of the financial burdens of the churches. In John Knox, for example, in 1846 there was an average attendance of about 500. This was not high but it was greater than the attendance at St Clement's and the North churches and was six times greater than the attendance at its own 'mother' parish church of Greyfriars under whose jurisdiction it still lay. Those who had remained in the Establishment were of low socio-economic status—the proportion of seats let to numbers attending was less than in any other congregation.[62] Indeed the sacrifice of all three ministers of these churches was probably far greater than anything experienced by the seceding ministers. One minister, because of the seriousness of the financial situation, was prepared to accept any stipend, however small, that the presbytery felt able to provide.[63] There was no need for such a 'heroic spirit of self-sacrifice for the sake of conscience'[64] in the Free Church.

In the nine *quoad sacra* parish churches, therefore, extensive secession from the Establishment took place. Five charges were abandoned and a sixth was lost after half-hearted attempts to hold what was left of the congregation. In the remaining three churches secession was also substantial, especially among the financially better-off and the Establishment was for several years confronted with serious financial problems concerning the maintenance of all three charges. Their survival, in fact, was largely the result of personal sacrifices made by certain individual ministers and elders.

3 The Pattern in the Six Kirk Sessions (*Quoad Civilia*)

In all six of the first group of churches—parish churches under the patronage of the town council—the Establishment survived despite substantial secessions in all but one of the congregations. The more prosperous the congregation the more successful was the Establishment in maintaining its support—secession was relatively less in the South and East churches and least of all impact was made by the seceders in the West Church. In the other three parishes containing the most destitute areas of the city—St Clement's, North, and Greyfriars—heavy secession took place to such an extent that the independent existence of the North and Greyfriars charges was seriously threatened. Indeed, but for the fact that the seceding congregation abandoned the parish and moved to a select residential area of the city the Greyfriars charge would almost certainly have been irretrievably lost. The suggestion was made following the Disruption that the North and Greyfriars congregations be united[65] and for several years the presbytery considered the possibility of closing Greyfriars permanently and transferring the endowments to John Knox or Trinity. John Knox Church was in the rather anomalous position of being under the jurisdiction of Greyfriars—a church with no minister, one elder, and insufficient members of the social status required to form a kirk session.[66]

In fact, the heavy secession among the eldership was just as serious a problem for the Establishment as the departure of the fifteen clergymen. The kirk sessions were more than instruments of religious and social discipline—they were composed of bodies of influential men whose presence was essential to the smooth-running of church affairs. Much of the subsequent success of the seceders was determined by the support they received from men properly qualified to serve on the kirk sessions; elders who, when so required, could either furnish sufficient capital from their own resources or borrow it on their 'good name'.[67] Following the Disruption, ten Free churches were erected largely on the financial support of such individuals. Of the ninety elders in these six parishes, however, only a little over a third remained loyal to the Establishment; just over half seceded, the position of the remainder being uncertain.[68] In only one session—that of the West Church—did the Establishment hold its own, in all the other sessions the seceders were in a majority. The problem for the Established Church was most acute in the three poorer parishes of St Clement's,

North, and Greyfriars where two-thirds of the elders went over to the Free Church. It was largely a reflection of the relative prosperity of the parish that the pattern of secession was also related to the status of the kirk session. Nearly three-quarters of the elders in the top three parishes were of a high social status[69] whereas in the bottom three parishes these amounted to less than a half—a number inflated, moreover, by the exceptional proportion of high status members serving on Greyfriars session.

Secession would also appear to be related to seniority within the kirk sessions although there does not seem to be any precise method of defining 'seniority'.[70] Certainly elders with long service on the session tended to remain. This was particularly true in the three more prosperous parishes where only six out of twenty-six seceded although in the three poorer parishes just over half left the Establishment (nine out of seventeen). The reverse was true, however, when one considers elders whose service was of short duration. Seventeen out of twenty-eight seceded in the top three parishes whilst in the bottom three support for the Free Church was overwhelming—sixteen out of nineteen seceding, and only one elder clearly committing himself to the Establishment. Overall it is evident that the Establishment was more likely to find support among the senior members of the kirk sessions, whilst the junior members tended to adhere to the Free Church.

Although the six kirk sessions were, in effect, composed entirely of middle-class members there was, nevertheless, a considerable range of socio-economic status within those recruited. It is necessary, therefore, to divide the eldership into two broad groupings approximating to a high and a low middle-class status. When one distinguishes between elders in this way it emerges that the propensity to secede was also related to status as well as length of service.[71] Whilst about half of the high status elders seceded (28 from 58) the proportionate secession amongst those of low middle-class status was very much greater (18 from 25). Overall, in fact only six low status elders remained in the Establishment.

When one takes this analysis a step further and links seniority on the kirk sessions with eldership status a clearer pattern emerges of the type of elder who remained in the Establishment, and the type one might expect to secede. By far the most important section to support the Establishment were the high status senior elders of the top three parishes in order of prosperity, viz. West, South, and East. Of the twenty-one high status senior elders identified in these kirk sessions no less than sixteen remained loyal to the Establishment; only two high status senior elders seceding from the West and South sessions. Among high status junior elders support was sparse for the Establishment even in the top three parishes and in less prosperous parishes of St Clement's, North, and Greyfriars, it was scarcely nominal. Outwith the top three sessions only two low status elders adhered to the Establishment.

Support for the Free Church was somewhat more widely and more evenly spread. Unlike the Establishment, however, a powerful section of the high status junior elders was to be found in the ranks of the new church (18 from 25), along with a large body of low status elders. A smaller but significant group of high status senior elders also seceded (10 from 28). The high status elders—senior and junior—were spread fairly evenly over the six kirk sessions; the low status elders on the other hand were predominantly drawn from the less prosperous parishes of St Clement's, North, and Greyfriars.

Within these six kirk sessions, therefore, the pattern of denominational adherence would appear to be determined to some degree by status and seniority of the elders. Certainly at one level it was a conflict fought out between the senior high status elders and the younger men of more recent ordination—whether of high or low status. Although, as we shall see in the next chapter, the differences between the two groups ran much deeper than simply that of age, it was not uncommon for contemporaries to portray it in this way. The doctrine of the Establishment was 'cold and lifeless moonlight' compared to the 'genial and fructifying sunlight' of the Free Church.[72] It was argued that the conflict was between the aged and worn-out and the young and virile:[73]

> Dry leaves, which the Church has lately been, produce nothing. They may nourish in their decay the young shoots from the old firm-rooted trunk, but they are dead leaves nonetheless.

Certainly much of the vigour of the Free Church was derived from the dynamism of its young and vigorous eldership. But they were not simply young men. They were men of sufficient socio-economic potential to see the new Church through its initial financial problems concerned with church-building and also to provide a large portion of the stipends for the seceding clergymen. However, in life styles and attitudes they were very different from their counterparts in the Establishment. Following the Disruption it was these men who were to stamp their mark on the Free Church and influence its development.

Conclusion: 'Dry Leaves and New Shoots'

In terms of loss of charges, clergy, elders, influential members, communicants, and general financial support, the Disruption of 1843 amounted to a disaster of the first magnitude for the Established Church in Aberdeen. All fifteen clergymen left the Establishment and ultimately no less than six charges had to be abandoned. The kirk sessions lost their younger influential and potentially most prosperous members —the 'new shoots' from which the Free Church in the city was to blossom.

If simple congregational survival is taken as a criterion the Establishment was most successful in retaining support in the three more prosperous parish churches of West, South, and East, where the sessions were composed predominately of high status middle-class elders. The Establishment was less successful in retaining support in the three poorer parishes of St Clement's, North, and Greyfriars where the eldership contained a much greater proportion of members of low-middle-class status. The Establishment failed completely in the six charges which were permanently lost and where the sessions were predominantly of a low-middle-class status as will be seen in the chapter following.

The 'dry leaves' who remained—long-serving high-status members of the West, South, and East sessions—did nourish more than the 'new shoots' who seceded in 1843. By their endeavours the congregational remnants of Holburn, Gilcomston, and John Knox churches were preserved. The great majority of those who remained loyal to the Establishment in these three congregations were poor—too poor in many cases to pay any seat rent—and certainly unable to raise funds towards the support of a minister for their congregation. In these three charges there were not half-a-dozen members remaining of the status necessary for the formation of a kirk session. In some ways the financial and administrative problems confronting the 'dry leaves' of the fragmented Establishment were every bit as great as those facing the seceders intent on building a new and better Church. Before looking at the method and the means by which these 'young shoots' influenced the course of the Free Church, it is necessary to study the conflicting groups in a wider chronological and societal perspective. This will be undertaken in the next chapter.

Notes

1   See ch. 2, pp. 28-9.
2   A. Gammie, *The churches of Aberdeen* (Aberdeen, 1909), p. 76. *NSA*, p. 33.
3   Gammie, op. cit., p. 11.
4   Ibid., pp. 21-3.
5   Ibid., pp. 69-70.
6   Ibid., p. 56.
7   Ibid., p. 39.
8   *NSA*, pp. 35-7.
9   Gilcomston was disjoined from Oldmachar and allowed to form its own kirk session in 1852; Holburn was likewise disjoined in 1867; John Knox remained in Greyfriars parish until 1880. These dates are given in *Fasti Ecclesiae Scoticanae*.
10 J. Bruce, *The Aberdeen pulpit and universities* (Aberdeen, 1844), p. 12.
11 *Register of General Session*, vol. 50, 12 January 1846.
12 Gammie, op. cit., p. 215. The chapels-of-ease were run by managers generally drawn from the parish church. Although they did not possess kirk sessions many were financially self-sufficient and had the right to appoint their own minister.
13 Ibid., p. 222.
14 Ibid., p. 149.
15 Ibid., pp. 92-3.
16 See ch. 8, pp. 195, 197.
17 Gammie, op. cit., p. 17.
18 Ibid., pp. 19-20.
19 Ibid., p. 32.
20 Ibid., p. 17.
21 *Est. Presb.*, 20 February 1844.
22 See Biographical Notes.
23 The attitudes of the clergy towards temperance societies provide an interesting example. All the clergy denounced intemperance, but some also condemned the temperance reformers as 'enemies of Christ' who put their temperance before the gospel. Murray of the North Church preached that 'the devil was the author of the Total Abstinence Societies'. Other ministers, such as Longmuir and Simpson, were active supporters of these societies; Simpson being described by Bruce as 'a ring-leader among the tee-totallers who infest this town'. See A. S. Cook, *Pen sketches and reminiscences* (Aberdeen, 1901), pp. 4-6, 20-1; Bruce, op. cit., pp. 72-3; report of the committee on temperance societies, *Est. Presb.*, 3 May 1842.
24 Extract from unpublished autobiography of Dr Foote, minister of the East Church in 1843. Reprinted in W. Alexander, *Free East Church reminiscences* (Aberdeen, 1893), p. 13.
25 Ibid.
26 Report in *Aberdeen Herald*, 11 March 1843.
27 The *Banner* (post-Disruption), *passim*. See also ch. 5.
28 *Selected portions from the diary and manuscripts of the Rev. Gavin Parker* (Aber-

deen, 1848), 1 June 1843. See the letter from Rev. A. L. Gordon, *Est. Presb.*, vol. 13, 28 March 1843.

29 See general discussion of this feature in W. Ferguson, *Scotland: 1689 to the present* (Edinburgh, 1968).

30 See ch. 5, pp. 104

31 *Est. Gen. Sess.*, vol. 50, 1 May 1843.

32 *Est. Greyf. Sess.*, 11 January and 1 February 1843.

33 The entire sum of a bequest, which had been made for the poor of the congregation some five years previously, was distributed. *Est. Trin. Sess.*, 9 June 1843.

34 *Est. Greyf. Sess.*, 3 May 1843.

35 See ch. 5, pp. 105-7.

36 Alexander, op. cit., pp. 7, 13.

37 *Selected portions from the diary and manuscripts of the Rev. Gavin Parker*, 31 December 1842 and 1 May 1843.

38 M. Angus, *Sheriff Watson of Aberdeen* (Aberdeen, 1913), p. 50.

39 R. M. W. Cowan, *The newspaper in Scotland* (Glasgow, 1946), p. 149. See also ch. 1, pp. 20-1.

40 Cowan, op. cit., p. 149.

41 *Aberdeen Herald*, 28 January, 11 February and 4 March 1843.

42 Ibid., 11 March 1843.

43 Ibid., 1 April 1843.

44 Ibid., 8 April 1843.

45 Ibid., 15 April 1843.

46 Ibid., 6 May 1843.

47 Ibid., 15 April 1843.

48 Ibid., 3 June 1843.

49 See ch. 5, p. 101, and Biographical Notes.

50 By 1850 consideration was given to the possibility of suppressing both churches or reducing them to preaching stations without a regular minister, but neither of these proposals was implemented. *Free Presb.*, vol. 1, 5 March, 16 July 1850.

51 *Est. Presb.*, vol. 13, 30 August 1843.

52 *Free Trin. Sess.*, 'Origins and history', p. 20.

53 For more detailed account see ch. 5, pp. 110-11.

54 *Free Trin. Sess.*, p. 19. *Est. Presb.*, vol. 13, 1 March 1844.

55 *Est. Presb.*, vol. 13, 19 June 1844; 27 April 1846. *Est. Gen. Sess.*, vol. 50, 12 January 1846.

56 *Est. Presb.*, vol. 13, 20 February, 3 May and 18 September 1844.

57 Ibid., 23 November and 21 December 1843.

58 Ibid., 30 August 1843. At a meeting on 4 June 1844 the stipend was fixed at £150.

59 Ibid., 20 February 1844.

60 Ibid., 3 May 1844.

61 Ibid., 6 August, 9 October 1844; 31 March 1845.

62 *Est. Gen. Sess.*, vol. 50, 12 January 1846.

63 The minister and ten elders seceded leaving only one member of the session. Thereafter the session was made up of a mixed group of elders from the West and St Clement's sessions, who attended infrequently and by February

1844 there was difficulty in forming a quorum. Elders were appointed towards the end of 1845: *Est. Greyf. Sess.*, 7 August and 5 September 1843; 5 February 1844; 11 September 1845.

64 R. Rait and G. S. Pryde, *Scotland* (London, 1954), p. 267.
65 *Aberdeen Herald*, 10 June 1843; *Est. Presb.*, vol. 13, 12 October and 19 December 1843.
66 See ch. 4, pp. 78-9.
67 See ch. 5, pp. 114-15.
68 See Appendix E(i).
69 See Appendix F.
70 See Appendix E(ii).
71 See Appendix E(iii).
72 James Martin, *Eminent divines in Aberdeen and the north* (Aberdeen, 1888), p. 181.
73 Angus, op. cit., pp. 43-4.

Chapter 4

An Analysis of Denominational Adherence

Dry leaves and new shoots.[*]

In Chapter 3 a significant trend was detected in the Disruption eldership with regard to the pattern of adherence to the Established and Free Churches. The support of the lower middle-class grouping for the Free Church was crucial in six sessions. In these churches the secession was so great that the Establishment were obliged to abandon permanently five of the charges soon after the Disruption and in the other—Trinity where they had a nucleus of support—to relinquish the charge at a later date. So great was the middle-class secession in three other charges —Gilcomston, Holburn, and John Knox—that although the congregations survived there were insufficient members of the necessary social status to form kirk sessions until 1852, 1867, and 1880 respectively.

In the six city parishes (*quoad civilia*) the Establishment came near to losing Greyfriars and North where, as we shall see, there was a marked shortage of eldership material after 1843. Indeed, although the Establishment recovered fairly quickly, secession was heavy in all but the wealthiest West Church congregation. However, to gauge the impact of the secession on the Establishment, and to understand the development of the Free Church after 1843, it is necessary to widen and to deepen the analysis to gain both a chronological and societal perspective. It is necessary to study not only the pattern of adherence as it was crystallised in 1843 but to look at the changes in social composition of the eldership which occurred in the years before and after the Disruption. By doing this one can sharpen the apparent social differences between the two groups in 1843 and reach a better understanding of what the divisions along the lines of status and seniority really entailed outwith the limits of analysing the static situation at the point of the actual schism.

It is the purpose of this chapter, therefore, to examine the pattern of denominational adherence within each kirk session where comparisons are possible, namely the six parish churches of West, South, East, North, St Clement's, and Greyfriars; and Trinity Church—the only *quoad sacra* parish where the remnant elders who adhered to the Establishment can be traced. All serving elders of these churches will

[*] M. Angus, *Sheriff Watson of Aberdeen* (Aberdeen, 1913), pp. 43-4. (Sheriff Watson's own words.)

be examined over the period from about 1831 to 1861.[1] These men will be dealt with in three main sections. The first section—'The Non-participants and the Uncommitted'—will look at those elders who ceased serving on the kirk sessions before the Disruption, and in the event itself did not commit themselves to either serving on the Established or Free kirk session. The second section deals with the pattern of adherence with regard to the 'Loyalists'; that is those elders who adhered to the Establishment in 1843 as well as those men who were co-opted to serve on the Established kirk sessions in the eight years following the Disruption. The third section deals with the pattern of adherence with regard to the 'Seceders'—those who went over to the Free Church at the Disruption as well as those who were elected to office in the eight years following. However, because of significant differences in the pattern of adherence in two of the kirk sessions— St Clement's and the East—these will be dealt with as entities. In the latter case of the East the analysis will include a discussion of the role of the minister in determining the pattern of denominational adherence on the kirk sessions.

The Non-participants and the Uncommitted

The increasing polarisation of the rival groups on the kirk sessions in the years before the Disruption did not lead to the emergence of a coherent 'middle' party which shunned the heightening conflict. In only one session—the East—can one detect elements of such a manifestation, and in only one session—Greyfriars—can one confirm *active* non-participation in that elders resigned and moved to another congregation. By far the greatest number of non-participants, and to a lesser degree perhaps the uncommitted, failed to align themselves to one or other group by reason of death or the frailty of old age.

Between 1831 and 1843 ten elders ceased serving on the West kirk session and of these as many as eight would appear to have died.[2] The two elders who could be described as non-participants were both wealthy members of families long established in the area and possessing country estates. Duncan Davidson had been admitted to the Society of Advocates as far back as 1794, and although he retired from the kirk session before 1836 he was still living at his country seat in 1845. The other elder, Alexander Duthie, was connected to the family firm of shipbuilders at Footdee. He left the session some time between 1838 and 1842 and was still alive in 1851. When the Disruption took place a further two elders in the West Church did not commit themselves to either the Established or Free sessions. Both men were in retirement several years before 1843 and may have died about that time as they cannot be traced after that date. Robert Forbes had been a teacher at the Grammar School (the rector, James Melvin, was an elder of the same session), and George McNaughton had been a partner in the old-established firm of Gordon, Barron & Co. Both men had been ordained before 1831. All four of these men were, as we shall see, typical members of an Established kirk session. Three were members of families with roots in the city going back to the eighteenth century and if Forbes's origins are less clear he was nevertheless associated with the oldest school in the city. Certainly all four were old men, ordained before 1831, and by 1840 in semi- or total retirement. Only two can be traced after 1843 as being alive and one, Davidson, must have been an octogenarian. Indeed in all four cases it would not seem unreasonable to see non-participation as resulting from the frailty of old age rather than a lack of commitment.

In the South kirk session the question of non-participation does not arise. Between 1831 and 1842 the session lost twelve members. Seven left in 1834 to serve with Trinity kirk session when that church was raised to a *quoad sacra* parish with its own session.[3] The other five would all have appeared to have died by 1842.[4] At the Disruption no elder remained uncommitted. The same was true of Trinity kirk session. Of the five elders who ceased serving between its inception in 1834 and the Disruption, all died before 1839 with the notable exception of one who was deposed in 1840 for 'unlawful intercourse with an unmarried woman belonging to the Episcopal church'.[5] Likewise in the North kirk session the evidence suggests that the three elders who ceased serving did so by reason of death.[6]

The remaining three kirk sessions—Greyfriars, St Clement's, and East—all exhibit distinctive patterns related to circumstances peculiar to each church or congregation. Although Greyfriars kirk session lost only five elders in the years before 1842 the circumstances concerning their removal tends to some extent to substantiate the claim by the Established Presbytery after 1843 that the real crisis in Greyfriars did not occur at the Disruption but was precipitated by the actions of the minister and certain elders in the years preceding it. Unfortunately, from the point of view of identification, three of the five elders who left the session bore the name 'Smith' and none can be positively identified.[7] Nevertheless there are clear links between two of the

Smiths and the East parish where one became an elder in 1838 and another probably was co-opted following the Disruption. The other two non-participants left Greyfriars session before 1836 and it seems probable that they had died about the time of the Disruption. Again there is evidence to suggest that one at least joined the East parish congregation. At the Disruption one elder remained uncommitted[8]—a retired small shopkeeper whose allegiance was not claimed by either the Established or Free sessions. He died before 1850.

The drift of elders from Greyfriars to the East parish was indicative of peculiarities inherent in the East congregation and the conduct of its minister. As we shall see later these factors had a profound effect in determining a more complex pattern of denominational adherence.[9] However, as far as non-participation was concerned, in the East parish no less than seventeen elders ordained before 1831 had left the session by 1842. Thirteen of these had ceased serving by 1836—as far as can be ascertained seven had died and the other six had left to join former chapels-of-ease which had been raised to *quoad sacra* status.[10] The remaining four, therefore, were the only real non-participants in the East kirk session. It seems likely that two of these men died or left the city shortly after 1843. The other two, however, were still alive in 1851 although they were not serving members of kirk sessions of either denomination.[11] At the Disruption itself a further four elders remained uncommitted.[12] It is an interesting and important feature of these eight elders who left before 1843 or remained uncommitted at the Disruption, that at least seven lived west of the Denburn area.[13] In this feature the East parish pattern differed significantly from the other sessions and the matter will be discussed at some length later in this chapter.

Finally there remains St Clement's kirk session where a high degree of occupational integration and relative geographic isolation were to play their part in determining a differing pattern of denominational adherence at the Disruption.[14] Two elders ceased serving before the Disruption—and it seems likely that both had died. At the Disruption three remained uncommitted; at least one of whom survived until after 1851.[15]

What emerges from this brief study of non-participation and non-commitment in these kirk sessions is that, on the whole, relatively few elders either quietly withdrew before 1843 or 'sat on the fence' in the event of the Disruption. (Some of the reasons for this remarkable denominational polarisation are analysed in Chapter 5.) Certainly one or two elders withdrew from the rancour of the Greyfriars session and took refuge in the East parish where the conflict would appear to have been less intense. It seems likely by doing so they themselves in fact contributed to the development of the Disruption alignments in both parishes. Generally, however, the loss of elders from the kirk sessions before the Disruption was largely the result of death, or in some cases old age.

As we shall see in the immediately following sections, 'fence-sitting' weakened the Establishment rather than the Free Church. If lack of commitment demonstrated doubts as to the claims of the seceders it had far more serious consequences for the Establishment confronted by the necessity of replacing the elders who had seceded and finding a near total deficiency of eldership material in some congregations. Ironically death also favoured the Free Church for it removed from kirk session membership the older statesmen who, statistically at least, would have adhered to the Establishment.

The Pattern of Adherence

1 The Loyalists

The West Parish The West Church, the senior parish of the city, was commonly described as the 'high church'. This was an apt title—reflecting as it did the high social status of its elders and congregation. In the Disruption years it was a citadel of the Establishment against the flood of non-intrusion. Certainly it was the congregation in which the seceders made least impact; the only congregation in fact where a majority of elders adhered to the Establishment. Although the minister took eight of the kirk session into the Free Church, fourteen remained to provide—with one or two others—the backbone of the Establishment in the critical years after the massive secessions in 1843.

Of the remaining eleven elders who were still members of the kirk session in 1851 a remarkable feature was their residential clustering. Only two men—James Edmond and John Whyte—lived west of the Denburn valley; one lived in a mansion outside the city; the remaining seven lived on the east side of the Denburn in the streets running off the east end of Union Street, particularly in Adelphi Court. Edmond and Whyte, moreover, had business premises in that area. All eleven men represented a cross-section of eminent middle-class families of long standing in the area. Seven were senior members of the session. All were professional men, or business-men dealing in high-class consumer goods. Alexander Cadenhead had become a member of the Society of Advocates as far back as 1809; James Edmond more recently in 1821. George Lyall was a silk mercer, and John Whyte a woollen draper—both firms being appointed to Her Majesty and Prince Albert. David Chalmers was owner-editor of the conservative *Aberdeen Journal*. George Henry was senior partner in an old-established firm of iron-mongers. William Walker was the owner of a high-class family grocers and wine merchants, with several branches in the town. The leading educational, medical, and financial institutions were also represented: James Melvin was rector of the Grammar School: William Laing the consulting surgeon at the Royal Infirmary; Arthur Thomson a stock-broker, and agent for the Bank of Scotland. Alexander Johnston was a country gentleman.

Of these fourteen, only three men—Thomas Blaikie, John Suther-land, and Robert Taylor—had ceased serving on the session by 1851. Sutherland and Taylor were still alive in 1847 but cannot be traced thereafter. Both were long-serving elders and it seems likely that they had died or left the city in retirement. Unfortunately Sutherland cannot be positively identified. Taylor had certainly given up his partnership in a music-selling business by 1851. Thomas Blaikie, on the other hand, was still very much alive in 1851. A member of a prominent and long-established family, he had extensive business and financial interests in the city. His elder brother, James Blaikie, had been an elder in the West Church until his death in 1836 and lord provost of the city between 1833 and 1836. He had been in a law partnership with Patrick Banner-man of the well-known Bannerman family. Thomas was a partner in his father's business—John Blaikie & Sons, and a partner-founder in his own firm—Blaikie Brothers. He played a leading part in obtaining the extensive redevelopment of the harbour and the harbour area, as well as various railway schemes. He was lord provost from 1839 to 1846 and 1853 to 1855. Not surprisingly he was not an active member of the session either before or after 1843 and his retirement from the West Church session would appear to coincide with his resignation from the town council in 1846 when certain sweeping city improvements which he had strongly advocated were rejected.

A feature which persisted was the marked reluctance of these families to move out of the old residential areas of the town across the Denburn divide into the new terraced houses being built in Crown Street, Dee Street, Bonaccord Street, Union Place and other areas of the west side. By 1861 most of these men still clung to the general area around

Adelphi Court although some had inherited or purchased country estates. Chalmers had an estate at Westburn and continued to use his town house at 13 Adelphi. Edmond had moved his business premises to a few doors away. Although Cadenhead had moved out of Adelphi to an estate at Seafield, Walker had moved into the house at 3 Adelphi Court. Lyall continued to live round the corner on Union Street throughout the period 1831-61 and no more than a stone's throw away lived Thomson in Castle Street. Laing had moved just across the Denburn from Belmont Street to Golden Square, but Melvin had moved into a house close to the one in Belmont Street quitted by Laing. Henry continued to live in his Gallowgate house until about 1860 when he moved to Rubislaw on the outskirts of the city. He died a few years later.

Whatever the social ties which bound these families to the same residential areas, it seems likely that, in these days before the introduction of the telephone, close residential proximity must have been a considerable asset in the conduct of business affairs. Certainly beneath the obvious ties of residential association there was woven a complex net of interlocking family and business interests binding these men even closer to one another. Many of these family and business ties must have been based on their understanding and implicit agreements. Below the great joint speculative ventures of the Blaikie and Bannerman families which already have been remarked upon, there lay a great number of smaller undertakings linked by kin and financial arrangements. The Cadenhead, Simpson, and Whyte families provide an excellent example of this process at work within the West Church eldership. By a series of complex partnerships and financial assistance these families furthered each other's interests over several generations.[16]

It was some four years after the Disruption before new men were co-opted on to the kirk session to replace the elders who had seceded. The eight men brought into service between 1847 and 1851 bore a striking similarity in life style to the eldership which had co-opted them. Although some of these new elders had recently taken up residence in the new west end the business, social, and professional ties with the existing session were strong. David Kerr, George J. Nicol, and Francis Ogston were medical practitioners associated professionally with William Laing, consultant surgeon, of the existing session. Kerr was a lecturer in surgery at the university and lived only a few doors from Laing. Nicol lived in the house immediately next to the house formerly occupied by Laing in Belmont Street. Ogston lived in Adelphi Court and was a member of the long-established local firm of soap and tallow manufacturers of the same name. William Bain was manager of the City of Glasgow Bank and lived in Castle Street—a neighbour of Arthur Thomson (of the existing session) who was an insurance broker and agent for Lloyds and the Bank of Scotland. James Black and James Burgess were in business together. Although they had both moved across the Denburn to the west side by 1851, Burgess was still living in Adelphi Court adjacent to their business premises in 1847, at about which time the firm claimed to be 'stock, share, and produce brokers, and forwarding agents to H.R.H. the Duchess of Kent'. As has already been noted two members of the existing session—Lyall and Whyte—claimed to be the Queen's silk mercer and 'clothier to Her Majesty and Prince Albert' respectively. Of the two remaining new elders Alexander Burness was a retired wholesale grocer and provision merchant formerly with premises at 7 Adelphi Court near William Walker (of the same trade and of the existing session), who lived at 3 Adelphi Court. James Brebner was an advocate and agent for various London assurance companies. Although he was one of the four who lived west of the Denburn he had only recently moved from Marischal Street (adjoining Castle Street and near Adelphi Court) where he had lived since before 1831. Of the eight new men only one appears to have had previous service as an elder.[17] As we shall see this was not the case in other Established kirk sessions where elders long since retired from active participation on the session were recalled to service. Indeed what was remarkable about the West kirk session was its ability to co-opt men of similar social standing as themselves albeit four years after the Disruption. In most of the other Established kirk sessions there was a marked shortage of eldership material in the years following 1843.

The South Parish Measured in terms of the liberality of the congregation and the social status of its kirk session the South Church followed the West in order of prosperity. The session was relatively small in 1843 (thirteen members), but the proportion of high to low status elders was similar to that of the West, although the elders themselves were socially less eminent in the community. At the Disruption the kirk session divided almost equally—six remained and seven seceded. The congregational secession was heavy, however—certainly more substantial than in the West Church—and it is clear from the sort of elders co-opted to replace the seceding session members that the younger and more vigorous elements of the congregation had gone over to the Free Church. This was clearly not the case in the seceding South Free congregation and it is obvious that the Establishment went through a critical period of shortage with regard to suitable eldership material of the sort remarked upon above. Certainly the six elders who remained loyal in 1843 were of fairly advanced years. Three of them had ceased serving on the session by 1847 and only one can be traced after that date. Robert Ragg, a paper manufacturer, had been a very infrequent attender in the years before the Disruption and his allegiance to the Establishment would appear to be little more than nominal in 1843. It seems likely that he died about the same time as John Dunn, a merchant tailor. On the other hand, David Gill—in business as a painter and glazier—was still alive although he had been ordained before 1831. All three had business and residential associations with the Netherkirkgate-Gallowgate area in the old part of the city.

The other three South parish loyalists still serving in 1851 were also old men. George Birnie—a 'foreign merchant'—had been in semi-retirement when he was ordained in 1833 and by 1841 he had retired to an estate outside the city. The remaining two elders, James Ferguson and Alexander Webster, were lawyers of long standing, admitted to the Society of Advocates as far back as 1816 and 1794 respectively. Both had business and residential associations east of the Denburn.

Following the Disruption ten men were co-opted to the session to replace those who had seceded or later died. The five who were co-opted in 1844 show just how hard pressed the session was to find suitable candidates. William Paterson was a leather merchant who had been ordained as far back as 1799 and who presumably had retired from active sessional activity some time in the 1820s. George Sim, a customs clerk, came from St Clement's parish and had been ordained in 1817. William Reid, a teacher, came from the near-defunct Trinity parish where he had been ordained in 1835. John Simpson was a wright—he died in 1850; and Peter Williamson was a druggist who outlived all the others by about nine years to die in 1859. None of these men lived in the fashionable areas west of the Denburn although Paterson did have a country estate. The men co-opted after 1847 followed a similar pattern. One was a retired army surgeon who had been an elder in the parish before 1831; two were advocates—one had been admitted to the Society of Advocates about thirty-five years earlier; one ran a blacksmith's business; and finally an elder who, in a sense, typified the life style of the South Church loyalists—Thomas Melville, head of an old but thriving family firm of ironmongers. He lived throughout his life on the business premises despite the obvious prosperity of the firm. All five, with the exception of the blacksmith, died before 1860.[18]

The startling dissimilarity between the life styles of the loyalists and the seceding elders can only be brought into focus by studying the pattern of adherence in the Free churches. Before doing this, however, it is necessary to complete the analysis of loyalist support in Trinity, North, and Greyfriars parishes. Certain peculiarities in the East and St Clement's parishes make a separate treatment necessary in their cases.

Trinity, North, and Greyfriars Parishes These three parishes can be considered together simply because of the similarity of the problems faced by the Establishment in each case, largely resulting from the heavy secession which took place. The Establishment came close to losing all three parishes permanently and in the case of Trinity it became necessary finally to abandon the charge. Out of the three kirk sessions only four elders of the existing sessions remained loyal. Two of them came from Trinity: Alexander Nisbet, a mason, and William Reid, a schoolteacher. Reid was later co-opted to the South kirk session as we have seen. No members of the remaining congregation could be found who were considered of sufficient moral and social status for the eldership. The two loyalists of the North and Greyfriars kirk sessions were remarkably similar in socio-economic terms. In the North session William Reid was a retired partner in an old-established firm of ship-builders which also had ship-owning interests. Although retired from business he continued to live in the harbour area. In Greyfriars the loyalist elder again typified the life style of the Established elder. George Thomson was a member of an old local family with mercantile and shipping interests. Like Reid he continued to live in the harbour area, near his premises and in the same house throughout the period under study.

Once again it is clear from the men brought into service on these sessions to replace those who had seceded, just how hard pressed the Establishment were to find men of eldership potential. In the North only three could be found: a retired farmer, a shoemaker living on his premises, and one man who cannot be identified.[19] In Greyfriars two years elapsed before six men were co-opted: a retired shipmaster, a small shopkeeper, a tobacconist living above his premises, a blacksmith, a clerk, and a retired businessman.[20] All the new elders in both North and Greyfriars lived east of the Denburn in the older parts of the city. There is no question at all that force of circumstances was the primary force behind the co-option of men of such low socio-economic status. When the fortunes of Greyfriars underwent a sudden and dramatic improvement around 1850 (partly as a result of the collapse of Grey-

friars Free Church) men of a very different sort were co-opted to
eldership.[21]

2 The Seceders

Whilst age clearly was a significant factor to be considered in determining patterns of denominational adherence it would be very misleading
to interpret alignments at the Disruption simply in terms of the
perennial youth/age dichotomy. There is no valid comparison between
the adolescent youth and his conflict with authority in the 1970s, and
the 'young shoots' of the 1840s who challenged authority in the
control of church affairs. The seceding eldership may have been generally younger than their loyalist counterparts nevertheless they possessed
all the experience, maturity, and indeed conservatism, associated with
men of their age group—men who were approaching or who had
reached the middle years of life. Indeed the most outstanding characteristics of the seceders, negatively defined as a dissimilarity with their
counterparts who remained in the Establishment, could only be linked
with a youth/age conflict analysis in the most mechanistic fashion. The
staidness, stability, security, and deep-rooted social origins of the
loyalists, contrasted vividly with the seceders' rapid social mobility,
with their eagerness to move across the Denburn at the first opportunity, with the ease by which they demonstrated their wealth
by continually changing houses and business premises, and with
their ability to enlarge and diversify and sometimes dramatically
change the nature of their business interests. However, if this sort of
social dynamism was a general characteristic of the seceding eldership,
and the men elected to the Free kirk sessions after the Disruption,
support did come for the Free Church from some of the older long-
serving elders although these men were less socially eminent in the
community.

Free West Church The greater 'social mix' of the seceding eldership
can be seen in the adherence to the Free Church in the West parish.
Of the eight seceders two were long-serving members of the session.
Both died a few years after the Disruption and, unlike their long-serving
loyalist counterparts, neither was prominent in the city.[22] Two of the
remainder were professional men. Francis Edmond was a young
advocate and younger brother of James Edmond, who was a loyalist.
Both brothers became leading members of their respective churches.
John Macrobin was a professor of medicine who although seceding
refused to accept office in the Free West for fear of endangering his

university post. The one common feature which distinguishes all of these men (and the four yet to be discussed) was the fact that they all lived west of the Denburn in the newly developed area of Crown Street, Dee Street, Bonaccord Street, or further west in the Albyn Place-Carden Place development. However, it is in the remaining four elders that one can most easily isolate the social characteristics of the Free Church eldership.

It is an interesting feature of the Free Church eldership that one of the occupations most closely identified with their rapid mobility was that of commission agent or commission merchant. It was an occupation which clearly demonstrated that, at least in the nineteenth century, small beginnings could lead to great things. It was an occupation requiring no specific qualifications, no entry fees, no fixed capital, and on a small scale relatively little liquid capital, and under no restriction from guild or incorporated trades societies. It was an occupation requiring considerable business acumen, as well as the ability to amass knowledge of where goods were to be obtained, and to glean information as to who would be willing to purchase. A man could start up in a small way operating from his own home or a small office with a limited area of interests. These interests could, however, be changed or diversified into other areas according to changing sources of supply and altering demands of the market.

At least three of the seceding elders in the West Church were commission agents: Neil Smith, jun., John Smith, and Alexander Thom. Neil Smith set up on his own behalf as a commission agent in 1837. He then lived in the Gallowgate. Within four years he had moved to a new house in Bonaccord Street. Between 1831 and 1861 he moved his house or premises on no less than nine occasions. By 1840 he was the agent for a number of ships and soon he diversified his interests to include insurance broking. Before 1852 he had become a director of the Aberdeen Fire and Life Assurance Company, and had also formed another company with premises in Marischal Street—at that time the centre of the city's principal finance houses. John Smith was one of the two long-serving elders who seceded. It is not clear whether or not he was related to Neil Smith although he certainly set himself up in business about the same time. Formerly an auctioneer living in the east end, by 1842 John Smith had his own premises, and a house in Dee Street. Alexander Thom, on the other hand, had formerly been a surveyor of taxes. He set up in business with his brother William (later an elder in East Free) about the same time as the Smiths. The business prospered and by 1851 he had occupied three houses in select areas west of the Denburn. About 1846 he had also been appointed Belgian consul in the city.

The other two seceding elders were Alexander Leslie, and Alexander Low. The latter was manager of a firm of woollen manufacturers in 1835, but within a few years he had become a partner in the enterprise and moved out of his Gallowgate house into the fashionable west end. Alexander Leslie was rather different from the others. He appeared to owe his income to colonial ventures—the family fortune being built in Jamaica. It is possible, although completely speculative, that Leslie may have been involved in providing finance for some of the other seceders' business enterprises. Certainly although he does not appear to have had any occupation he was successful in making his money work. By 1861, although continuing to live in Bonaccord Terrace, he had also purchased an estate at Banchory.

A remarkable feature of the seven men elected to eldership in the Free West in the year after the Disruption was the fact that only two of them had not seen previous service on other kirk sessions, and at most only three were derived from the original seceding congregation. This phenomenon is more important than it might at first appear as it illustrates the kind of problem which was to determine the development of the Free Church generally after the Disruption.[23] The three elders from the seceding congregation were: John Macrobin who now considered his university post secure (see p. 79); David Mitchell—a young lawyer recently admitted to the Society of Advocates; and James Aiken, a retired man who later became the church missionary. It would perhaps not be too harsh to speculate that the elders who came from the other city congregations were more ambitious than pious. John McLaren had a remarkable career which followed a similar pattern to that of Neil Smith and Thom of the seceding elders. A flesher in 1837, living in a street described as 'the very centre of slum-land, and the abode of all manner of evil characters',[24] McLaren became a commission agent and within five years had moved to Crown Street. A few years later he again moved house, to Dee Street. John McLaren had been ordained elder in Greyfriars parish in 1840 despite spirited protests from members of that congregation who had threatened to take the matter to the city presbytery.[25] Two of the other elders elected to the Free West were tax collectors: James McLaren (he would appear to be an elder brother) also from Greyfriars, and William Brown, an elder from the North parish. The other elder elected in 1844 was John Catto, also from Greyfriars. He had interests in shipping and insurance.

One does not have to look far for reasons why these men were attracted to the Free West. Three of the elders came from Greyfriars kirk session—a congregation with a record of internal strife which, if anything, was exacerbated by the Disruption. Within ten years Greyfriars Free Church was bankrupt and the church building had to be sold and certainly much of the blame must be laid upon those elders who deserted the congregation in the critical years after 1843.[26] Their attraction to the Free West cannot be given much credit. Following the Disruption the Free West found itself playing the role of the 'high church' in the Free Presbytery as indeed the West Church was in the Establishment. Membership of the Free West Church held considerable attractions to ambitious men. It was said at the time that 'the height of a merchant's ambition in Aberdeen was a house in Crown Street and a seat in the Free West Church.'[27] Many of these men had already achieved a fashionable residence—it was but a short step to seek control over the most fashionable church. It was also the case that the seceding elders from the West parish were probably glad to receive them. Whilst eight elders had seceded only two were senior members—both of advanced years—and one elder's allegiance (Macrobin) was uncertain. There was a need for men of proven capacity and if these men were also prosperous their presence on the session was all the more desirable.[28] The need for such men was not of course peculiar to the Free Church—what was different was that the Free West found it necessary to recruit suitable elders from outside their own seceding congregation.

South Free Church Of the seven elders who seceded from the South parish five exhibit to varying degrees the characteristics associated with seceding as opposed to loyalist members. Robert Brown, the only long-serving elder to secede, had worked his way up in a firm of wine merchants to become a partner in the business. Of these five elders he alone continued to live east of the Denburn. George Yeats was a silk mercer who occupied three different houses and two different business premises between 1831 and 1841, finally settling in Crown Street. John Hay was a carver and gilder who lived next-door to his business premises in 1831. Before 1841 he had expanded his interests to include optical instruments and plate glass and had erected an additional warehouse and workshops. By the latter date he had moved out to a house at Broomhill. James Abernethy was the elder son of a family business of ironfounding which in this same period underwent similar expansion and diversification into the fields of engineering and machine-making, and later undertook work as blacksmiths and boilermakers. He lived in Ferryhill. William Keith was a doctor who later became surgeon at the Royal Infirmary and a lecturer at the university. He lived in the west end of Union Street.

No less than fourteen new elders were ordained in South Free Church in the eight years after the Disruption. The addition of these men to the existing eldership made the South Free session the largest among the city churches in 1851. The new elders contrasted strongly with their counterparts in the Established South session introduced in these same years and certainly confirm that the younger, more vigorous middle-class sections of the congregation had seceded in 1843. Although they were a remarkable 'social mix' almost all shared the same restless energy despite their considerable occupational differences.

Of the fourteen only five had been communicants in the South Church in 1835. Two of these were small craftsmen-businessmen,[29] and three were lawyers admitted to the Society of Advocates between 1829 and 1831.[30] The three lawyers (two of whom were in partnership) occupied no less than six different business premises and twelve different houses before 1861.

Three of the other nine new elders were also members of the legal profession—one of them standing out from the others simply by the fact that he appeared to be content to remain in the same 'large dwelling-house' throughout the period.[31] One of the others, James Bryce, was a writer with a firm of law agents at the time of the Disruption and lived in a rather seedy area of the Denburn valley. Eight years later by a series of residential leapfroggings he had purchased a mansion house in Fonthill.

Of the remaining six, one was a schoolteacher (who must have been infected by the restlessness of the others as he moved house four times) and the others were businessmen.[32] All lived in the west end and all to varying degrees were socially, occupationally, and residentially mobile. Two are worth singling out by way of examples. William Smart at the time of the Disruption was a clerk with a firm of family grocers. He rose rapidly in the business and within eight years had moved from a modest house in the east end of the city to a fashionable west-end residence. John Urquhart, on the other hand, followed a different path although one closely associated as we have seen with social mobility in Free Church elders. A druggist in 1830, he was involved in a series of partnerships in the years before the Disruption. In the mid 1840s, however, he abandoned his former occupation and formed a new partnership as a commission agent and wholesale tea and coffee dealer. From the east end in 1830 he moved house on five occasions finally settling in a mansion house in the fashionable suburbs in 1860.

Trinity, North, and Greyfriars Free Churches   The pattern of adherence in Trinity and North Free churches was very similar to that of the South. Indeed the account almost reads like repetition. Of the nine elders who seceded in Trinity[33] four lived west of the Denburn, one lived in the upper Denburn itself, two moved to the west soon after the Disruption, and the two who continued to live in the east had both died by 1850.[34] The careers of the elders were also similar. One was a textile manufacturer who between 1831 and 1851 diversified his interests and expanded his premises at least five-fold. Another was an employee with a firm of rope manufacturers and rose to become manager. Thereafter he moved house three times, finally settling in Dee Street. Two other elders occupied three houses in that area in ten years, and one of them was a commission agent. Finally, one was a haberdasher, who also moved house three times, and in the course of his career, changed his business interests and formed a firm of clothiers and furnishing tailors.

As in the South Free kirk session all five of the new men elected were young in years. Each was to serve on the session for thirty years or more —one in fact was an elder for more than fifty years.[35] Four of the five were professional men and one was a businessman. All five exhibited the propensity to move into ever more fashionable houses and in the case of the businessman to alter radically and diversify his interests. One was a schoolmaster; two were young lawyers recently admitted to the Society of Advocates who between them occupied seven houses before 1861. Another was an accountant who moved house three times—again all in fashionable areas. The businessman perhaps requires special mention. A hairdresser, and son of an east-end hairdresser, he occupied two premises and three houses between 1831 and 1841—all in the east end of the city. About 1843, however, as was so typical of the seceding businessman, he changed course and converted his hairdressing premises to a wholesale and retail warehouse. Soon after, he moved into a house in the Crown Street area. Later he opened new premises and extended his interests to photography and the supplying of photographic equipment.

The secession in Trinity parish had been so heavy that the Establishment, as we have seen, were finally forced to abandon the charge. They came very near to doing so in North and Greyfriars and at one point it was suggested that the two churches which were adjacent should be conjoined although this was not acted upon.[36] In the North, of the seven elders who left the Establishment two had ceased serving on the North Free session by 1851.[37] The remaining five were a mixed social and occupational group. There was a small shopkeeper, a bank cashier, and the owner of an expanding firm of ironmongers. The other two seceding elders, and the two new members elected after the Disruption, all possessed the Free Church characteristics previously remarked upon. One began as a tea, wine and spirit dealer living in the east end of the city. Between 1831 and 1851 he built up the business by means of a partnership and considerably expanded his premises. Thereafter he entered the wholesale trade and opened an additional warehouse. Before 1846 he had occupied three houses finally settling in Crown Street. The other seceder had built up his business in a similar fashion. Beginning as a builder he extended his interests to the supply of timber and other building materials. By 1861 he described himself as an architect and had by then occupied three houses. The two new elders exhibited similar career patterns. William Birnie was a painter and glazier who expanded his interests to interior decoration. Before 1851 he had occupied three different houses and three premises. Alexander Morrice was an ironmonger in a firm which in the 1830s and 1840s underwent rapid expansion and diversification. By 1841 the firm undertook work as blacksmiths, coppersmiths, and tinsmiths, as well as ironfounding. Later additional premises were opened to undertake the manufacture of bone manure. He occupied at least five houses before finally settling in Albyn Place.

Alexander Morrice had been an elder in Greyfriars at the Disruption and left to join the North Free at about the same time as the two McLarens and Catto moved to the Free West session. Another elder, William Connon, also moved to the Free West, but was not elected to the session and declined to accept a lesser office. He had a familiar career pattern. Formerly an employee in a firm of grocers and spirit merchants, he became a partner about 1837; thereafter he moved house three times and, like Morrice, finally settled in Albyn Place. Of the other four Greyfriars seceding elders only one was still serving on the session in 1851—R. J. Brown, a university professor who lived in fashionable Golden Square. The careers of the three others was less spectacular. One was builder, one 'an agent', and one a bookbinder. All three had died or left the city by 1851.[38]

By 1851 the session consisted of only three elders, Brown and two others of low socio-economic status of whom only one can be positively identified.[39] We have already seen that the dramatic decline of

Greyfriars Free congregation was to some extent related to events in the Free West. Other factors concerned with the choice of site for the new church, and the role of the minister, will be dealt with later.[40]

Whilst the pattern of denominational adherence in the West, South, Trinity, North, and Greyfriars kirk sessions shows marked divisions along social lines, this is less the case in the two kirk sessions which remain to be discussed—St Clement's and the East. In both these churches new patterns emerge which, especially in the case of the East, require lengthier explanation. In St Clement's the reasons for the differences are much more apparent and as we shall now see are tied up with the nature of the parish itself.

St Clement's: 'A Community of Its Own'

The most distinctive feature of St Clement's parish was its close association with the seafaring trades and professions. The parish contained the harbour area, and most members of the kirk session were drawn from occupations associated with the mercantile and fishing industries, and were actually resident in the parish.[41] This situation partly resulted from the relative isolation of the parish, which was least exposed to the residential attraction of the areas west of the Denburn valley—the entire city lying between these residential developments and St Clement's parish. The area making up St Clement's parish took the form of a rough triangle enclosed by the sea on one side, the river on the south side, and the largely working-class sections of the North and East parishes on the city side. The high occupational integration of the parish, largely centred on the old fishing village of Footdee, tended to increase this relative isolation as the parishioners looked to the sea for their livelihood rather than the industrial centres of the city which lay outside the parish. Likewise, whilst the business interests of elders in the other parishes tended to overlap and interlock with elders outwith their own particular session this was not the case in St Clement's where such interests tended to be confined within the parish itself. The site of St Clement's Parish Church is in fact illustrative of the inward-looking orientation of the community. Whilst all the other parish churches lay close to one another in the centre of the city—and on the periphery of their particular parish—St Clement's Church was situated in the middle of its own parish.

At the beginning of the twentieth century it was lamented that St Clement's district was not what it had been and that migration had scattered church members throughout the city weakening their bonds of association with the parish church. It was a cause for regret that 'we are far from the days when the Church of St Clement's was in the heart of a community of its own, and readily found a response from the fishers of Footdee, whom it was primarily designed to serve'.[42] In 1843, however, St Clement's was still a community on its own— within the city but apart from it and still largely protected from the forces which were at work in the other city parishes. This is revealed to a considerable extent when one studies the social base of denominational adherence where, in fact, no marked dissimilarity is apparent.

We have already seen that three elders remained uncommitted at the Disruption—all three worked in occupations associated with the parish.[43] This was also true of the four elders who remained loyal to the Establishment: one was a customs clerk, one a fisherman, one a shipping company manager, and one a ship agent.[44] Only the ship agent was serving on the session by 1851. The six new men ordained after 1843 followed the same occupational pattern. There was an engineer, a ship-master, a baker, a clerk, a grocer and ship chandler—all of whom lived in the parish—and one man who has not been occupationally identified.[45] Of these six new elders only two were still serving in 1851. This heavy loss of post-Disruption elders must be put down to the un-savoury publicity surrounding the deposition of the St Clement's minister and the fairly substantial legal costs that elders were expected to pay towards the deposition proceedings.[46]

Of the nine elders who seceded only one did not live in or near the parish. Occupationally they were very similar to those who remained loyal. There was a ship bread baker and shipowner, a clothier and haberdasher, a master boatbuilder, a shipmaster and two men who were probably shipmasters, a shipowner, a baker, and a retired ship agent. Of the ten new elders ordained after 1843, two have not been occupationally identified, but most of the others had obvious sea-going connections and only one was clearly residentially removed from the parish.[47]

The East Parish: a Notable Exception

The East parish lay in the centre of the city and was bounded by all the other city parishes. In this parish the pattern of adherence to

Established and Free churches differed critically from all the parishes already discussed. An important feature noted earlier was the large number of non-participant elders and, at the Disruption, a proportionately higher number of elders who remained uncommitted—almost all of whom lived west of the Denburn. This same pattern is also apparent amongst the loyalist elders who, in other kirk sessions, would predictably have lived in the older residential areas east of the Denburn.

Of the five elders who remained in the Establishment all had at one time lived east of the Denburn. However, before 1841 two moved into the fashionable west end and within the next decade they were followed by another two. Only one elder—Rev. Alexander Straith, a schoolteacher—continued to live in the east. He died before 1851.

The other four were all members of well-known middle-class families. Donaldson Rose (his younger brother seceded and became an elder in East Free) was a shipowner and timber merchant. Alexander Simpson was a retired clothier closely connected in business with the Cadenhead and Whyte families who were Establishment figures of the West Church. William Melville was a partner in an old-established firm of wholesale ironmongers (his brother, Thomas, was a loyalist elder in the South Church). David Fairweather, a cabinetmaker and son of a cabinetmaker, also had interests in the importing of fine quality timber.

Whilst occupationally these elders were typical of loyalist sections in the other city parishes they were markedly different in their early move across the Denburn as compared to the members of other Established kirk sessions. This difference in the East parish becomes even more apparent when one looks at the men co-opted to replace the elders who had seceded. In the eight years after the Disruption ten new men were introduced. They were Francis J. Cochran, a member of the Society of Advocates since 1831; John Galen and William Leslie who were both medical practitioners; William Lumsden, a grocer and spirit merchant; David Marshall and William Webster who were both tradesmen shopkeepers—the one a painter and glazier, the other a baker; James Middleton whose occupation has not been traced; William Reid, a ship and insurance broker; James Roy, jun., a seedsman and nurseryman; and John Smith who was the city architect. By 1851 not one of these men lived east of the Denburn—all were settled in the new fashionable west-end areas.

Unlike the new elders of the other Established sessions these men were all fairly young and with the exception of Smith were all engaged in business in 1861. Lumsden, Cochran, Galen and Leslie were all young members of long-established middle-class families. Middleton's origins before 1841 are unknown. Tradesmen such as Marshall and Webster were found in both Established and Free churches. Reid and Roy, however, exhibit the sort of characteristics which in other sessions were closely associated with the seceding sections. Reid carried out his business as ship and insurance broker from his house, but by 1851 he had taken premises in Marischal Street—the centre of such operations—and had occupied two houses in the Crown Street area. Roy's interests were wide. He was a seedsman, nurseryman, florist, and fruiterer, and later became an agent for paving-stones. He had two nurseries and occupied several houses—the first being a cottage attached to his nursery and his final house being Rotunda Lodge, Ferryhill.

Despite Free Church claims to the contrary[48] it is clear that the East Church held the support of many of the younger members of long-standing families as well as some of the newer and vigorous elements making their way upwards in middle-class society—elements which tended in other sessions to be committed to the Free Church.

With regard to the seceding elders from the East kirk session it seems likely that about half were of advanced years. Certainly four of these men were no longer serving on the session by 1851, namely, Arthur Dingwall Fordyce, jun., an advocate and member of a well-known family possessing several country seats; Alexander Martin, a clothier and haberdasher; and William Beattie and Alexander Smith whose occupations have not been traced. It is significant that all four, as far as can be ascertained, had died before 1851. Smith had been ordained in Greyfriars parish before 1831, and Fordyce and Martin had served in the East parish for as long a period. Beattie had been ordained in 1836.

The four elders who were still serving on the session in 1851 were William Henderson, James Ledingham, William Rettie, and John Ross. Ledingham was a schoolteacher and Ross was a civil servant. Rettie was a younger partner in an old-established firm of lamp manufacturers which throughout the period greatly expanded its premises and diversified its interests to include silverware, jewellery, and watches. Rettie lived in fashionable Bonaccord Street as early as 1831 and moved house on several occasions in the next two decades. Rettie's father (senior partner in the firm) was an elder in North Free Church. The other seceding elder was William Henderson, a builder. Like Rettie, Henderson continually extended his interests and the scale of his operations. By 1861 he was head of a firm described as 'architects and builders' and with three premises in the town. The Disruption brought Henderson a great deal of work and he built a large number of low-cost churches in the highland areas to the specifications of the General Assembly for the Free Church. In 1841 Henderson had lived on his premises. Ten years later he lived in one of the most fashionable houses in Carden Place.

Of the six seceding elders who have been identified two lived east of the Denburn in 1851—Ledingham and Ross. Ross occupied five houses in the old areas of the city between 1831 and 1841.

Between 1843 and 1851 eight elders were ordained. They were Alexander Dingwall Fordyce, jun.—another member of the well-known local family—captain in the Royal Navy and local M.P. from 1847 to 1852; James Fraser, grocer, wine and spirit dealer; James Garden, a young lawyer admitted to the Society of Advocates in 1842; Alexander Gibb, civil engineer; Alexander Machray, superintendent at the House of Refuge; John Mitchell, builder; William Rose, a younger brother and partner of Donaldson Rose, shipowner, a loyalist elder of the East Church; William Thom, commission agent—a brother and partner of Alexander Thom, elder of the Free West.

By 1851 only two of the above lived east of the Denburn. Machray lived in the House of Refuge, and Rose continued to live in the firm's premises in Footdee until about 1861 when he moved to the family house in Golden Square. Of the others, Fordyce and Garden, each occupied at least two houses in fashionable areas west of the Denburn in the 1840s and Thom at least three. Fraser surpassed the record of any Free church elder in the city. Between 1837 and 1850 he occupied at least six houses in the fashionable west end—Bonaccord Street, Rubislaw Den, Albyn Place, a Deeside mansion, Bonaccord Street (a different house), and finally Dee Street.

A 'Timid Schismatic': the Role of the Minister

It is clear that the East Church differs critically from all the other sessions which have been examined. Unlike the West, Greyfriars, South, Trinity, and North elders there is no clearly discernible trend in the pattern of adherence to either denomination. In these other sessions a distinction can be made between the elders belonging to long-standing middle-class families, pursuing staid professional or commercial occupations, and tending to 'cluster' in the old residential areas of the city; and the elders belonging to a 'new' and emerging middle class, prepared to switch occupations or diversify and expand their business interests, and generally in line with the expansion of these interests to occupy any number of houses in the new residential areas developing west of the Denburn valley. In the East session, however, the pattern of adherence cut across these social distinctions and support for both denominations could be found in either social group. This was particularly the case regarding residential situations. Loyalists showed no marked reluctance to move westwards and seceders were to be found in the older residential areas. Elders co-opted after 1843 in the Established session showed that the allegiance of some of the younger and more dynamic middle class had been retained.

Whilst the differing pattern of St Clement's is readily explicable in terms of the inward-orientation of the parish resulting from its comparative isolation from the residential west end, and its peculiar occupational specialisms, it is not possible to explain the differing pattern of adherence in the East Church in such a way. The one factor, however, which is present in the East parish and absent from all the others is the character and influence of the minister—the Rev. James Foote.

In the previous chapter it was seen that Foote was a 'timid schismatic' whose decision to secede from the Establishment was reached with considerable apprehension regarding the possible social consequences.[49] Born in 1781 he had been a minister in the parish since 1824. Unlike the ministers of the West and South churches who 'vied with each other which should be the more evangelical'[50] Foote owed the respect of his congregation 'more to his character as a gentlemanly, good man in private life, than to the eloquence and ability of his preaching'.[51] He disliked the in-fighting on the Presbytery between the Evangelical and Moderate factions and though he voted with the Evangelical group he advocated conciliation rather than conflict. Prior to the Disruption he was described as 'a man readily disposed to conciliation, it may be with safety said, that if all his evangelical brethren were such as he is, we would not have got into difficulties from which we now groan to be delivered'.[52]

Foote, therefore, stood by the principle of non-intrusion believing or hoping to the last that conciliation was the best means of achieving such an end. Whilst other ministers intensified the differences between the factions by castigating those who were uncommitted and aiding the Evangelicals on the kirk session, Foote pursued an entirely different line and sought to balance the two groups. It was said at the time that 'he was strongly opposed to allowing his congregation a voice in the choice of elders'.[53] Certainly no elders were ordained after 1837 and those brought into service before that date maintained a careful balance between the two factions; this balance only being maintained by a rather drastic reduction in the number of elders from twenty-seven in 1831 to seventeen in 1843. Although in the event of the Disruption, Foote carried a majority of his session and his congregation into the Free Church by his conciliatory policy, he did leave a far greater number of uncommitted elders and presumably uncommitted congregation than was the case in any of the other churches.[54] As we have seen he also failed to carry a considerable number of the younger middle class of the congregation who after the Disruption provided the new elders for the East parish. It is somewhat paradoxical, and in some ways illuminating, that the minister who filled the place left by Foote was 'decidedly evangelical in preaching' and was one of the few outstanding non-intrusionists who remained in the Establishment.[55]

Whilst Foote's influence on the pattern of adherence in the East parish might be regarded as critical it would be wrong to see the role of the ministers generally as being of critical importance. This is not to say that the minister did not exert considerable influence on his session and congregation, but that it is evident that the extent of his success was closely related to other factors in the congregational situation. A strong evangelical preacher supported by powerful non-intrusionist elements on the session could expect considerable success. The same preacher without such support could make little headway. Indeed if the non-intrusionist elements were strong enough the role of the minister was of far less importance and a relatively weak preacher, or aged minister, could achieve an apparently high level of success in carrying the congregation over to the Free Church.

Thus we find that Simpson of Trinity Church—a fervent evangelical preacher—supported by the bulk of his session carried almost all the congregation whilst Davidson of the West Church—an equally fervent preacher—made little headway against the entrenched moderatism of the session and congregation.[56] Then again in the South Church where the minister 'had no opportunity of making any special impression'[57] there was a clear division between 'old leaves' and 'new shoots', and no elder remained uncommitted. The two ministers most directly comparable to Foote in terms of length of service—Gordon of Greyfriars and Murray of the North Church—also illustrate the same point that sessional and congregational support was the crucial factor. Gordon, a fiery and aggressive evangelical, backed by powerful members of the session, drove out the more moderate elements some of whom removed themselves to the East Church where they must have found the ministrations of Foote to be more congenial.[58] Murray, on the other hand, had been an 'evangelical at a time when there was not much of that doctrine in the town'. By 1843 he was an old man who had lost much of his fire and was specifically mentioned by the *Aberdeen Herald* as a minister who would be more careful than most about endangering his stipend by seceding.[59] Yet in both these congregations secession was virtually entire, only one elder remaining in each session.

Although committed to the principle of non-intrusion, Foote had never been a fervent evangelical. His long pastorate bridged the period known as the 'ten years' conflict' which led up to the Disruption. In the event itself he stood by his principles and left the Establishment reluctantly. A 'moderate' among evangelicals, one wonders whether, had the general climate among the ministry been less evangelical and the attacks of the *Herald* been less caustic, he might have remained in the Establishment. Foote had little influence outside the East Church, but within that congregation his personal esteem and his desire to avoid open conflict would appear to have been sufficiently strong so as to confuse the factional alignments which were the norm in other churches.

Conclusion

The social pattern which emerges from the study of these fourteen kirk sessions over four decades shows a clear distinction between the sections of the middle class who adhered to the Establishment and those who left to join the Free Church. Support for the Establishment was drawn largely from long-standing middle-class families who had in the past governed the church in oligarchic fashion, controlling the kirk sessions by successive co-option. By the 1830s, however, this strategy was becoming increasingly difficult to maintain because of the general expansion in the urban population and the resultant stresses in the social structure of the middle class. The families tended to cluster in specific residential areas of the old town[60] and were not immediately attracted to the new residential areas developing west of the Denburn valley, although some of the older families did have estates in the country as well as town houses. The prosperity of these families was based on the pursuit of relatively staid business and professional careers and there were considerable interlocking economic interests among the families themselves.

Those who seceded and formed the Free Church tended to contrast sharply with the stability and security which characterised the loyalists who remained in the Establishment. Mobility typified the seceders both in terms of occupation and residence. Their eagerness to move across into the fashionable areas west of the Denburn and occupy any number of residences was only matched by their readiness to switch occupations and alter or diversify their existing business interests. Less socially coherent than the loyalists, their business partnerships were often more transient than permanent. Derived from relatively new middle-class families with obscure origins, the fact that they were to some extent bolstered by the presence of a few younger dissident members of the older-established families did not save them from being regarded as socially inferior by the loyalist oligarchy, who regarded the Disruption as another example of the disordering of society:[61]

> It is far from desirable for the world at large that distinction of rank should cease, either in civil or religious matters. It has been ordained since the beginning of the world, that the superior and educated intellect should control the inferior and uneducated. Rules do not alone form the superiority which the poorer person fancies, if once levelled would render the earth a paradise.

The seceding clergymen, however, had pandered to these fancies of the uneducated and 'excitable portion of the people' and had encouraged 'thoughts and feelings of envy towards those who may be possessed of more of this world's goods'. By so doing each had become a 'hired tradesman, to whom patronage is only extended so long as he suits his customers'.[62]

Despite such attitudes of the ruling oligarchy towards the seceders it is unlikely that the problem would have been so serious if the numbers of the 'new shoots' had been less formidable. Given the undoubted ability of these men to make money, and some demonstration of their readiness to conform, a relatively speedy structural assimilation into the old ruling order might have taken place. But the numbers involved were too great to allow assimilation without changing the whole basis of the old order, and as such they constituted a challenge to its continued existence. Indeed it was in this numerical superiority yet relative social isolation, obvious wealth yet general feelings of inferiority or insecurity, that one discerns the key to the understanding of the subsequent development of the newly emergent Free Church in Aberdeen. This theme will be developed and analysed in the chapter following.

Notes

1 Biographical details of the ministers and elders of the ten Established and fifteen Free churches (including all elders mentioned in this chapter) are contained in the Biographical Notes.

2 They were William Black, James Blaikie, James Calder, John Chree, Duncan Davidson, Alexander Dingwall, Alexander Duthie, Arthur Dingwall Fordyce, Robert Reid and Robert Simpson. Five of these men would appear to have died before 1842, and three of them, Calder, Simpson and Reid, had ceased serving on the session before 1836 and cannot be traced.

3 John Barron, James Bentley, James Fraser, Alexander Harper, John Mennie, Alexander Nisbet and James Williams.

4 James Laing, John Leith, Thomas Rennie, George Smith, Robert Sutherland. The first four had left the session before 1836. Sutherland died in 1842.

5 Thomas Clark, Alexander Harper, John Mennie, James Robb. The elder deposed was James Williams: *Est. Trin. Sess.*, 21 May 1840.

6 George Mollison, Francis Webster, Thomas Robertson. One other elder remained uncommitted in 1843—Alexander Allan. Unfortunately I have been unable to trace either his occupation or place of residence.

7 Robert Davidson, Robert Garden, Alexander Smith, James Smith and John Smith. Robert Garden's son, James, later became an elder in the East Free Church so it seems probable that when Robert Garden left the Greyfriars kirk session he joined the East congregation.

8 William Chalmers.

9 See pp. 87–93.

10 The seven who would appear to have died were Gilbert Falconer, Alexander Dingwall Fordyce, John Gibbon, William Johnston, jun., James Nicoll, Joseph Norrie and William Still. John Cameron, Alexander Cowie, James Harper, Alexander Watt and John Will became elders in Union Parish; and James Robb served in Trinity parish until his death in 1838.

11 William Copland and Peter Duguid had been ordained before 1831. Copland had been retired for a number of years; neither of the two can be traced after the Disruption. William Allardyce, wine merchant, and George Leslie, shipowner, were still alive in 1851.

12 They were Harry Lumsden, John Murray, Andrew Philip and William Smith.

13 William Smith cannot be positively identified. His place of residence therefore cannot be ascertained.

14 See pp. 86–7.

15 The two who left before the Disruption were Alexander Mackie (sen.) and James Mitchell. The three who remained uncommitted were Alexander Fiddes, William Knowles and James Riddel.

16 See entries in Biographical Notes.

17 Alexander Burness had been an elder in Greyfriars from about 1831 to 1841.

18 Their names, respectively, were Alexander McDonald, William Simpson, Robert Ledingham, John McHardy and Thomas Melville.

19 Alexander Gildawie, James Greig and William Smith.

Notes

20 Alexander Martin, Alexander Paterson, George Miller, George Robertson, Ferguson Smith and James Wilson.

21 Five new elders were co-opted—three were professional men: James Collie was an advocate; William MacGillivray and William Pirie were university professors. The other two were William Duguid, an ironmonger (with a country estate), and Robert Johnston, timber merchant.

22 John Smith was an auctioneer. The fact that the other elder, James Brown, has not been positively identified demonstrates his relative social insignificance.

23 See ch. 5, pp. 113-16; ch. 6, pp. 121-6.

24 A. Gammie, *The churches of Aberdeen* (Aberdeen, 1909), p. 238.

25 *Est. Greyf. Sess.*, 20 September 1840. In the Free West McLaren was elected to the kirk session only after the eight men above him in terms of votes declined to accept office. *Free West Sess.*, vol. 1, 27 June 1844.

26 See ch. 5, pp. 110-11.

27 A. S. Cook, *Old time traders and their ways* (Aberdeen, 1902), p. 39.

28 See ch. 6, pp. 122-6. Not all of those who deserted Greyfriars were successful in obtaining election. See William Connon.

29 William Ironside was a builder, and David McHardy (who would appear to be a brother of John McHardy, South Church) was a blacksmith and bell-hanger. Tradesmen had been strongly represented in the pre-Disruption kirk session but had declined in numbers before 1843. The two seceding elders not discussed above also fell into this category; George Fullerton, baker, and Robert Simmie, retired reed-maker.

30 Nathaniel Farquhar, Andrew Murray and William McCombie.

31 John Webster who lived in King Street. His house was large enough to be used at a later date as a school for the North Free Church: Gammie, op. cit., p. 41. It is possible that Webster may have been marked out from his fellow elders for other reasons. Between 1846 and 1849 an advocate of that name was disciplined by the kirk session. The matter was handled very delicately and the nature of the offence was not recorded although it was serious enough to lead to his being denied communion during these years: *South Free Sess.*, vol. 1, 4 April 1849.

32 Rev. Robert Gray was the schoolteacher. The others were Thomas Gordon, George Rennie, William Smart, John Urquhart and David Wylie.

33 They were John Barron, James Bentley, James Fraser, John Gray, Thomas Laurie, William Mirrielees, Alexander Pearson, Andrew Sutherland and George Watson.

34 Bentley, a university professor, died in 1846. His position would appear to be somewhat similar to that of Macrobin in the Free West as his official status on Trinity Free session is not clear. His death was recorded by the kirk session however. James Fraser was a boot and shoemaker who died in 1850.

35 Robert Collie resigned in 1866; George Tulloch died in 1873; George Marquis died in 1875; William Hunter resigned in 1881: *Trin. Free Sess.*, vol. 1, roll of elders. George Grant was still alive in 1894 when he was described as having as 'elastic a step as any man of thirty': *Centenary celebrations of Trinity Free Church* (Aberdeen, 1895), p. 33.

36 It was also suggested that Greyfriars be conjoined with either Trinity or John Knox: *Est. Presb.*, vol. 13, 19 December 1843.

37 The seven elders were William Brown, Robert McCombie, John Bisset, James Henderson, William Littlejohn, Middleton Rettie and William Sievewright. Brown joined the Free West session in 1844, and McCombie would appear to have left the city before 1845.

38 James Cobban, Lewis Stewart, John Philip respectively.

39 Robert Fenton was a bookbinder; Alexander Scott may have been a shoemaker.

40 See ch. 5, pp. 110-11.

41 Although certain members of other sessions resided in St Clement's parish, e.g. Thomson (Greyfriars), Reid (North), William Rose (East Free) the St Clement's session was composed almost to a man of residents of that parish.

42 Gammie, op. cit., p. 58.

43 Alexander Fiddes was a collector of customs; William Knowles a timber merchant; and James Riddel was treasurer to the harbour trustees.

44 George Sim, George Brands, Robert Mitchell, Charles Runcy respectively.

45 Thomas Brown, Alexander Davidson, Alexander Eddie, Alexander Ross, George Spark, Robert Thomson. Eddie and Ross were still serving in 1851.

46 In 1848 a libel was served on Rev. James Newlands by the Established Presbytery. He was accused of intemperance and fornication with a certain Ann Duguid and the Presbytery's description of the libel filled no less than twenty-four pages of the minutes. He strenuously denied the charges, but after the evidence of forty-eight witnesses had been heard he was deposed. See *Est. Presb.*, vol. 14, 20 October 1848. All members of the Presbytery were required to share the legal costs of the proceedings. In August 1850 it was recorded that four elders had not yet paid their share. It is just possible that these are the same four men who had ceased serving on the session before 1851 (ibid., 4 August 1850). See also ch. 6, n. 11.

47 Alexander Mortimer, Alexander Slight, James Thain, Alexander Watson, John Walker and James Horn, Alexander Hay, James Inglis and Alexander Mackie, jun., who lived outside the parish. The new elders were George Allan, a young lawyer (admitted to the Society of Advocates in 1844) and son of a shipmaster; Peter Buyers, a grocer and ship's chandler; William Inglis, baker; Alexander Pittendrigh, former beadle of St Clement's Parish Church and now a wright and funeral waiter; Peter Riddel, clerk at harbour office; Alexander Robertson, ship's engineer; Robert Thain, teacher at Mariners' School; Alexander Troup, grain merchant on Blaikie's Quay (lived outside parish); James Middleton, James Stuart, whose occupations and residences cannot be traced.

48 It was claimed afterwards that 900 of the 1,176 communicants had seceded: W. Alexander, *East Free Church reminiscences* (Aberdeen, 1893), p. 13. This figure is suspiciously well rounded and, in view of the recovery of the East Church after 1843, probably considerably exaggerated.

49 See ch. 3, p. 54. Foote was obviously a wealthy man. When he applied to the Presbytery for ministerial assistance in 1848 he offered to make over his entire salary to the assistant. His decision to secede may well have been made the more difficult by the fact that he had contributed liberally towards

the building of the East Parish Church: *Free Presb.*, vol. I, 18 January 1848;
J. Bruce, *The Aberdeen pulpit and universities* (Aberdeen, 1844), p. II.

50 Bruce, op. cit., p. 28.

51 Ibid., p. 13.

52 Ibid., p. 16. See also the tone of his overture to the general assembly on the question of patronage in the church, which he submitted to the Presbytery. *Est. Presb.*, vol. 13, 29 March 1842.

53 Bruce, op. cit., p. 22.

54 Between 1830 and 1836 six elders died and six left to form the new session of Union Church when it was raised to *quoad sacra* status. This left three elders who were to remain loyal to the Establishment (Simpson, Rose and Fairweather); four who were to secede (Fordyce, Martin, Rettie and Ross); and five who remained uncommitted (Allardyce and Leslie left immediately prior to 1843, and Lumsden, Murray and Smith ceased serving at the Disruption). The last ordination of elders before the Disruption was in 1836-7, and the balance began to move slightly in favour of the seceders although the number of those uncommitted remained exceptionally high. Seven new elders were introduced: two remained loyal in 1843 (Melville and Straith), four seceded (Beattie, Henderson, Ledingham and Alexander Smith) and one was uncommitted (Andrew Philip). This pattern, as we have seen, was totally dissimilar to other sessions. In all the sessions considered a total of only ten elders were uncommitted in 1843 (two in the West, two in St Clement's, one in Greyfriars, one in North). In the East Church four remained uncommitted in 1843, and two dropped out immediately before the event.

55 James Martin, *Eminent divines in Aberdeen and the north* (Aberdeen, 1888), pp. 235-7.

56 When Davidson transferred from the South to the West Church many people believed that he would then temper his sermons according to the Moderatism of the congregation. But they were mistaken and Davidson's sermons attracted 'swarms of evangelicals from different quarters'. Bruce, op. cit., p. 28. This view is confirmed by James Riddell, who cites an example of a lady who ceased attending afternoon services because many of those present belonged to a lower class of society whose habits were disgusting: *Aberdeen and its folk* (Aberdeen, 1868), pp. 81-2.

57 Gammie ascribes his failure to his relatively short pastorate (four years), but from Gammie this is thinly veiled criticism. For example elsewhere he describes a three-year pastorate as being characterised by 'thrilling and masterly sermons' and a minister who had served less than six months as a 'young man of exceptional promise'. Rev. James Stewart was a Disruption minister (ordained to the South parish in October 1842). For Gammie to dismiss him in this way is an indication of his inadequacy. (Op. cit., pp. 207, 212, 228.)

58 Prior to the Disruption there had been a steady decline in the size of the congregation. See the report of the committee about Greyfriars Church, in *Est. Presb.*, vol. 14, 14 July 1846.

59 See ch. 3, p. 57.

60 Long after the Disruption certain areas of the city were remembered for their Establishment associations. 'One almost fancies, in walking through

the long narrow streets, fringed on each side with mouldering houses . . .
that the very air is laden with the breath of the old "moderate" times.'
Martin, op. cit., pp. 194-5.
61 *Observations on the relative positions . . . by a lady* (Aberdeen, 1844), p. 10.
62 Ibid., pp. 8, 10.

Chapter 5

The Development of the Free Church
after 1843

We must carry on a war . . . with all the force of a duty.*

As we have seen from the religious census carried out in 1851 the Free
Church by that date had clearly established itself in the city as the
largest single denomination.[1] Although it might seem by hind-sight
from the situation of 1851 that the numerical and financial prosperity
of the Free Church assured its success from its inception in 1843, it is
misleading to regard the development of the seceding body in the years
after the Disruption from such a standpoint. Indeed the reasons for the
decay in vigour of the Free Church in the 1850s is best understood by
examining the source of the dynamism and energy of the 1840s. In the
immediately preceding chapter support for secession was seen to be
drawn from sections of the middle class characterised by aggressive
individualism, economic opportunism, rapid social and physical
mobility, and yet relatively insecure within the social structure because
of their shallow roots in bourgeois society. Support also came from
clergymen who feared the loss of social status which might result from
leaving the Establishment but were carried over into the new church
by principle and by force of circumstances. The threat that presented
itself after the Disruption was peculiarly potent to those who had
openly committed themselves to secession. It was, simply, the threat of
failure, the fear that the new body would make little general impact on
society beyond the immediate sensation its demonstration of principle
had created. The new Church would be a seven-month wonder which
after the immediate interest had passed would be swallowed up by the
wealth, power, and organisation of the Established Church and would
disappear into the sectarian wilderness as indeed other such demonstra-
tions had done in the past.[2] Indeed subsequent developments suggest
that for many of the seceders the success or failure of the new church
became a measure of their own ability; a measure of their own
acceptance by, and integration within, the totality of middle-class
society.

It is important to recognise, however, that fear of failure was not
merely a reflection of the general social insecurity of many of the

* *Banner*, 13 May 1843.

seceders; in the months following the Disruption these fears were certainly based on a real, and critical, appraisal of the situation. In these months many church members and a number of elders adopted a cautious 'wait-and-see' attitude towards the new Church. Although this attitude revealed itself in a variety of forms fundamentally these all involved a degree of non-commitment to the emergent Free Church. Some church members whilst contracting to hold seats in the new Free churches when built, continued to hold seats in the Established body, and certain well-known business families divided their support numerically and financially between the two churches.[3] A number of elders failed to sign the Deed of Demission from the Establishment which was circulated in May 1843 and, as a result, for some time were claimed as elders in both churches. Others signed but were slow to take up their offices in the Free Church and those that did occasionally had second thoughts on the matter when it appeared that their careers might suffer if they left the Establishment.[4] As late as November 1843 the Established Presbytery were uncertain as to whether Principal Dewar of Marischal College had seceded. Despite his written denial of having signed any document withdrawing from the Establishment it was believed that by his actions he had continually implied 'adhesion to the Separatists'.[5]

For those men totally committed, however, the issues at stake were clear. There must be no backsliding, no fence-sitting, or the Free Church would slip down 'from [its] high position into that of a mere sect, impotent and unassisted. . . . It depends on what course we propose to ourselves now, what is to be the fate of the Free Church, whether it is to sink into the littleness of a puny Scotch sect, or to make itself felt as a force in Europe.'[6] The *Banner*, local organ of the seceders, expressed these fears and proposed the remedies. It flayed those who were unprincipled enough to practise dual seatholding as supporters of moderatism but at the same time warned those disposed to the Establishment to wait 'for a twelvemonth' before taking seats so that 'they see what sort of minister they are to get'.[7] Arguing that the Free Church was now the true Established Church it was maintained that 'honestly, and in plain speaking' we must carry on a war against the residuary Establishment:[8]

It will be the policy of our enemies to do all they can to crush the rising Church . . . we must carry on a war. . . . To our mind this suggests itself with all the force of a duty. We are not at liberty to do it, or not to do it, according as we shall think [it is] an absurdity to imagine that we shall not aim at its destruction, and a sin to intend not to do so.

This was the ideology which was paramount in shaping the early development of the Free Church in Aberdeen. It was a force which has been observed in the Free Church at a national level in Scotland and which has been described as sectarian bitterness which poisoned religious life and diverted spiritual energies away from their proper course into needless denominational competition.[9] Such a view, however, fails to grasp the nature of the dynamism which was an essential feature of the early Free Church, certainly in the city of Aberdeen. Whilst applauding the 'heroic spirit of self-sacrifice for the sake of conscience' exhibited in the actual secession it condemns the bitter denominational rivalry which resulted. Given the nature of the social support for the new Church it is misleading to view the action and the subsequent development as exhibiting differing characteristics. The seceders carried into the new Church the very attributes which had led to their own economic success. The Established Church was associated with a way of life of which they personally were not yet part. The new Church was cast in their own image—it was aggressive, competitive, and run on the lines of a business organisation. It was not simply sectarian or denominationally competitive—the new Church must be bigger, better, exhibit greater prosperity, and must demonstrate their ability to be socially as well as economically successful.

The New Men and Their New Church

The Nature of the Ideological Conflict and Its Effects

The war against the residuary Establishment which the *Banner* advocated as the only possible course in May 1843 had effectively commenced before that date. It was the policy of the seceding clergymen to use the pulpit as a means of convincing, or even frightening, the uncommitted members to rally to the support of the emergent Free Church. One eminent citizen, and seceding member of the West Church, recorded in his notes that the Disruption sermon preached by Rev. A. D. Davidson from the text 'But if the gospel be hid, it is hid to them that are lost' was such 'that most of us quailed under the flashes of his vivid illustration'.[10] Elsewhere, congregations were told that 'there was no efficacy in the blood of Jesus to save an adherent of the Establishment, nor could the Holy Spirit bless his own Word, preached by any of its ministers. The wine drunk at the communion, in the Established Church was *dog's blood*.'[11]

The fact that all fifteen ministers in the city were committed to non-intrusion, albeit to varying degrees, and that all were in the event to secede, must have considerably hampered the development of a counter-agitation on the part of the Establishment.[12] Certainly protagonists of the Established cause lacked the fire of their Free Church counterparts and much of their work was marked by the 'cold formality' which the non-intrusionists condemned as the principal characteristic of the Moderate churchman's sermon. Whilst the Free Church supporter would portray the conflict as one of Jehovah versus Leviathan,[13] defenders of the Establishment's position saw the issue simply as the work of troublesome agitators who lacked due respect for the just laws of the land:[14]

> But above all, fellow-Christians, do we deprecate disobedience to the laws. The evils of such disobedience must in every case be enormous. But how much more so when exhibited by clergymen . . . bound in faith, in truth, by the very terms under which they hold their appointments, to show an example of peace and good order, by recommending ready and respectful obedience to the laws of their country?

Even after the Disruption when the supposed illegality of the prior actions of the seceders was scarcely a live issue the Establishment continued to make this a central theme in their attacks on the new Church. A typical pamphlet circulating in the city in that year declared that 'Patronage, however objectionable some may think it is, is certainly a civil right, which cannot be either abolished or limited by the ecclesiastical courts without the sanction of the British Parliament.'[15] Such excessive concern for the illegality of past actions was misconceived and as a propaganda measure was totally misdirected in its appeal. As the supposed illegality of the action had not prevented secession it is illogical to believe that it could now frighten seceders back into the Establishment. It was also unlikely to prevent any further congregational drift from the Established Church because it could not deny the legality of the seceders' actions after they had broken from the Establishment. Arguments like these could only have reassured the hard-core adherents of the Establishment from whom of course they owed their origins. Such appeals were the work of men still staggering under the impact of the secession and unable to comprehend that the whole plane of the conflict had now shifted.

Whilst accusations of illegality regarding their actions had been countered by the seceders' claim that the Free Protesting Church was now the true Establishment it seems highly probable that the continuation of this theme by Established adherents must have driven the committed seceder to greater efforts to ensure the success of the new denomination. Certainly, as the next section will show, it must have become clear by the effort and capital expended by the seceders as well as the heavy financial obligations entailed in church-building that the Establishment was to be seriously challenged for the first time. Realisation of this induced a near panic in certain pro-Establishment propaganda and just as the Free Protesting Church had claimed to be the 'true' Established Church the Establishment sought to prove that it was the 'truly *free* church' particularly after attempts were made by Parliament to reform some of the worst abuses concerning the patronage issue.[16] Established Church members were reminded of the 'substantial privileges' they possessed as compared to the 'visionary advantages of a misnamed Free Church':[17]

> And for *what*, after all, have those who have gone out left the Establishment? What, after all, is to be gained by joining the 'Free Church', as it has been so arrogantly called? In the Establishment you have all the privileges and blessings without money and without price; but in what is called the Free Church you must *pay* for everything. When a minister of the Establishment appears among his people it is as a friend, with something where it is needed to give away. But when a minister of the 'F.C.' comes among you, probably it is to *claim* some *arrears* of your *penny-a-week subscriptions*. Let your toils and your honourable struggles to support yourselves and your families be what they may, your money, if you belong to the 'Free Church' *must be forthcoming*. Money! money! with the 'F.C.' is everything.

Perhaps the most important aspect of this type of propaganda is that it was aimed at preserving the post-Disruption membership in the Established Church—it was an attempt to prevent further secession to the Free Church. It was also an implicit recognition of the fact that the Free Church propagandists had succeeded in polarising the issues into one of Jehovah versus Leviathan and were winning over those who had for various reasons been wary in committing themselves to the new church.[18] The Establishment had lost the ideological debate. Far from crushing the emergent church, it had by the nature of the excessive legalism of its propaganda and the social peculiarities of the seceders, probably contributed to the success of the new body. The crudity of the appeal based on the material benefits of membership of the Establishment is a rather startling withdrawal from the initial condemnation of illegality. Nevertheless it was based, as we shall see later in this chapter, on a fairly accurate observation of developments taking place within the new Church and which were to be important in determining its economic organisation and social relationships.

Churches and Church-building

Whilst the ideological conflict was fought and won as a means of justifying their actions and rallying the uncommitted, other equally important and essentially 'practical' problems presented themselves to the seceders. First, temporary church accommodation had to be acquired in order to provide religious services for those who had left the Establishment. Sites had to be found for the new Free churches; the purchase had to be negotiated and cash and credit had to be raised. Lastly, there were the continuous ever-present problems of paying off the debt on the church buildings, and maintaining the ministers' stipends.

The speed and relative ease by which the seceding congregations were able to solve the immediate problem of arranging temporary accommodation suggests that some sort of informal agreement had been reached prior to May 1843. The West, South, East, North, Greyfriars, Bonaccord, and Union churches made arrangements to share Congregationalist and dissenting Presbyterian church buildings, meeting at different times or at alternative services.[19] St Clement's seceding congregation erected a temporary wooden building which was in fact completed before the return of their minister from the Disruption Assembly in Edinburgh despite an attempt by the Established Presbytery to prevent its erection by means of an interdict.[20] Holburn congregation also erected a temporary wooden building. Both congregations later erected stone churches.[21] John Knox and Gilcomston congregations obtained temporary accommodation in public halls.[22] The Melville Free congregation had a constitutional right to retain their church on leaving the Establishment and after the Disruption they provided temporary accommodation for Trinity Free.[23] The Gaelic and Mariners' congregations were small and it would seem that they continued in their former churches at least temporarily as the very high secession in each case led the Establishment to abandon each charge permanently.[24]

The finding of suitable sites for the building of the new Free churches was also accomplished surprisingly quickly. Although there were fifteen seceding congregations in the city only eight sites had to be found immediately. Melville congregation owned their church building and there does not appear to have been any immediate attempt by the Establishment to evict the Mariners' and Gaelic congregations. In the case of the Union and Bonaccord churches the policy adopted by the seceders was to advertise the church building as being for sale and then to purchase it on behalf of the seceding congregation. As the Establishment was reluctant to be saddled with the large debts still outstanding on the buildings no effort was made to prevent the sale taking place.[25] The Established Presbytery, however, strongly resisted efforts by the seceders to auction the Holburn and John Knox churches and after a lengthy legal wrangle succeeded in proving that the seceding group had no claims whatsoever on the buildings. The erection of new churches to house the seceding congregations was not sanctioned by the Free Presbytery until November 1843 in the case of John Knox and August 1844 regarding Holburn.[26]

The John Knox and Holburn Free churches when built were located close by the parish churches from which respectively these congregations had seceded. Of the eight churches for whom sites were found and churches erected and occupied before March 1844, namely West, South, East, North, Greyfriars, St Clement's, Trinity, and Gilcomston, only Greyfriars and Trinity were not in the immediate vicinity of their Established counterpart. Sites were obtained apparently without difficulty and no real attempt was made by the Established Presbytery to hinder the Free Church building programme.[27] There is no doubt that it was a deliberate policy on the part of the seceders to site the new Free churches as close as possible to the parish churches. The Free Presbytery were reluctant to sanction the building of Trinity and Greyfriars Free churches in fashionable Crown Street and regretted that these congregations had been unable to obtain sites 'in the immediate neighbourhood of their former church'.[28] The policy of building as close as possible to the parish church was, of course, a national rather than a local phenomenon. At the local level, however, it seems clear that it comprised an important part of the 'war against the residuary Establishment'. Siting the Free church close to the parish church was a practical demonstration of the numerical and financial strength of the new body. Certainly it must have made dual seat-holding difficult to conceal, and clearly indicated commitment. Perhaps above all it was a means of causing obvious embarrassment to an Establishment seriously depleted in terms of members, finance, and morale.

The greatest problem for the Free Church, however, was not the finding of temporary accommodation or the acquiring of building sites but the question of how to finance the ambitious and costly building programme and to maintain guaranteed stipends for Free Church clergymen. The great bulk of the money required for the building of the churches and provision of stipends was raised from the individual congregations concerned and, as we shall see, the need to maintain a constant flow of money for such purposes had far-reaching consequences for the structure and organisation of the Free churches. As far as building costs were concerned the amounts required were substantial. The building of a church involved outlays of anything between £1,000 and £2,000 per congregation[29] and the desire for additional interior comforts and external ornament often added considerably to these basic costs. Thus the South Free session committed the congregation to a considerable number of additional expenses in order to make the church more 'elegant and commodious' and because of 'their anxiety for the comfort of their fellow worshippers'.[30] These additional expenses totalled nearly £450 and included the provision of seat-doors (£38), velvet for the seats (£47), the erecting of partitions with 'obscuring glass' (£60), and a wall clock and other incidentals. A church spire which had not been included in the original estimates was also constructed at a cost of £383.[31] Similar internal improvements were undertaken by other Free kirk sessions.[32]

Free Church congregations, therefore, were required to raise very substantial sums of money for the running of their own churches as well as contributing to the national needs of the Free Church in the form of the Sustentation Fund. Large sums for such purposes were raised by city churches. The Free West from the Disruption down to 15 March 1845 paid off all but £204 of the church-building debt, raising a total of over £3,656. By the end of 1845 the East Free congregation had raised £5,382 for all church purposes. By the time Trinity Free church was completed in March 1844, £760 had been collected towards its total cost of about £1,200 and by the end of the year very little debt remained. By March 1844 South Free session had raised over half the cost of the £2,000 church.[33] Almost all the vast sums that were raised by the congregations were utilised in debt repayment and other similar commitments of the church both locally and nationally. Thus of the £3,656 raised by the Free West only £125 found its way to the 'communion poor of our own and other city congregations' whilst £701 was paid to the national committee administering the Sustentation Fund.[34] Unlike the Establishment the Free Church, simply to survive, was required to organise itself to undertake fund-raising activities on a large scale and on a long-term basis.

The Economic Organisation of the New Church

The realisation by Chalmers that 'we can look neither for stability nor enlargement' unless a steady flow of financial contributions was maintained led him to argue that the Free Church ought to be organised on a sound business basis:[35]

> It is, therefore, of the utmost importance to our financial prosperity, that we should have a superintendent of thorough business ability and habits, under the contract, at the same time, and surveillance of a Committee mainly composed of business men.

In Aberdeen the seceding eldership was largely composed of successful businessmen and there was no delay in organising on a profit-and-loss criterion the two main sources of church revenue, namely income from the letting of seats, and financial contributions to the schemes of the church. The need to organise church finances on a sound basis was, of course, not a new problem. Congregations which were not supported fully or in part by state or town council endowment or private patronage, such as Bonaccord, Union, Melville, and Trinity, had always faced the problem of building debts and running costs.[36] The charging of seat rents which bore some relationship to the extent of these outlays was certainly not a new feature of church finances.[37] What was new was not the charging of economic seat rents but the extent to which the concept of 'each according to his means' was followed.

As far as seat-letting was concerned this concept was adopted by drawing up a complex scale of rents relating the situation of the seat within the church to as many as eight or ten different prices.[38] A considerable amount of both direct and indirect pressure was applied to ensure that members of the congregation undertook the renting of seats.[39] Seat-holders were committed to a three-year contract in the South Free church although it was recognised that rent might have to be collected half-yearly 'from such members as found it inconvenient to take them for a longer period'. Of the 1,296 seats in this church only 30 were allotted as gratis sittings, and the same sort of proportion was observed in other congregations.[40] The effects of the scale of charges and the pressure on members to become seat-holders was to allocate social status according to ability to pay. The result (which is considered in more detail in the next chapter) was that the poorer members tended to be excluded whilst the richer status-seekers quarrelled over the rights of individuals or families to hold the prestige sittings.[41]

Whilst the scale of seat rents implied a recognition of the belief that each individual must commit himself to supporting the church according to his means, this concept was made explicit as far as financial contributions to the schemes of the church were concerned. By far the most important scheme was the Sustentation Fund and it is in the operation of the contributions to this fund that the most influential long-term results can be observed concerning status differentiation both among the churches and within each congregation. Contributions to the scheme were covenanted—a fixed sum being paid each week—and although the ideal of continuous contributions was not always realised the belief that it was wrong 'to neglect or under-rate the mites of our artisans and labourers'[42] was a central part of the scheme. Scales were drawn up listing what proportion of each congregation might be expected to contribute anything from a shilling to a farthing weekly.[43] The elders were considered best able to assess the potential contribution of each family unit. Although they were warned to be circumspect and show discretion when visiting 'those on a level with or above themselves in worldly circumstances' they were supplied with a note-book in which they were expected to record precise details of the domestic economy of working-class families.[44]

Whilst the claim by an Established Church propagandist that 'your money, if you belong to the "Free Church" must be forthcoming. Money! money! with the "F.C." is everything'[45] was on the whole an exaggeration in 1844, certainly the ability of a congregation to raise or maintain its contributions increasingly became an important criterion of the status of a congregation. It was self-evident that the more wealthy members a church could attract the better would be its financial position and its resultant status in the community. It was early realisation of this simple fact which undoubtedly played a large part in influencing the choice of building sites for both Greyfriars and Trinity Free churches. Both of these congregations deserted what were primarily working-class parishes and built their churches within fifty yards of one another in fashionable Crown Street. The decision to build in Crown Street in the case of the seceders from Trinity was almost certainly dictated by the minister and elders, who raised most of the cash, rather than the congregation itself. The old church, built in 1794, was situated in what had become an unfashionable area near the harbour. The great majority of the congregation lived in the parish or in the vicinity eastwards of the church although the minister and six of the nine seceding elders either lived in Crown Street or its vicinity, or moved there soon after the building of the new church.[46] The seceding elders found that they 'could not procure a site within the parish or its immediate vicinity' and settled with no apparent regrets on a site in Crown Street.[47] As a speculative venture the choice was a sound one. The church prospered and appeared to attract members from the Crown Street vicinity.[48] In the case of Greyfriars Free congregation, however, the choice was an unhappy one because of the scandal which ensued over the choice of site and it seems clear that Trinity Free Church benefited in terms of members from the dissension within the Greyfriars Free congregation. Greyfriars Church lay in a parish described as the poorest in the city,[49] and the desertion of the parish certainly was an embarrassment to the Free Presbytery, who were reluctant to sanction the building of the new church in Crown Street which was far removed from the Greyfriars vicinity.[50] Of the minister, Rev. Abercromby Gordon, and the session, it was openly stated that 'their ambition drove them to the west end among the gentry'.[51] This allegation, which was a particularly serious one for Gordon, was never successfully refuted. One cannot but accept the view that it was the basic reason for Gordon resigning the charge and leaving the city in 1845.[52] Prior to the Disruption, Gordon had been an active worker within the Greyfriars mission field, particularly concerning the provision of working-class education, and had maintained that there was 'a very great deficiency of church and school accommodation' in that parish.[53] In 1840 he had been forced to appeal generally for financial assistance for his work because 'the congregation had done what they could, the parish is too poor to give much help'.[54] Although the careers of certain members of the Greyfriars session might cast some doubt as to their motivation in choosing the Crown Street site[55] the explanation offered by Gordon to the Free Presbytery amidst the scandal was a rational enough appraisal of the circumstances:[56]

> In going to a new locality farther west . . . he was serving the interests of church extension. . . . He had hoped that by raising a strong congregation in this new locality he might be able with their support and co-operation to give more effective service than ever in east end mission work.

If Gordon had offered a less rational, less worldly explanation regarding the choice of site he might have been more successful in refuting the allegations. However, in 1844 the idea of a church being sited according to the requirements of the financial balance sheet was not yet generally acceptable. The heavy costs of running the Free Church had not yet become the financial drain which later would make the cause of church extension sufficient explanation for any choice of site in the west end of the city.

Gordon's realistic appraisal of the situation and his recognition of the need for building a financially strong and liberal congregation was not immediately reflected in the attitude of the other city sessions. No doubt many congregations regarded the large sums of money being raised after 1843 as once-and-for-all efforts which following the building of the church and the clearing-off of the debts would diminish to a more manageable scale. A gradual disillusionment developed in the kirk sessions and deacons' courts, faced by the demands from the Sustentation Fund Committee in Edinburgh. The disillusionment, which eventually permeated the congregations, can be traced by the changing attitude of church officials towards congregational contributions. The Free West congregation soon after the Disruption was the wealthiest Free church in the city. In 1845 it was decided by the court to send a tactful reminder to all seatholders regarding the need to increase their contributions to the Fund:[57]

> While the Deacons are anxious to do all in their power to increase the Sustentation Fund, yet they look only to those for doing so whom God has enabled. . . . They wish none to give who cannot afford to do so; nor any to increase the rate of their present contribution, except they are convinced, that it is disproportioned to their present means.

By the end of the same year, however, it was clear that a tactful approach had failed to achieve the necessary response and a tone of admonition crept into the congregational report—a reminder that the Free West must uphold its position as the wealthiest city congregation. After all the Sustentation Fund 'so far as any human means can be so [was] the pillar of the Church's strength and efficiency and should it not be adequately supported by such a congregation as this, what is to be expected of the poorer congregations'.[58] By 1848 the congregation were reminded that 'what they possess they have received from God in the way of mercy, they ought in the way of duty, to return to God a portion for the support of his house'.[59] The same year the continual reminders from Edinburgh concerning the need for increased contributions drove office-bearers into open conflict with the superintendent of the Fund and a unanimous resolution was sent to the Edinburgh Committee declaring that his salary was excessive as his 'services might be obtained for a far less sum'.[60] But faced by a fall in contributions the Free West committee were soon forced to take urgent action and it was decided that elders should be asked to report on their visits particularly 'if any of their contributors shall appear to be contributing in any considerable degree below their means'.[61] By 1850 all tact was abandoned and a circular letter was sent to all whose contributions were considered insufficient:[62]

> Do you hold the principles of the Free Church? . . . Let us ask you, if all the Members had acted as you have done what would have been the position of the Free Church to-day? Need we tell you that it *would* and *could* never have existed except in the cities and larger towns of the country. What would have become of the warm and liberal hearted, but poor, adherents in the other portions of the land? The Lord, doubtless would have taken care of them that were his own, and have fed and nourished their souls in his own way; but they could not have enjoyed ordinances in a communion the principles of which they could approve. . . . If you do not think that you are required to help in this matter, then you do not hold the principles of the Free Church, and we must plainly tell you that you would be acting in a more consistent manner by withdrawing from the communion, than by continuing. . . .

The Free West Church had the wealthiest Free Presbyterian congregation and perhaps was the most prosperous congregation in the city by 1850. In terms of liberality only seven other congregations within the Free Church contributed more to the central Sustentation Fund in Edinburgh,[63] and yet by 1850 the pressure was so great that there was a clear attempt to make contributions to the Fund a necessary part of membership. This was a serious enough development for a wealthy congregation such as the Free West but the same pressures coming to bear on poorer congregations resulted in crises which raised the whole question as to whether the congregations could continue to survive. Two such congregations were the Mariners' church and the Gaelic church. Both were small congregations with 200 and 114 communicants respectively, and were able to contribute so little to the Sustentation Fund that in 1850 serious consideration was given to closing down both churches.[64] The Edinburgh committee had estimated that the Mariners' church was 'contributing less than it ought to do' and it was also clear that in the case of the Gaelic church there was an 'unwillingness on the part of the people to give'.[65] Following reports from committees set up to consider the finances of the churches the Free Presbytery decided to appeal to the general Sustentation Fund Committee against their closure on the grounds of their special services rendered to specific sections of the community, and the possibility that in the future additional contributions might be forthcoming. The committee in Edinburgh decided to refer the matter to the General Assembly.[66]

Neither the Mariners' nor the Gaelic churches were closed down, but by 1850 it was clear that their continued existence was based on the fact that they were special cases owing to their peculiar social function. Moreover, whilst there always had been status differentiation among the city churches the differences formerly had been linked only indirectly to the overall wealth of any one congregation. The presence of well-known long-standing professional and commercial families in the West Church had made that church the élite among the city churches prior to the Disruption. After 1843, however, status in the Free Church was dependent directly on the ability of a congregation to maintain or to increase its financial contributions to the schemes of the Church especially the Sustentation Fund. The fact that each was expected to contribute according to his means—however inadequate the income—meant that there was a definite incentive to attract a prosperous middle class into membership. This was true just as much for east-end as west-end churches; just as much for those who sought to carry the Word forth to the heathen working class as those who regarded them as beyond redemption. Thus Gordon, active in the mission field but hampered by shortage of funds, sited his church as a grocer with an eye for future business would site his shop.

Comparability in all Things

Following the Disruption the Free Church in Aberdeen as a result of internal and external financial pressures increasingly became a Church catering for the prosperous middle class. Led in 1843 by members of a dissident, newly wealthy middle class these men speedily made their mark on the new Church which in itself became a measure of their own status within bourgeois society. Although constitutionally the Free Church was more democratic than the Establishment, in effect this came to have little or no influence in determining the social structure of the eldership.[67] In the Free Church to a greater degree than in the Establishment it was necessary for elders to be men of considerable socio-economic status in the community. From the inception of the Free Church it was necessary for elders to be able to obtain on the basis of their 'good name' bridging and long-term finance at favourable rates of interest to meet the immediate and urgent requirements of church-building. Moreover, the overwhelming desire of the seceders to demonstrate not only their respectability to the wider society but also their superiority over the residuary Establishment, drove them into attempting comparability in all things. Thus the measure of a man's suitability for office was to no small extent determined by a scale of comparability with the socio-economic status of elders in the Established Church. By 1851 an analysis of the eldership of both denominations reveals a convergence in the social composition of the rival sessions. Where comparability did not arise—namely in the former *quoad sacra* kirk sessions which the Establishment abandoned or discontinued—the lower middle-class grouping continued to predominate.[68] In all the other Free kirk sessions, however, there was a significant shift in the balance of the eldership which brought the social composition much nearer that of the Establishment; the lower middle-class representation declining in favour of the higher social grouping. Over the six Established churches of West, South, East, North, St Clement's, and Greyfriars, and their Free Church counterparts the percentages of high and low status elders were: Established 70·3 per cent high, 26·6 per cent low; Free 65·7 per cent high, 31·3 per cent low. However, if one takes into account the fact that by 1851 Greyfriars Free Church was on the point of closure and to all intents and purposes had been replaced by the neighbouring Trinity Free Church, the similarity between the social composition of the eldership of both denominations is startling. In fact, if the Greyfriars Free figures are excluded and replaced by Trinity Free the Free Church percentages are virtually identical with those of the Establishment, viz. 70·7 per cent high, 26·7 per cent low.[69]

However, the similarity in the social structure of the eldership was only one factor among others which illustrate the changes which had taken place within the Free Church and the general level of acceptance of society itself of the new denomination. By 1851 the Aberdeen *Directory* had ceased describing the new Church as the 'Free Seceding Church' and referred to it simply as the 'Free Church' and about the same time the city *Almanac* which had published lists of the Established kirk sessions began also to publish similar lists of the Free sessions.[70] It was by then indisputable that the Free Church was not transient but had a permanent place among the city's religious denominations. Although an element of competitiveness continued between the two denominations much of the original animosity had declined. When Greyfriars Free Church was rebuilt after its bankruptcy and removal from Crown Street it was one of the formerly bitterest opponents of the Free Church in the city who undertook negotiations and building specifications for the purchase of a site within the parish the congregation had deserted in 1843.[71] The similarity in the social structure of the eldership in both denominations may well have been an important factor inducing concomitant changes in what had formerly been attitudes fundamental to the Free Church. The Free Presbytery refused to recognise or assist independent missionary endeavours whose popularity threatened to remove members from neighbouring Free churches.[72] There was also a marked reluctance on the part of the Free Presbytery to allow mission charges to form their own kirk sessions and disjoin themselves from the Free Church congregation under whose jurisdiction they lay. The continual refusal of the Free Presbytery to sanction such a development in one mission church led to the secession of the minister and congregation from the Free Church and the forming of a United Presbyterian charge.[73] The issue of the chapels-of-ease and their right to form their own kirk sessions had, of course, been of paramount importance for those who had been involved in the conflict with the Establishment before 1843 and who finally seceded at the Disruption.

It is clear that much of the evangelical fervour which had characterised the Free Church in 1843 had declined by the 1850s and in some congregations the Disruption-seceders themselves had fallen from favour.[74] The decline in the old attitudes which accompanied the changing balance in the social composition of the kirk sessions and the increasing similarity in the views of the Established and Free presbyteries on certain issues must have created some confusion among Free Church members. Certainly it became necessary to launch a series of lectures entitled 'the distinctive principles of the Free Church' and a committee was formed by the Presbytery to consider the whole matter of how the public could best be told of these distinctive principles. It is perhaps significant that this committee found great difficulty in defining these principles and ultimately the problem was passed on to the ministers who were told to preach on the subject once a year and to ensure that all new office-bearers, communicants, and members, were instructed on the nature of the Free Church.[75]

The decline of the former vigour combined with the confusion over basic principles led to a falling-off in the readiness of congregations to contribute to the financial schemes of the Church. One Disruption elder, deploring the changes, asked:[76]

> Is the cause of God less worthy of our support now than it was at the time of the disruption, or are we less able now than we were formerly to give for that cause?

Certainly this congregation—the Free West—was not in any way less able to contribute than it had been eight years before and the subsequent history of the church suggests that the reverse was the case.[77] What had changed was not the ability to contribute but the cause itself and the motivation which had supplied the dynamics of the cause. By 1851 the war advocated by the *Banner* as the only possible course had been fought out. The Residuary had not been destroyed but the Free Church had established itself in the city and nationally it was clear that there was no fear of decline into yet another 'puny Scotch sect'. In Aberdeen the Church had grown from nothing into a denomination with fifteen congregations all of whom were installed in their own church buildings. The Establishment had shrunk to nine congregations and lagged far behind the Free Church in numerical support. The seceders had demonstrated their ability, and the success of the new Church was a reflection and a measure of their own success in bourgeois society. It was a victory which had been won, however, at no small cost in terms of changes in attitude, organisation and function—what the seceders had claimed as the 'Church of the People' might now be more accurately described as the Church of the middle class.

Notes

1 See ch. 2, 44–5.
2 For earlier secessions see ch. 2, pp. 26–7.
3 *Banner*, 13 May 1843. For example, see Francis and James Edmond, David and John McHardy, Donaldson and William Rose (Biographical Notes).
4 See Act of Demission by elders, *Free Presb.*, vol. 1, p. 15. A considerable number of elders were listed in pencil as having seceded but did not sign the actual Deed. Macrobin (West) and Mirrielees (Trinity) were apprehensive concerning their university posts at Marischal College. At King's College only Doctors Tulloch and Fleming 'dared the consequences of secession'. M. Angus, *Sheriff Watson of Aberdeen* (Aberdeen, 1913), p. 56.
5 *Est. Presb.*, 3 October 1843; A. Gammie, *The churches of Aberdeen* (Aberdeen, 1909), p. 23; James Martin, *Eminent divines in Aberdeen and the north* (Aberdeen, 1888), p. 225; see also Principal Dewar (in Biographical Notes).

6 *Banner*, 13 May 1843.

7 Ibid. In the Free West dual seat-holding led to the formation of a committee to deal with the problem. A number of seat-holders were requested to give up their sittings and rules were drawn up to regulate future seat-letting: *Free West Deac.*, vol. 1, 7 November 1844.

8 Leader article in *Banner*, 13 May 1843.

9 R. Rait and G. S. Pryde, *Scotland* (London, 1954), p. 266.

10 Angus, op. cit., p. 49.

11 Seceding ministers also preached that those who did not sign the Lists of Demission would be sent to hell on Judgment Day. See *Facts not falsehoods* (Edinburgh, 1845), p. 37.

12 The Established Presbytery was forced to rely on the work of ministers and supporters in outlying rural parishes, on the circulation of unsigned pamphlets, and the distribution of pamphlets produced in Edinburgh or elsewhere. A large number of such works have been assembled in the *Herald Collection*, King's College Library, Aberdeen. Presumably they were collected by James Adam, editor of the *Aberdeen Herald* and devastating critic of the Free Church.

13 *Selected portions from the diary and manuscripts of the Rev. Gavin Parker*, 31 January 1843.

14 Rev. J. Paul (Tullyneale) and Rev. W. R. Pirie (Dyco), *Letter in explanation . . . addressed to the people of Scotland* (Aberdeen, 1840), p. 26.

15 *Reasons of adherence . . . addressed by a minister to his parishioners* (Aberdeen, 1844), p. 3.

16 Objections to presentees by patrons were heard under certain circumstances after the passing of Lord Aberdeen's Act on 17 August 1843.

17 *The Established Church of Scotland: the truly 'Free Church' and friend of the people* (Edinburgh, 1844), p. 7. This pamphlet was circulated in Aberdeen by Alexander Mitchell, bookseller and stationer, 20 Upperkirkgate.

18 By 1845-6 the Free churches were attracting many new members, e.g. see *Free West Sess.*, 20 March, 6 October 1845; *Free Trin. Sess.*, 20 April, 19 October 1846.

19 Arrangements were made to share Blackfriars Congregational Chapel, John Street Secession Church, Frederick Street Congregational Church, St Paul Street Relief Church, Skene Terrace Secession Church. The Bonaccord congregation also held an open-air morning service. (*Free West Sess.*, 18 January 1844; Gammie, op. cit., pp. 109, 157, 131; *Selected portions from the diary . . . of the Rev. Gavin Parker*, 18 June 1843.)

20 The first sermon was preached in the new building on 4 June 1843. The tradesmen worked throughout the night to complete the building before the interdict could be served. See Gammie, op. cit., p. 183.

21 St Clement's Free Church was opened on 8 October 1843. Holburn Free session, owing to a legal wrangle over possession of the old Holburn church, did not get the sanction of the Free Presbytery to begin building until 19 August 1844 (*Free Presb.*).

22 At the Temperance Hall, George Street, and the Assembly Rooms, Union Street, respectively. The John Knox Free congregation disputed occupancy of the parish church but the Establishment successfully resisted this move. The erection of a new church building was finally sanctioned by the Free

Presbytery on 7 November and the church was completed by March 1844:
Free Presb., vol. I, 10 October, 7 November 1843; Gammie, op. cit., pp. 146, 126.

23 Ibid., pp. 149-50. *Free Trin. Sess.*, June 1843.

24 See correspondence between Established Presbytery and the Gaelic chapel managers: Gammie, op. cit., p. 189. The Mariners' Free congregation later sought and received permission to erect a new church in Commerce Street: *Free Presb.*, vol. I, 21 November 1843, 6 February 1844.

25 There was a debt of £1,200 in the case of Union Church and substantial debts on Bonaccord Church. See report of the committee on chapels-of-ease, *Est. Presb.*, vol. 13, 20 July 1843. W. Robbie, *Bonaccord Free Church; a retrospect, 1828-87* (Aberdeen, 1887), p. 23.

26 There was a debt of only £12 on John Knox Church: *Est. Presb.*, vol. 13, 20 July 1843. See also *Free Presb.*, vol. I, 10 October and 7 November 1843, 19 August 1844. The Holburn congregation had, of course, erected a temporary wooden building. John Knox seceders continued to occupy the parish church until 23 July 1843: Gammie, op. cit., p. 146.

27 The West, South and East Free churches were built on the same site about a hundred yards away from the parish churches. John Knox, Holburn, Gilcomston and St Clement's Free churches were also erected close by their Established counterparts. North Free was built directly opposite the parish church, only 25 yards distant. The first permanent Free Church to be occupied was St Clement's on 8 October 1843; East followed on 31 December; South on 7 January; North on 22 January; West on 28 January; with the exception of Holburn the others were completed by March 1844. (*Free Presb.*, vol. I, 19 April 1844; J. O. Skea, *The Free West* (1963), p. 19; *Free South Sess.*, 28 December 1843; Gammie, op. cit., pp. 184, 109, 157.) When the site for the building of the West, South and East Free churches was purchased it was revealed that a solicitor who was a well-known adherent of the Establishment had also signified an interest in it. There is no evidence to suggest that his interest was anything other than private however. (Ibid., p. 109.)

28 *Free Presb.*, vol. I, 25 July and 8 August 1843. 'Origins and history of the congregation', *Trin. Free Sess.*, p. 20.

29 For example Trinity Free cost about £1,200. The West, South and East Free cost their respective congregations more than £2,000 each: *Free Trin. Sess.*, 31 March 1844; *Free West Deac.*, vol. I, 17 December 1845; *Free South Sess.*, 15 March 1844.

30 *Free South Sess.*, 15 March 1844.

31 Ibid.

32 The total cost of building the West, South and East Free churches was £5,213 11s. 3d. but additional comforts for the congregations brought the final cost up to £6,704 17s. 7d.: *Free West Deac.*, vol. I, 17 December 1845.

33 Ibid.; W. Alexander, *East Free Church reminiscences* (Aberdeen, 1893), p. 13; *Free Trin. Sess.*, 28 November 1844; *Free South Sess.*, 15 March 1844.

34 *Free West Deac.*, 17 December 1845.

35 Rev. Dr Chalmers, *Earnest appeal to the Free Church of Scotland on the subject of its economics* (Edinburgh, 1846), pp. 8, 18-19.

36 As did earlier secession churches where there were often continual financial crises. See the case of Charlotte Street U.P. Church, ch. 6, pp. 121-2, 133-4.

37 For example, it was hoped that Bonaccord Chapel, opened in 1828, would be able to balance income and expenditure because of the high prices charged for sittings: *Aberdeen Journal*, 30 July 1828.

38 A joint meeting of committees from the West, South and East Free churches was held and the following scale of charges was approved: Body; back seats 8s., table seats 3s., fourth row from pulpit 4s., seats removed at communion 5s., all other seats 7s. Gallery; front seats 10s., second row 5s., third 3s. 6d., all other seats 2s. 6d. These charges were altered slightly by the East Free session at a later date: *Free South Sess.*, 30 November 1843.

39 The pressure was so great at first that the Free West later found itself obliged to refund money it had taken in seat rents from paupers. By 1850, however, demand for seats exceeded the supply: *Free West Deac.*, vol. 1, 17 December and 3 December 1845.

40 *Free South Sess.*, 25 January 1844.

41 See ch. 6, p. 134-5.

42 Rev. Dr Chalmers, op. cit., p. 9.

43 Forty were to give 1s., fifty 6d., two hundred 2d., four hundred ½d. and two hundred and sixty ¼d. to ½d.: *Free South Sess.*, 15 March 1844. See also *Free Trin. Sess.*, 10 March 1845.

44 *Free South Sess.*, 15 November 1843.

45 See n. 17.

46 The elders' visitation lists indicate the areas in which the congregation lived: *Est. Trin. Sess.*, 21 March 1837. See also ch. 4, pp. 83-5.

47 'Origins and history', *Free Trin. Sess.*, March 1844.

48 Elders ordained after the Disruption came from the Crown Street area. See ch. 4, p. 84.

49 *Est. Greyf. Sess.*, 22 December 1840. Attached sheet.

50 *Free Presb.*, vol. 1, 4 July 1843. The Trinity Free site was sanctioned on 8 August 1843.

51 A considerable section of the Free Presbytery were opposed to the Crown Street site. Captain Shepherd of Kirkville, Skene, was reported as having made the above allegation. Gordon's letter of denial was subsequently published: see Gammie, op. cit., pp. 131-2.

52 Gordon resigned, claiming that owing to the 'illness of a member of my family' it was necessary to move to an area with a warmer climate: see *Free Presb.*, vol. 1, 29 July 1845. He later requested a letter of introduction to the Presbyterian Church of England: ibid., 25 September 1845.

53 *Est. Greyf. Sess.*, 22 December 1840. Attached sheet.

54 Ibid.

55 See ch. 4, pp. 81, 85.

56 Gammie, op. cit., p. 131.

57 *Free West Deac.*, vol. 1, 27 February 1845.

58 Ibid., annual congregational meeting and report 17 December 1845.

59 Ibid., 31 January 1848.

60 *Free West Deac.*, vol. 1, 30 June 1848.

61 Ibid., 15 March 1849.

62 Ibid., 22 July 1850.

63 Ibid., annual congregational meeting and report, 31 January 1848.

64 See 'Reports of the committee anent Mariners' and Gaelic churches', *Free Presb.*, vol. 1, 26 March 1850.

65 Ibid., and 16 July 1850.

66 Ibid., 26 March 1850.

67 See ch. 6, pp. 121-6.

68 See Appendix G(iii).

69 See Appendix G(i) and (ii). The change in the social structure of Free kirk sessions is measurable, but other more subtle changes were taking place in the life styles of elders which are more difficult to quantify. For example, Alexander Thom of the Free West became Belgian consul in 1846; after his death in 1856 his nephew William S. Thom succeeded to the post. Dr Keith (South Free) became a university lecturer—the university had been a stronghold of moderatism. Numerous other elders bought country mansions (e.g. Bryce, South Free, moved to a Fonthill mansion after living in several other west end properties). Gradually these men were adopting the life styles of the residuary Establishment. For other examples see Biographical Notes.

70 See the Aberdeen almanacs and Post Office directories for these years.

71 *Free Greyf. Deac.*, 4 and 11 September 1854.

72 See ch. 8, pp. 172-6.

73 *Free Presb.*, vol. 2, 2 December 1856, 1 December 1857, 1 February 1859, 1 March 1859, 7 February 1860, 21 February 1861, 4 February 1862. In January 1863 the missionary and a substantial portion of the congregation left the Free Church after repeated requests to be set up as a separate charge: ibid., 3 February 1863.

74 See ch. 6, n. 18. (Some of the 1843 seceders scarcely gained a nominal number of votes in the election of elders in 1855—being squeezed out by new members of the congregation.)

75 *Free Presb.*, vol. 2, 10 and 31 March, 5 May 1857. The lectures were subsequently published. See *Lectures on distinctive principles of Free Church* (Aberdeen, 1858).

76 *Free West Deac.*, vol. 1, annual report by treasurer, 6 November 1851.

77 The most prosperous of the Free Church congregations, the Free West, was the first congregation to desert their Disruption-built church and erect a new building—'one of the best examples of ecclesiastical architecture in the city'—in the west end. A substantial portion of the congregation refused to leave the old building and both congregations prospered thereafter. *Free West Sess.*, vol. 2, 1 October 1866. Gammie, op. cit., pp. 228, 136-7.

Chapter 6

Kirk Sessions and Church Attendance

The veriest trifle will keep them away from church.*

As we have seen in the two previous chapters the Established and Free kirk sessions were controlled by the middle class. Although by 1851 there was a remarkable similarity in the social composition of the six city parish sessions and their Free Church counterparts it remained true nevertheless that the Free sessions, overall, were derived from social groups of significantly lower status than one would expect to find in the Establishment. Whilst by 1851 virtually all members of Established and Free sessions could be traced in the six city parish and Free churches, and also Trinity Free, a significant portion of the remaining eight Free church sessions could not be positively identified regarding social status.[1] The fact that out of the seventy-four elders of these churches, nine could not be traced at all does suggest that they might have fallen below the lower-middle-class status grouping. Only one elder, however, can be positively identified as not belonging to one or other middle-class grouping and this man does appear to have been regarded as something of an exception by his contemporaries.[2] What is more significant concerning the social structure of the Free Church eldership is that a substantial proportion—not less than 25 per cent—were derived from the small merchant and self-employed tradesmen section of the lower middle class. This section in fact was predominant in seven of the fifteen sessions of the Free Church. In this aspect the Free Church was similar to the United Presbyterian Church which with five congregations was the only other Presbyterian denomination of any numerical importance.

Compared to the Establishment, and indeed the United Presbyterian Church, the Free Church was constitutionally more democratic. In the Establishment elders were openly co-opted by the existing kirk session. In the U.P. churches, however, despite or perhaps because of their self-supporting financial organisation, control of church affairs tended to become the property of particularly wealthy individuals in the congregation, who either carried the burden of debt on the church building or could be relied upon in the not infrequent financial crises to see the church through its difficulties. Thus in the year of the Dis-

* *Selected portions from the diary and manuscripts of the Rev. Gavin Parker* (Aberdeen, 1848), p. 149.

ruption when the 'each-according-to-his-means' principle was being put into effect in the new Free Church one finds similar moves being successfully opposed in one United Presbyterian church by the principal creditor as 'it ultimately would have bad effects' and in the same month it was explicitly stated that the mode of electing elders lay, not with the congregation, but entirely with the existing kirk session. In actual fact the power lay with certain wealthy men on the session.[3]

Concomitants of Office

However democratic the constitution of the Free Church might appear in relation to the Establishment, and indeed the U.P. Church, severe social and economic limitations were attached to its democratic function. The official directive from its general assembly, the interpretation of which was a favourite theme of pre-election sermons, left the existing kirk session members sufficient scope:[4]

> The General Assembly appoint the Judicatories of this Church, to take good heed that none be admitted to, or continued in the office of an Elder, but such as are tender and circumspect in their walk, and punctual in their attending upon ordinances, and strict in their observation of the Lord's Day, and in regularly keeping up the worship of God in their families.

Although all communicants were given the opportunity 'to exercise the right of voting, if they should think proper to avail themselves of that privilege'[5] the voting procedure was not such as would encourage active working-class participation. Those who desired a voting list were required to apply to kirk session members at the church door on the Sabbath preceding the election.[6] The ballot was not secret—all papers had to be subscribed with the voter's name and place of residence, and then returned to a member of session. Although there is no evidence of eligible persons being denied a voting list if they sought one, there is reason to believe that many who were entitled to vote refrained from so doing. In one election of elders held in 1855 fewer than 300 participated although there were about 1,000 communicants.[7]

Moreover, although theoretically all male communicants in a congregation possessed the right of election to office, various practical requirements restricted the possible choice within fairly narrow limits. Certainly a measure of educational competence was required, though in effect this was a relatively minor problem. A greater limitation was perhaps the fact that the presbytery and certain kirk sessions met generally in the mornings and afternoons, weekly and fortnightly, and not at times when working men could be expected to participate.[8]

But if social factors such as these must have limited the possibility of working-class men serving on the session, the economic requirements associated with the eldership were more important in restricting working-class participation on the kirk sessions. We have already seen the pressures which were exerted on the congregations regarding contributions to the Sustentation Fund.[9] Elders were expected to make substantially greater contributions to the schemes of the churches than were the rest of the congregation. This was true of all three presbyterian denominations. In the Free Church specific enquiry was made by the central committee regarding office-bearer's contributions to the Sustentation Fund. Pressure was frequently applied to individual members of the session and the court that they increase their contributions.[10] In the Established Church, elders were held responsible for the legal expenses of the presbytery.[11] In both Free and United Presbyterian Churches the elders were in effect (morally if not in fact legally) the guarantors of the building debts and other liabilities of the church.[12] Similarly, certain Established Church elders found themselves morally obliged to furnish sufficient funds to maintain the chapels-of-ease over a fairly long period.[13] The smooth working of each individual church's finances was closely related to the socio-economic status of its elders in the community—elders who, when so required, could either furnish sufficient capital from their own resources or borrow it on the basis of their 'good name'. Indeed, so astute were certain Free Church elders in the field of finance that occasionally they could raise money on terms more favourable than the fairly low interest rates charged by the local banks.[14]

The financial obligations attached to office-holding and the economic requirements of the church were, therefore, serious obstacles to working-class participation in church government and as a result such participation was neither expected nor desired. This was true, not only of the Established Church where the sessions co-opted new elders, but of the other Presbyterian denominations. Even where co-option was the method of selecting elders difficulties could be encountered in finding men 'qualified for so highly important an office'.[15] When the South parish session 'began to look around for an addition to its members' they were confronted by the problem of 'the amazing multitude of removals, on the part of the middling, not to speak of the higher ranks, towards the new or West part of the city' lying outside the parochial boundary. 'It was found impossible to procure a sufficient number of men properly qualified for the office' and 'acting in the conscientious discharge of its duty' it co-opted men from the neighbouring Oldmachar parish where they were by then resident.[16] In the constitutionally more democratic Free and United Presbyterian Churches the existing sessions also acted as the guardians of the socio-economic status of the eldership by using their power of deciding when additional elders were required and when the most socially satisfactory results of an election were likely to be obtained. It was explicitly stated by the Free West session in 1844 that they alone would determine 'whither and at what time another election shall take place' to fill any vacancies and despite pressure from the congregation the existing session 'found obstacles in the way of proceeding immediately'[17] and no elections were in fact held until 1855 when there was obviously no shortage of eligible members.[18]

But if elections could be delayed indefinitely and, as we have seen earlier,[19] the electoral system itself was open to possible abuse, other more direct pressures could be applied by the existing session. Ordination of the new elders could not take place until the existing session approved those who had been elected by the congregation. It was customary following the election to visit the men so chosen and it is clear that this was a convenient means of eliminating those considered unsuitable for the office. Occasionally the existing session found it necessary to ordain less than the number of elders that they had originally intended.[20] An elder was of course elected for life and it was the duty of the existing eldership to maintain the standing of the office. Nevertheless it would seem that objectives became confused and that the morality of the individual was generally insufficient in itself as a qualification for office. Although constitutionally any communicant could object to the ordination of a man whom he considered unsuitable for office the possibility of objection from working-class members was not seriously considered. Indeed after some elections the result was considered so much a foregone conclusion that no real provision was made for possible working-class objections. These were heard at a time of day which ruled out working-class attendance—although adequate provision was made by the same session to allow the signing of a petition against Sabbath desecration at an evening hour.[21] Other sessions were less scrupulous than this, however, and instead of attempting to manipulate elections to obtain the most acceptable elders they simply by-passed the elective process completely. It seems virtually certain that the seceding elders from the South Parish Church co-opted additional elders in October 1843, and the following year they ignored the democratic process completely and openly co-opted two men to the eldership whom they considered eligible for the office although there is some evidence to suggest that the congregation did not share this view.[22] Certainly in terms of socio-economic status both were welcome additions to the existing session.

This need for men of sufficient socio-economic status on the kirk sessions tended to create a situation whereby election to eldership itself became a recognition of a man having pursued a successful business or professional career which in turn was a visible sign of his worth in the eyes of God.[23] The men to be 'set apart' by the church were usually men who were successfully setting themselves apart economically from their neighbours in the community. Failures did not become elders. In fact, as we shall see later in this chapter, failures could find it difficult to remain communicant members of the congregation.[24] Those who were elected (i.e. obtained a majority of the votes) but declined to accept the office may well have done so as a result of a realisation of the social limitations and economic requirements attached to eldership, or simply by kirk session persuasion. A refusal to accept office based solely on terms of religious principle was so unique as to be a matter almost of embarrassment to one session.[25] To those of the smaller merchant class whose presence was so much a feature of the Free and U.P. sessions the office of elder may have appeared as an acceptable alternative, or for many a stepping-stone to higher things. 'Public work, such as a member of the Police Board, or a Town Councillor, was looked upon as a waste of time, a kind of service which should only be undertaken by idle or wealthy men.'[26] Eldership, on the other hand, although an office possessed of considerable prestige, required only a minimum of attention. Membership of the kirk session not only reflected an individual's undoubted social respectability, it was both a recognition and a warranty of his financial integrity.[27] That church office might bring material benefits to a businessman one can only postulate. Certainly for some the office would appear to have brought at least a modest financial return.[28] However, to suggest that the kirk sessions were made up entirely of self-seeking individuals would be as unfair as it would be foolish to insist that these men were all 'set apart' purely on the basis of their spiritual qualities. The important and unifying feature was not whether particular individuals holding office were suitable or even capable, but the fact that these men were all drawn from distinct middle-class social groupings. It followed by a close interaction of cause and effect that a situation was perpetuated whereby institutional difficulties, and social and financial requirements, made working-class participation in the affairs of the kirk session impracticable. Nevertheless, it is quite conceivable that such a situation was accepted by the working class as an inevitable economic necessity, and the fact that middle-class members completely dominated the kirk sessions need not by itself be seen as a factor deterring working-class attendance at church services. The attitude and actions of these sessions were an important factor, however, and these must now be considered along with other features of church-going which were a recognisable deterrent to working-class participation in public worship.

Church Attendance and the Kirk Session

We have already seen in an earlier chapter the problems involved in analysing the official census of religion which was undertaken in 1851.[29] Whilst the attendance figures clearly demonstrate the numerical superiority of presbyterianism in the city and also provide a fairly reliable indication of the relative strength of active support received by the various denominations, it would be totally misleading to regard attendance figures alone as a gauge of 'religious feeling' or to see them as a means of determining whether the community remained even 'nominally Christian'.[30] An earlier census carried out by the Aberdeen kirk sessions in 1837 and based not on attendance but on what was termed 'connection' revealed that only some 8 per cent of the population were not 'connected' to some church or other.[31] Although the situation obviously did not remain unchanged throughout the fourteen years between the two investigations, it would be a mistake to exaggerate the extent of change. Certainly in one important aspect—the proportion of seats to population—practically no change at all had occurred.[32] The problem of reaching some sort of working definition of what exactly was meant by 'connection' is less serious than might at first appear. 'Connection' implied a nominal allegiance to a church; an allegiance which shaded through various degrees of commitment by regular attendance, intermittent or occasional, or even rare attendance, to a simple realisation that one ought to be connected to a religious body. There was a general recognition at the time that it was the working class who were not the regular attenders. Two questions therefore naturally arise from this situation: First, why they chose not to attend

church; and second, given their lack of attendance, why they nevertheless continued to hold an allegiance—a 'connection'—however tenuous,
with a religious body. The second question, which is obviously closely
associated with the first, is the more complex and will be dealt with in a
later chapter.[33]

The problem of non-attendance can only to a limited extent be
explained by religious apathy which in many ways is a symptomatic
rather than a causal factor. Certainly in many Presbyterian churches in
the 1840s there was no lack of enthusiasm, if at times it descended to
little more than inter-denominational rivalry. As we have seen there
was a wave of church-building led by the Free Church and followed
to a lesser extent by the United Presbyterians. All of the presbyterian
churches appeared to be aware of their shortcomings regarding the
participation of the masses in public worship, and particularly in the
Free Church the matter was a subject of annual debate.[34] Nevertheless,
little if anything was accomplished, and the trend overall would appear
to be one of deterioration rather than improvement.

The connection between non-attendance and lack of suitable clothing
among poorer members has often been advanced as a reason for the
failure of the churches to attract working-class participation.[35] Many
who might otherwise have attended were undoubtedly deterred from
doing so for this reason. One elder, looking back over nearly fifty
years, commented thus on a revival meeting held in the church:[36]

> One peculiarity of these meetings we have never observed in other
> gatherings of the kind. . . . It was that many men attended in their
> working clothes, and crowds of young women without bonnets
> or caps, but with little shawls about their shoulders, which they
> put on their heads when they left church.

A gathering such as this in a Presbyterian church would appear to be
virtually unique, and it might be argued from this occasion that where
ragged rather than respectable clothes were the general rule the lower
classes were prepared to participate. Few working people, however,
were prepared to risk ridicule, and even kirk session censure perhaps,
by attending thus on a normal occasion. Indeed, lack of suitable clothes
was accepted by some sessions as sufficient reason for non-attendance.[37]
Agencies were set up by female members of congregations to provide
clothes for respectable members of the lower classes.[38] In one church
the session arranged that two girls share the same clothes at alternate
services.[39]

But if lack of suitable attire undoubtedly deterred many from attending church it is perhaps equally true to say that it provided a ready and acceptable excuse for not doing so. Respectability of dress was in fact only a visible conformity to all the other requirements of religious respectability which was an integral part of church attendance. Any hint of violation of a whole catalogue of moral crimes brought the censure of the kirk session upon the individual.

Presbyterian kirk sessions were well organised and integrated instruments capable of imposing a pattern of social, economic, and moral behaviour upon the church-going sections of the community.[40] Although the actions of these bodies were felt most profoundly by church-goers, their influence extended far beyond the immediate congregational bounds and tended to have the reverse effects of encouraging middle-class participation and deterring working-class attendance. Those who did not attend church but continued to believe in church 'connection' did not escape kirk session censure. A request for the sacraments of marriage or baptism led to moral enquiry by the session, which must have inhibited many from seeking more than this basic connection with a church. Working men and women were continually before the sessions on matters of moral behaviour, particularly with regard to the 'gross sin' of what was termed 'antenuptial fornication'. The child of such a premarital union was regarded in the same way as a bastard and unfit for baptism until the parents had fully submitted themselves to the discipline of the session.[41]

Such discipline could be, and often was, a lengthy process extended on the slightest pretext for an indefinite period. Cases were 'continued' because of irregular attendance at public worship, or because the sinner feared the temporal rather than the spiritual consequences, or more usually the offender was not reduced to a 'state of mind suitable to the circumstances'.[42] The Free and United Presbyterian Churches were particularly active in the pursuit of such offences and occasionally parents undergoing discipline rebelled against the harshness of the enquiry and had their child baptised by ministers of other communions.[43] Moreover, enquiry by the elders was not restricted to those guilty, or considered guilty, of a moral offence. Elders would verify statements made before the session by visiting relatives and neighbours and questioning them on the subject.[44] Testimonies would also be sought from the accused person's employer affirming previous good character, present shame, and capacity for hard work.[45] Hearsay would appear to be the basis of prosecution in such cases and occasionally the enquiries carried out would lead to the citing of other individuals suspected of the sin of association. The South Free session denied communion to a member who admitted that she had 'accommodated in her house, for a short time, a female of disreputable character'.[46] Where paternity could not be clearly established it was customary for a session to continue discipline indefinitely in the hope that further evidence would eventually come to light.[47]

But if the various types of fornication ranked highest on the list of offences dealt with by the kirk sessions the sin of intemperance followed closely behind. Intemperance was used to describe all shades of addiction to intoxicating liquor—from the undertaker who admitted partaking prior to his placing of dead bodies in their coffins, to the occasional reveller unfortunate enough to have been seen in an inebriated condition by a church elder.[48] Many of those called to appear before the session on such charges claimed themselves to be innocent and undoubtedly some who claimed to be suffering from physical disabilities were not guilty. Nevertheless all were placed under the scandal of the accusation. Appearance before the kirk session was, in itself, a censure. One individual, after five months of questioning and enquiries from 'other parties likely to know about the matter', was found innocent of the charge brought against him and dismissed from further discipline, although he was exhorted 'to walk circumspectly so as to give no occasion to unfavourable reports being carried against him'.[49]

No sphere of conduct was free from kirk session interference. Those who walked for pleasure on the Sabbath, as opposed to walking to church, were severely censured as Sabbath desecrators. One individual found himself before the session for 'keeping untimely hours in his family'. A teacher of music was exhorted to 'betake himself of some respectable calling for the support of himself and his family'.[50] An hotel waiter was instructed 'to abstain from such an objectionable occupation in future'.[51] Anyone involved in legal proceedings was required to give an account of the matter to the session. Relatively minor offences against property rights were treated severely. One girl called before the session admitted 'appropriating for her own use a bolster or pillow belonging to a person residing in the same house' and was denied communion until further enquiries were made regarding the state of her mind.[52] Suspicion of guilt was enough to raise enquiries and bring forth comment. A man who requested a certificate of membership was granted the same with the following inscription included: 'certain charges were made against him by some of the public authorities but which the Session understand were subsequently abandoned'.[53] On another occasion enquiries were instructed to be made on whether a man reported in the local press as having been found guilty of disorderly conduct was a man of the same name who was a member of the congregation.[54] A church member who appeared on being cited by the session and 'acknowledged the fact of his having received payment of Accounts from some of his master's customers, and had not paid over the money in regular time' was struck off the communion roll despite certain admitted 'extenuating circumstances' with regard to 'the harshness of his master's dealings towards him'.[55]

With the general exception of church office-bearers where any hint of scandal tended to lead to investigation, and deposition was not altogether uncommon,[56] the middle class do not appear to have undergone any extensive disciplinary action concerning sexual morality and alcoholic intemperance. This does not mean that they did not indulge in such excesses but simply that they were more prudent in the manner of their indulgence, and offences which did come to light were handled discreetly by the session. There was a marked reluctance on the part of the kirk sessions to proceed against individuals of socio-economic status in the community and who lived in respectable residential areas. Where sessions were compelled to act on the matter through force of circumstances, technical reasons would be found for not pursuing the case. Thus one session readily accepted a blatantly false explanation as to the paternity of a child borne by a domestic servant who was a member of the congregation, but later were forced to take the matter up again partly as a result of the 'notoriety of the case in the parish'. The real father was not a shoemaker who 'had left Aberdeen to avoid the consequences' but the girl's employer—a lawyer living in fashionable Bonaccord Street. The session found it could not proceed as the 'guilt was committed in the parish of Oldmachar, Bonaccord Street being in that parish'. The Oldmachar session subsequently denied responsibility and the matter was shelved.[57] Similarly another session 'found that they could not interfere' in the case of a seat-holder in the church who lived in fashionable Springbank Terrace and who 'had acknowledged himself . . . the father of an illegitimate child of which the mother had been under discipline' to another kirk session.[58] The same session also found itself forced to refuse communion to an advocate and later to expunge his name from the roll without recording the reason for his removal or indeed the fact that his name had been removed. The matter only comes to light in the records when the advocate sought re-admission. Because of the 'excellent spirit manifested' by the applicant he was re-admitted without appearing before the session for discipline and his offence, which must have been a serious one, was never actually recorded.[59]

But if the middle class were generally able to avoid the rigours of kirk session discipline regarding matters such as sexual morality and alcoholic temperance, in one field in particular they were subject to close scrutiny. Any hint of unsound business practice led to immediate enquiry although here again one suspects that it was not so much the crime as the exposure which was regarded as the sin. Suspicion of financial insolvency could lead to immediate investigation. A member of Trinity Parish Church who had the audacity to declare, when approached and questioned regarding his financial stability, that 'Public Business and Kirk Sessions has little or no connection one with the other', was struck off the communion roll.[60] Even after meeting his creditors satisfactorily a bankrupt did not expiate his sin in the eyes of the session. One bankrupt who was a Sunday-school teacher was left by the session to determine for himself 'whether or not he should *immediately* resume the duties', the inference being that it was unbecoming for him to do so. Moreover, the stigma of bankruptcy was attached not only to the bankrupt but also to his family. One undischarged bankrupt in 1860 was refused the sacrament of baptism for his child until he gave a more satisfactory account of his failure to the kirk session.[61] Another in 1865 was refused a certificate of church membership until he produced a written testimony from his creditors, although the session after due consideration agreed that they now had no objection to the granting of a certificate to the bankrupt's wife.[62]

The social controls brought to bear by the kirk sessions on the middle class therefore differed radically in type from those exerted on the working class. Not only were they different in type however; one can easily see how they would differ greatly in their effects. Church membership to the Victorian businessman was in many ways a mark of his continuing financial stability and social respectability. No such positive advantages were attached to working-class membership, where fear of exposure or of mere perverted accusation acted as a disincentive to membership, as it inevitably resulted in humiliation and disgrace before a watchful session composed largely of employers acting in their capacity as elders.

Obligations Associated with Membership

Whilst as we have seen the kirk sessions showed considerable readiness to take upon themselves the task of enquiring into the spiritual condition of the working-class members, they were perhaps less able, and certainly less eager, to undertake responsibility for the material needs of the poorer members of the congregation. After the enactment of the new Scottish Poor Law in 1845 the sessions continued to provide a measure of outdoor relief which was drawn from the interest on endowments set aside for that purpose and also from the half-yearly communion collection. Recipients were almost entirely females, generally widows, and relief was given either on a 'permanent' or 'occasional' basis. The sums distributed were small—few recipients were allowed more than £2 per year. Some sessions attached conditions to how the money was to be spent—whether on food, clothing, school fees, and so on.[63] Payment in kind rather than money was adopted by one U.P. church, where a recipient was supplied with 'two common shirts, two flannel shirts, and two pairs of drawers; these being the property of the Session, and given only as a loan, paying some one to call once a week with a clean suit, and bring away the dirty ones; and if at any time any of these articles be pawned, no further relief shall be given'.[64] Another U.P. church appears to have made distribution only in times of exceptional hardship, using the sacramental collections as a means of paying the seat rents of the poor.[65]

Notwithstanding that the funds of the churches were limited and that the sessions were bound by necessity to use the money to its best advantage, it could well be maintained that neither the method of assessment nor mode of disbursement was likely to promote this. On the death of a recipient, or their removal to the Poor's House, the question of who was to take the vacant place on the roll very often would appear to have become a matter less of assessment than kirk session politics, the individual with the most influential backing being most likely to succeed. When pressure for admission to the roll was great, visitation of recipients occasionally took place leading to a 'generous renunciation' of a claim—the most independent, the least servile, and perhaps the most needy being the sufferers in such an arrangement.[66]

It was also the case that working-class members, unable to rely on receiving financial assistance in sickness or old age, were expected to contribute to the various schemes of the church. This was particularly true of the Free and U.P. churches. As we have seen, contributions to the Sustentation Fund were a burden on many Free Church congregations, and increasingly contributions to the fund came to be regarded as an obligation of membership—a fact which was not ignored by Free Church critics.[67] Dr Chalmers, champion of such principles, saw the question of working-class subscriptions to the fund in rather a different light:[68]

> There cannot be a falser principle, than that the poorer offerings should be declined or dispensed with. Under the guise of sentiment, there is in it all the grossness of materialism. To neglect or under-rate the mites of our artisans and labourers because of their insignificance, is to rate the moral value of a sacrifice at nothing, and to make the monied value all in all.

The real position regarding membership and subscriptions was probably nearer to indirect compulsion than to Chalmers' high-flown concept of the 'moral value of sacrifice'. The kirk sessions themselves were continually pressed by the central committee operating the fund and occasionally found themselves receiving directives concerning the correct utilisation of the congregational finances:[69]

> In the circumstances in which the Church is now placed, the main and primary object of the ordinary church door collections must necessarily be the supplementing of Ministers' Stipends, it being for the most part more expedient that the relief of the poor members of the Church should be provided for by occasional and extraordinary appeals ... [and] no sum whatever (even for objects that are highly laudable in themselves) ought to be paid out of funds arising from ordinary church door collections.

Thus, if the Free churches pressed for increased contributions from members of their congregations, they did so generally because of central direction and often, it would seem, with considerable reluctance.[70] Certainly despite the threatening tone of such circulars, there is no evidence to suggest that any working-class member was actually called upon to resign his membership because he failed to contribute to the Fund, although this type of pressure, exerted generally, may well have led to a decline in working-class membership.

The United Presbyterian Church, on the other hand, had less scruples with regard to those who failed to contribute to the support of the church. The Charlotte Street U.P. managers, having previously agreed that 'every member of the Congregation should pay for a seat', decided, on finding that not all the congregation had done so, 'to devise some plan in order to get them to pay ... [and] in the event of not getting satisfactory reason from them, that they shall be called before the Session, and reasoned with in a friendly and Christian-like manner'.[71] Considerable ingenuity was used in other plans for the raising of church funds and ensuring that those who did not contribute would be humiliated before the congregation. On one occasion the minister was instructed to preach a special sermon regarding the debt on the church building, and it was decided 'that Subscription lists should be prepared so as to ascertain what each member may be inclined to give and that the mode of getting the Subscription names should be by making the members come out of their seats by the Minister's room and through the Vestry, and put down their names for what they are willing to give and then pass through the Vestry to the Church'.[72] A careful watch was kept over church door collections, all managers and elders remaining by the plate until the collection was taken up and, moreover, whilst they were prepared to 'make allowance for poverty and want of employment . . . surely an extra penny-a-week could never be felt by anyone . . . and might this not be more than saved on some articles of superfluity?'[73]

A whole series of cases of non-payment of seat rents appeared before Charlotte Street kirk session. One party was grieved enough to appeal to the presbytery regarding his case, but the presbytery accepted the session's judgment of the matter and instructed them 'to proceed therein according to the rules of the Church'.[74] A member who pleaded inability to pay because of unemployment was told that he had formerly been earning high wages and that he must 'now that he has got employment . . . begin to pay the first instalment of these arrears'.[75] The session were, however, prepared in some cases to accept payment by service—one widow, unable to pay her arrears, undertook the task of 'washing and dressing the Table cloths connected with the church to the amount of her own and her mother's seat rents'.[76]

Neither the Established nor the Free Church took matters to such a length as this with regard to the non-payment of seat rents. The principle of providing gratis sittings for the poor was accepted by both bodies. Occasionally compromise arrangements were made. In one Established church certain seats were held conjointly, 'one party occupying them at one diet, and another at another, while the price of one seat goes to the chapel'.[77] Seat rents were reimbursed in one Free church when it was found afterwards that the circumstances of certain members made it necessary.[78] There is no reason to believe that such compromise arrangements were not entered into willingly enough by poor members who preferred to pay a nominal rent rather than suffer the social indignity attached to holding a gratis sitting, although even those seats held at a low rental lay under a degree of social stigma. At a congregational meeting of one Free church in 1851, when it was proposed that a reduction be made in the present seat rents, it was pointed out that there was 'a considerable number of sittings so low as one shilling and three pence . . . not so fully let as higher rented sittings'.[79] The demand on certain seats in the Free West Church was such that a committee was formed to regulate seat-letting of vacancies and to recommend to the session who were to receive them.[80] Those holding desirable sittings in some churches were pressed, sometimes rather high-handedly, to give up their seats and have others allocated to them and bitter disputes arose concerning the rights of individuals or families to occupy certain pews.[81]

Status Differentiation within the Congregation

The extent to which graduated seat rents in the Free Church confirmed the internal stratification of congregations has already been demonstrated.[82] Social differences among members of the same congregation were consolidated by a host of other factors through which the institution of seat-letting was associated with the sanctity of property and the enforcement of status differentiation. Doors were erected in the more desirable pews and official 'pew openers' were closely instructed that 'care is to be taken, that strangers be not admitted until the seat holders are accommodated'.[83] 'Partitions and obscuring glass' were utilised presumably as a means of providing special privacy for certain pews.[84] Beadles were warned that at all times they must 'attend first to the rights of seat holders' and special cupboards were provided in order that Bibles might be locked up after each service.[85] Even in the smaller Presbyterian churches status differentiation of this sort is all too apparent. In Charlotte U.P. Church, whilst some members were being interrogated concerning their inability to pay seat rents, others were engaged in covering their sittings with crimson cloth 'as a pattern to other individuals who may be inclined to cover their seats'.[86]

If features such as these may have discouraged working-class attendance, at a more general level there was also a failure to integrate working-class members within the congregation on a basis of equality. This was certainly true of the practice of visitation by elders. It was 'understood that in regard to a considerable proportion of the members of the Church the Elders visits and advice must be solicited before they can be tendered . . . particularly with those on a level with or above themselves in worldly circumstances'.[87] This solicitation was not required from the 'humbler classes' belonging to the church who were 'more than any other exposed to temptation'.[88] Discrimination of this sort led almost inevitably to the basis of contact between office-bearers and working-class members being restricted to investigation or appearance before the sessions on matters of moral discipline. Visitation by elders other than that for the investigation of reported moral misbehaviour, or in order to assess or propose increased financial contributions, was seldom carried out. The Free Church was particularly aware of its shortcomings and failures with regard to visitation. A committee reporting on the state of religion in Aberdeen in 1850 found that 'the one great cause of the low state of religion prevailing within the Church is the careless and perfunctory manner in which many of the office-bearers perform the duties devolving upon them. . . . Some elders visit not at all, most visit seldom.'[89] The failure of the elders to fulfil the obligations of their office is most clearly seen in the larger Free Church congregations. Although there is little evidence to suggest the Established Church elder was more ready to undertake these obligations, constitutionally he remained bound to the ideal of visitation on a parish basis. This was not true of the Free Church, which abandoned the parish as an area of ecclesiastical administration after the Disruption and concentrated on the congregational unit. Moreover, seatholding, not membership, sometimes became the criterion for regular visitation.[90] In one Free church the congregation was 'divided among the Elders according to the Pews they occupy', it being hoped that Christian men might 'occupy the districts not provided with Elders'.[91] It followed that elders were required to visit only those holding pews adjacent to their own and consequently of the same social status as themselves. The fact that domestic servants usually sat in or near their employers' pew created problems for some elders. The kirk session found in 1855 that 'as it had been found inconvenient for the Elders, in visiting, to see females engaged in domestic service, and at Manufacturies, in their respective dwellings, it was agreed that the Elders should meet from time to time with females so employed, sitting in the division of the church under Elders charge respectively,—in the Session house, on week-day evenings'.[92] It would be unfair, however, to maintain that all session members were complacent regarding the obligations of office. Indeed there appears to have been a fairly general recognition at session level that the extent of visitation was inadequate. In an election of elders in 1859 one session stressed that the acceptance of office would be viewed as an express declaration of the individual's resolution to carry out visitation of a portion of the congregation.[93]

Beyond vague and general recognition of their failure in this matter, however, few sessions were prepared to go although some did contribute to the support of full- or part-time congregational missionaries.[94] One kirk session did attempt to prick the consciences of elders by sending cards reminding them that visitation was now due, and requiring reports to be given of their reception whilst visiting working-class members, but even this direct approach proved ineffective.[95] On the whole, measures such as these are more symptomatic of the lack of contact than of any really earnest endeavour to alter the situation. The conscience of one session, in fact, did not extend beyond instructing the Sustentation Fund collectors to report to them any case of sickness or 'apprehended death' where their services or that of the minister were requested. The same collectors were also required to observe and report if 'any of their contributors shall appear to be contributing in any considerable degree below their means'.[96] Indeed with the exception of churches such as the Mariners' and Gaelic Free churches where the smallness of the congregation, combined with certain occupational, cultural and linguistic features tended to aid social integration,[97] there was little direct contact between office-bearers and working-class members other than on the basis of moral enquiry and financial obligations.

Conclusions: the Problem of 'Connection'

We have seen that beyond attendance at public worship working-class participation was negligible in so far as church government was concerned. Desire for social respectability and recognition by the wider society, as well as simple financial expediency, determined the composition of the kirk sessions. Although a middle-class eldership need not in itself have been a deterrent to working-class attendance it seems clear that social discrimination was practised and there was little integration or cultural contact within the congregation. Partly as a result of the social and economic requirements of the office, men called upon to serve on the sessions were often unwilling, or unable, to fulfil certain of the obligations of eldership. Nevertheless the Presbyterian churches were not unaware of their moral and religious obligations—particularly regarding those who seldom or never attended church. Their failure to integrate the respectable working-class church members, however, was magnified a hundred-fold when they sought to embrace the spiritually destitute and found their way barred by material poverty whose causes they could not fully comprehend.[98] Those whom they sought to help 'generally sneered at any attempt to help them',[99] and yet, as we have seen, there was a widespread and continuing belief in church 'connection' which, however defined, involved a degree of attachment to a religious body. Presbyterian churchmen worried over the problem: it was feared that 'some of them have not even rational knowledge of the fallen state of man. . . . Many of them become Chartists or Roman Catholics, or Unitarians, or have no profession of any definite religion.'[100] The same minister found himself 'grieved and discouraged' by the attitude of 'labouring men' because 'the veriest trifle will keep them away from church'.[101] Some of the reasons why these men chose not to attend have been revealed in this chapter. Most of the reasons can be ascribed to the class-conscious nature of the presbyterian churches. The reasons for the continuing belief in church 'connection' involves a more complex analysis of a concatenation of factors and this will be undertaken in the chapters immediately following.

Notes

1 See Appendix G(iii) for details of these and other figures cited in this chapter.

2 A fellow-elder describes his life in some detail almost by way of explanation: Hector McKay, born 1807, died 1860; immigrant from Sutherland about 1816; became ropemaker 'and continued in same employment until the end of his life'—such a statement from this author meaning that, had he so desired he could have bettered himself; McKay's 'visits to the sick and dying were numerous, and not by any means confined to the congregation with which he was connected' (W. Robbie, *Bonaccord Free Church, Aberdeen: a retrospect, 1828-87* (Aberdeen, 1887), pp. 88-90).

3 See *Charl. U.P. Man. Min.*, August 1843. (For the sake of convenience this church has been described as 'United Presbyterian' in 1843. In actual fact it was not 'U.P.' until the amalgamation of 1847.)

4 *The practice of the Free Church in her several Courts, published by authority of the General Assembly* (Edinburgh, 1871), p. 9.

5 *Free Trin. Sess.*, 11 December 1843; *Free West Sess.*, 1 November 1859.

6 *Free West Sess.*, 18 February 1855.

7 Ibid., 26 February 1855. *Free West Deac.*, 16 January 1851, records number of sitters as being 1,150, of whom 950 were communicants.

8 Session records occasionally reveal cases where offenders were unable to submit themselves to discipline because they could not be released by their

employer at that particular hour, e.g. *Est. Trin. Sess.*, 20 February 1887; *Est. Greyf. Sess.*, 11 June, 2 July 1866. One session found it necessary to change to alternate afternoon and evening meetings largely, it would appear, because of this problem (*Free Trin. Sess.*, 17 December 1853). See also *Est. South Sess.*, 3 April 1848.

9   See ch. 5, pp. 111–13.

10   See *Free Trin. Deac.*, 12 March and 12 August 1850, 13 December 1854. *Free West Deac.*, 16 January 1851.

11   These at times were fairly heavy. In one protracted case when a minister was deposed on a charge of intemperance, one of the ruling elders of the Established Presbytery went so far as to point out that after the expiry of his term of office 'he would not hold himself responsible for any expenses incurred after that date' (*Est. Presb.*, 23 October 1860). See also ch. 4, n. 46.

12   Greyfriars Free Church, facing bankruptcy with only £30 in funds, was pressed for £100 in debts by a creditor who claimed that 'it is true that the Deacons Court are not personally liable for the amount of the Bill, but it is in their interest to see it paid' (*Free Greyf. Deac.*, 30 June 1854; this Court was made up entirely of elders). Similarly, Greyfriars parish session were required to borrow 'on their personal security' in order to build a new school (*Est. Greyf. Sess.*, 8 June 1863). Loans and gratuitous professional services were common (e.g. *Free West Sess.*, 20 February 1866). In some congregations the obligations of elders and congregation were precisely defined (*Charl. U.P. Man. Min.*, 19 May and 8 November 1841).

13   *Est. Presb.*, 3 May 1844, 27 September 1853.

14   *Free West Deac.*, 17 December 1845.

15   *Est. South Sess.*, 30 January 1832.

16   Ibid. (Oldmachar kirk session raised objections as these men were residents of that parish. The South session justified their action in a six-page letter to the Presbytery.)

17   *Free West Sess.*, 29 February and 27 June 1844, 26 November 1851, 8 March 1853.

18   In 1844 only sixty votes had separated the first from the fourteenth on the voting list, but in 1855 this gap had widened to 202. The prestige attached to holding a seat in the Free West (see p. 82) had led to an influx of a large number of men suited to the office. In 1844 two men had been ordained because of the 'refusal' to accept office of others and yet had received only thirty-one and twenty-seven votes. In 1855 the lowest number of votes was ninety-two. None of the men who narrowly missed election in 1844 received anything near this figure in 1855. Only one man increased his share of the votes (by six); the others suffered a very substantial decline in both absolute and relative terms (e.g. one man who had received seventy-eight votes in 1844 and had been eighth on the voting order received only two votes in 1855). See *Free West Sess.*, 4 June 1844, 26 February 1855.

19   See p. 122.

20   For example, see *Free Trin. Sess.*, 20 March and 16 April 1852; *Charl. U.P. Man. Min.*, May–June 1848.

21   *Free West Sess.*, 1 March 1855.

22   The elders admitted to the South Free session in October 1843 were declared as having been 'elected by their suffrages' but there appears to be

no record of an election by the congregation having taken place. It seems likely that the seceding elders themselves were those who voted on this matter. Certainly the following year two men were co-opted by the kirk session—Sir William Seaton of Pitmadden, and William Stephen who had financial interests in cabinet making and upholstery as well as building. Both men had taken part in a congregational election for the office of deacon that same year and had been eighth and eighteenth respectively in terms of votes received. See *South Free Sess.*, 30 October 1843, 8 April 1844.

23 The language of the kirk sessions clearly indicates that integrity in business was linked to religious piety. Bankruptcy was, therefore, a particularly serious offence in the eyes of kirk sessions.

24 See p. 131.

25 After an election in Trinity Free Church one of those elected declined office as he could not bring himself to sign the confession of faith. He was pressed to reconsider, but later declined once more (*Free Trin. Sess.*, 20 March 1852).

26 A. S. Cook, *Old time traders and their ways* (Aberdeen, 1902), p. 42.

27 See discussion of extent of elders' visitations (pp. 135-7) and the attitude of churches regarding financial insolvency of members (p. 131).

28 For some, church connection brought contracts for work on their own or other churches, although session politics could make tendering a hazardous business (*Free Trin. Deac.*, 10 August 1852, 12 September 1864).

29 See ch. 2, *passim*.

30 Two eminent historians have suggested that the attendance figures could be used for these purposes. See H. Pelling, 'Religion and the nineteenth century British working class', *Past and Present*, no. 27 (1964), p. 131; and G. S. Kitson Clark, *The making of Victorian England* (London, 1962), p. 150.

31 *NSA*, p. 35. The writer, Rev. A. L. Gordon, doubted the authenticity of the figures on the basis that many were included who never attended church. This does not detract from the importance of enquiry as a means of gauging religiosity.

32 Largely because of the disruption in the Established Church and the spate of Free Church building which resulted (ten churches), the proportion of sittings to population remained at about 48 per cent. The United Presbyterians also erected three churches in the 1840s.

33 See ch. 7, *passim*.

34 For example, see reports of the committee anent the state of religion (*Free Presb.*, 7 May 1850, 13 December 1859).

35 For example, see K. S. Inglis, *Churches and the working classes in Victorian England* (London, 1963), pp. 59, 116, 130; Kitson Clark, op. cit., p. 149; Asa Briggs, *The age of improvement, 1783-1867* (London, 1959), p. 466.

36 Robbie, op. cit., p. 121.

37 *Est. Greyf. Sess.*, 5 September 1864; *Free Trin. Sess.*, 19 November 1854.

38 The Free Church were active in this field. However, it was a Congregational church which claimed to have founded the first of these societies 'before 1843'. G. King, *Brief historical sketch of the Congregational Church . . .* (Aberdeen, 1870), p. 20.

39 *Free Trin. Sess.*, 18 December 1854.

40 The kirk sessions co-operated on a national as well as a local level in matters

of moral discipline and in exerting pressure over issues such as national education and Sabbath violation by railway companies. By 1850 denominational animosities had cooled to the extent of allowing limited co-operation over the problem of the moral investigation of members who had changed their denominational allegiance. In other matters, however, the sessions acted independently. For examples of their extensive sphere of interest, see *Est. Trin. Sess.*, 21 January 1839; *Est. Greyf. Sess.*, 2 December 1850, 4 October 1852; *Free Presb.*, 26 March, 16 April, 3 December 1850; *Est. Presb.*, 10 February 1847, 1 February 1848; *Est. Gen. Sess.*, 23 April 1849.

41 All kirk session records abound with such cases—baptism being refused until discipline was complete. The discipline itself was no mere formality. One session found it necessary, by continual visitation and prayers, to 'forcibly impress' on the mother that 'marriage subsequently cannot do away or atone for that sin': *Free Trin. Sess.*, 31 July 1845.

42 *Free Trin. Sess.*, 28 November 1844, 18 March 1850; *Free West Sess.*, 27 February 1850, 4 May 1852.

43 *Est. Trin. Sess.*, 15 September 1840; *Free West Sess.*, 13 February 1849; *Free Trin. Sess.*, 17 June 1850.

44 For example, *Free Trin. Sess.*, 19 November 1849; *Est. Greyf. Sess.*, 17 November 1864.

45 *Free West Sess.*, 23 October 1860; *Est. West Sess.*, 25 February and 15 July 1863; *Est. Greyf. Sess.*, 5 September 1853, 7 November 1864; *Est. South Sess.*, 9 March 1848; *Free South Sess.*, 5 December 1849.

46 *Free South Sess.*, 11 July 1849.

47 For example, in the case of a young girl raped by 'one of two persons unknown to her' the Greyfriars session refused baptism and, despite appeals for leniency, submitted the matter to the Presbytery. After lengthy enquiries over a period of eighteen months the session finally relented and decided that she would no longer 'be subject to church discipline although in a scandalous situation'. (*Est. Greyf. Sess.*, 1 March, 3 May, 7 June, 6 September 1852; 5 September 1853.)

48 *Free Trin. Sess.*, 21 February 1848, 3 October 1859.

49 Ibid., 11 September 1861.

50 *Free Trin. Deac.*, 23 January 1845.

51 *Est. South Sess.*, 9 September 1847.

52 *Free Trin. Sess.*, 25 March 1847.

53 Ibid., 24 October 1864.

54 Ibid., 19 November 1849.

55 *Free South Sess.*, 12 March, 25 March, 1 April 1830.

56 For example, see *Est. Trin. Sess.*, 21 May 1840; *Free West Sess.*, 26 October 1863; *Free Trin. Sess.*, 21 July 1845.

57 The girl, Isabella Laurie, had gone back to her parents' home in the rural parish of Leochel Cushnie to have the child. The South parish kirk session were forced to take action when the Leochel Cushnie session reported the matter to them after having obtained a full confession from the girl who was being financially supported by the real father. Oldmachar refused to proceed against the father on an even flimsier pretext than the South session, claiming that Leochel Cushnie session ought to undertake the case as she was a resident of that parish. The girl, however, had returned to

live in the city two months earlier and both South and Oldmachar sessions had been made aware of this fact by the Leochel Cushnie kirk session clerk who had written giving the girl's address in Blackfriars Street: *Est. South Sess.*, 9 May, 13 June and 8 August 1850.

58 *Free South Sess.*, 13 January 1846. The clerk of Gilcomston Free kirk session reported the matter to the South Free session who recorded the correspondence and were required to make a ruling as in the case (see above) of Isabella Laurie. But for the need of a written reply it seems doubtful if either of these cases would have been recorded.

59 The man concerned 'stated his entire willingness to submit to the authority of the session' but this was not thought necessary—a small committee dealing with the matter privately: *Free South Sess.*, 4 April 1849.

60 *Est. Trin. Sess.*, 12 September 1842.

61 *Free Trin. Sess.*, 15 September 1851, 4 June 1860.

62 *Free West Sess.*, 16 October 1865.

63 For example, *Est. Greyf. Sess.*, 4 October and 6 December 1847; 3 December 1849, 5 August 1850, 3 March 1851. This session did give consideration to giving relief in kind rather than attaching conditions to the spending of the money so given (ibid., 2 November 1846). The South session did discriminate between those who were suitable objects for the receipt of money and those who were not—the majority of recipients received 'clothing and provisions only'. *Est. South Sess.*, 14 May 1846, 14 January 1847.

64 J. Johnston, *History of Carden Place Church, Aberdeen* (Aberdeen, 1959), p. 54.

65 *Charl. U.P. Man. Min.*, 16 December 1846, 8 February 1849.

66 *Free Trin. Deac.*, 16 October 1854, 27 April 1857.

67 See ch. 5, pp. 111-13 and n. 17.

68 Rev. Dr Chalmers, *Earnest appeal to the Free Church of Scotland on the subject of its economics* (Edinburgh, 1846), p. 9.

69 *Free Trin. Deac.*, 12 June 1848.

70 For example, see ch. 5, pp. 111-12.

71 *Charl. U.P. Man. Min.*, 8 December 1842, 14 November 1843.

72 Ibid., 16 January 1844.

73 Ibid., 1 November 1848.

74 *U.P. Presb.*, January 1849.

75 *Charl. U.P. Man. Min.*, 7 June 1848.

76 Ibid., 7 June and 10 May 1848, 1 August 1849.

77 *Est. Presb.*, 14 July 1846, referring to John Knox Chapel.

78 *Free West Deac.*, 3 January 1845.

79 *Free Trin. Deac.*, 1 July 1851.

80 *Free West Deac.*, 7 November 1844, 3 December 1845, 2 April 1846.

81 *Free Presb.*, 5 January, 2 February, 2 March, 30 March 1847; *Est. Presb.*, 2 July 1842; *Free West Deac.*, 3 December 1846, 31 May, 28 September, 22 December 1847, 31 January 1848; *Free Trin. Deac.*, 17 January 1845, 19 January and 16 July 1846.

82 See ch. 5, pp. 108-9.

83 *Free West Deac.*, 27 February 1845.

84 *Free South Sess.*, 13 March 1844.

85   *Free West Deac.*, 17 December 1845, 17 April 1865.
86   *Charl. U.P. Man. Min.*, 11 July 1843.
87   *Free South Sess.*, 15 November 1843.
88   Ibid., 15 November 1843.
89   *Free Presb.*, 7 May 1850.
90   Ibid., 7 May 1850.
91   *Free West Sess.*, 2 December 1844.
92   Ibid., 23 January 1845.
93   Ibid., 1 November 1859.
94   See ch. 8, pp. 179-87.
95   The response was poor. Only three of the sixteen elders appear to have fulfilled their obligations: *Free Trin. Sess.*, 13 September 1858, 21 February and 5 September 1859.
96   *Free West Sess.*, 15 March 1859.
97   See ch. 8, pp. 195-7.
98   See ch. 8, *passim*.
99   A. S. Cook, *Pen sketches and reminiscences of sixty years* (Aberdeen, 1901), p. 188.
100   *Selected portions from the diary and manuscripts of the Rev. Gavin Parker*, p. 116.
101   Ibid., p. 149.

Chapter 7

Social Control and the
Belief in Church 'Connection'

*Look carefully at these sharp little fellows, and think of your own
safety, if nothing else.**

In earlier chapters we have noted the overwhelming numerical
superiority of presbyterianism in Aberdeen. We have also seen that the
predominantly middle-class kirk sessions were not slow to censure
individuals guilty, or even thought to be guilty, of a whole catalogue
of moral crimes. Despite the social humiliation involved in the appearance before the session few people were prepared to challenge the
authority of the elders and, although the majority of the working-
class population attended church infrequently or not at all, there was a
continuing strong belief in church 'connection'.[1] Whilst this was
scarcely a satisfactory situation from the standpoint of the Church, it
was recognised by churchmen that even this tenuous attachment had
important stabilising effects on society.[2] Some of the reasons for the
continuing attachment are no doubt to be found in conscious and sub-
conscious fears as to the possible spiritual consequences of disbelief.
Assumptions inherited from parents and grandparents regarding the
propriety of church attendance may have played their part, especially
perhaps for those of recent rural origin who made up a large part of
the total population.[3] It seems likely that the hellfire preached by the
Presbyterian home missionaries may have strengthened the belief that
a minimal attachment to a church was advisable.[4] Fears such as these,
however, by themselves do not provide sufficient explanation. The
continuing belief in church 'connection' was determined by a com-
plexity of interrelated factors rooted in the nature of Presbyterian
society and the forms of social control exercised by the Presbyterian
churches. Perhaps the most important area of social control was that
of the provision of working-class education. Indeed it is in this area of
working-class education—in the facilities and form of education
offered—that one can establish the source of the belief in church
'connection'.

---

* *Aberdeen Herald*, September 1844; cited by A. Cormack, *Poor relief in
Scotland* (Aberdeen, 1923), p. 98.

Education and the Belief in Church 'Connection'

The Presbyterian churches were particularly active in providing educational facilities as education was seen not as a threat to a well-ordered society but as an assurance that the working class would become 'more decent and orderly . . . each individually more respectable, and more likely to gain the respect of their lawful superiors'.[5] Despite the low degree of working-class participation in public worship it would appear that the church schools were attended intermittently, if not regularly, by a majority of the working class.[6] This is especially true after 1843 when Established and Free churches competed with one another in the field of education. In 1846, with one notable exception, every Established church provided at least one school for its parish.[7] It was generally the case that the poorer the district the greater number of schools were provided. The Established Church schools run by Gilcomston and Holburn chapels in 1846 were attended by children whose parents belonged 'almost exclusively to the very poorest class'.[8] The schools run by the Establishment in the South parish also claimed the attendance of a substantial number of children of poor parents.[9] Greyfriars Established Church, situated in perhaps the most destitute area of the city, provided a school for children of the congregation and three district schools in 1854 and in the following year opened another two district schools.[10] These schools housed over 600 pupils in 1857, and by 1864 a new parish school had been opened with two qualified teachers and several probationers.[11] Although the kirk session claimed when applying for a government grant to build this school that 'hundreds of children are on the streets uncared for and uninstructed',[12] there were at least two other schools in the parish at this time run by the Free Church, one with accommodation for 400 children.[13]

The Free Church had abandoned the parish as an administrative unit in 1843, but the churches continued to accept a measure of educational responsibility for the neighbourhood in which they were situated. By 1846 more than half of the fifteen Free churches had opened session schools, some having both infant and junior departments.[14] The South Free Church had a session school with two paid teachers as well as numerous district Sabbath and week-day evening schools taught by about thirty voluntary teachers; and for those sufficiently advanced in reading and writing a special class was run on Sabbath evenings where participants were required to discuss and write on topics such as 'On the choice of companions' and 'On the value of time'.[15] The Free Presbytery was particularly careful regarding the appointment of teachers to session schools. These were required to be graduates or to have attended 'some university for one session at least'; they were also required to sit a written examination set by the presbytery and undergo an interview with regard to their 'aptness to teach' and their 'religious doctrine'. Similar, although perhaps less exacting, tests were required by the Established Presbytery.[16]

There were, however, substantial educational and social differences between the parish and session schools, which provided courses in Latin and mathematics and had qualified teachers, and the various other types of school which provided only a very limited education. Educational facilities were stratified on the assumption:[17]

> that men will be better servants, labourers and artisans, in proportion as they are instructed in the duties of their respective stations; and that all the gradations of society will be better supplied, when moral and religious motives lend their powerful aid to the requisitions of interest, and the obligations of duty.

Education was provided for 'all the gradations of society'. The parish or session school offered education to the children of shopkeepers, artisans, and other respectable members of the congregation. The fees charged were relatively high and were clearly aimed at providing an alternative to the local Grammar School where the quarterly bill came to a half-guinea. For example the South Free session school charged for 'reading, three shillings and sixpence per quarter; for reading and writing, six shillings; and for reading, writing, arithmetic, seven shillings'. Fees were also required to be paid quarterly in advance.[18] The district schools, as their name suggests, were sited in working-class areas and provided education of varying quality. At best they could be day schools run by a competent teacher, but it was more usual for them to be Sabbath or weekday evening schools run by a miscellaneous body of ever-changing congregational volunteers.[19] It was the latter type of school, however, which provided an essential link between the churches and the non-churchgoing sections of the community. It is clear that these schools were regarded by the churches as missions for children who in the future might be brought into the church:[20]

> In order to reform, reclaim, and save the young—before evil habits are formed in them—or wicked practices be pursued by them—let us take and educate them. But we ought not to be

content with merely sending them to school—we must endeavour if possible to get them to come to the House of God.

In Aberdeen in 1851 there were 62 Sabbath schools and about 800 teachers; 45 of these schools were run by Presbyterian churches.[21] The running of these schools raised the recurring problem of the children of the disreputable poor outnumbering the children of the respectable members of the congregation. The problem was solved by formal and informal social segregation. The South Established Church ran Sabbath schools at different hours for children of the congregation and for what they described as 'others'.[22] The South Free Church operated schools at the same time but in different buildings and the kirk session was pleased to note regarding the non-members' children that 'their outward appearance both as to cleanliness and clothing has been much improved since the school was opened' and that 'the scholars were most attentive while in School and seemingly interested'.[23] Trinity Free Church had a congregational school and two district schools in nearby poor neighbourhoods. These district schools catered for a population 'of a very low description', the children were generally 'a rough lot', some being particularly 'dreadful' and 'ungrateful' in the eyes of their teachers.[24] These rough elements were not welcomed at the congregational school which was intended for the children of Trinity Free Church members. Even if there is no evidence of deliberately conceived segregation, such a process was furthered by differing life styles. The congregational school was closed for the summer months when the 'greater number of scholars' had left the city on their annual vacation. Those whose habit it was not to go on annual holiday were presumably absorbed by the district schools, which in the same period increased their attendance figures. This process was continued in the following year, when a decline in attendance was noted at the congregational school 'arising through a change of hour of meeting by which the stranger children could not attend so that the scholars were now mostly all belonging to the congregation'.[25] But (as has been already noted)[26] even within the congregational membership, considerable social segregation took place. The Free West Kirk found that this was necessary with regard to congregational Sabbath school and recommended 'that a class should be opened, chiefly for female servants in connection with the congregation'.[27] Similarly, the South Free Church ran a separate Bible Class 'for factory girls connected with the Congregation'[28] and the South Established Church had separate classes for 'factory girls' and 'factory and apprentice boys'.[29] Generally, however, formal segregation of this sort must be seen as attempts to solve problems peculiar to specific congregations; the more informal features as observed at Trinity Free Church were undoubtedly of greater consequence in the process of segregation.

It has already been noted that social distinctions, whether by the lack of suitable clothing, graded pews, or other more subtle forms of discrimination, played their part in deterring working-class participation in religious worship; it is in some ways paradoxical that social segregation carried into the educational field should lead to a belief in church 'connection' The district day, evening, and Sabbath schools were for many parents the only means by which the barest basic education could be obtained for their children. Attendance at the district schools does not appear to have implied support for any particular denomination.[30] Moreover, since the children attending were collectively 'a rough lot', consequent lack of suitable clothing would not lead to social ostracism; neither were the parents exposed to the moral questioning of the kirk session nor were they obliged to pledge their financial support to a church whose members so often displayed an opulence immeasurably greater than their own. Nevertheless a tenuous 'connection' was established—between parents, children, and a church; and when one investigates the form of education provided, one realises the importance of education in maintaining a belief in such a 'connection'.

The Presbyterian churches looked on schooling as a means of promoting 'the interests of religion and education'.[31] It was maintained that:[32]

> Religion is beyond all comparison the most important part of education. . . . When properly taught it includes every moral and social duty; and among others, industry, temperance, and economy.

Education was regarded as a vehicle by which religious doctrines were 'instilled into the minds of the young', and care was taken to select teachers who were capable of doing this.[33] Both Established and Free presbyteries were prepared to accept a state-aided system of education—the Free Church on the condition that 'the Bible and Shorter Catechism [were] being taught in the schools receiving these grants';[34] the Establishment on the basis 'that religion shall be the main thing, and shall pervade all'.[35] This attitude was exemplified in the district schools. It was found in 1848 that many of the young persons attending Trinity Free Church District Sabbath School were unable to read, and so the following year a weekday evening school was opened:[36]

The object and origin of the School . . . was to communicate the elements of a secular education to the young persons attending the District Sabbath School . . . who from the inability of most of them to read could derive but little spiritual benefit from their attendance at Sabbath School.

Similarly, as early as 1836 Greyfriars parish kirk session ran an evening school where 'a great number of girls from the Factories had been instructed *chiefly in religion*'.[37] By 1840 another school was proposed and later opened, where 'besides the ordinary branches of *education on religious principles*' an attempt was made to train young people in industrious habits.[38] The methods used by the teachers are also important in understanding the source of the belief in church 'connection'. The Bible and the Shorter Catechism were the recognised, basic text books. Indeed the main preoccupation of teachers in some schools would appear to be the maintenance of order and the recitation of scriptural memory tests.[39]

One can see how the type and content of the education provided by the churches would tend to foster a belief in 'connection' and would lead to a desire for the sacraments of baptism and marriage which would further cement the attachment. For the churches, however, the intractable problems of the disreputable poor remained—those who 'generally sneered at any attempt to help them'.[40] It was no small problem. The rapid increase in population in the first half of the nineteenth century threw together diverse groups of rural migrants ill-equipped to deal with the stresses of their new urban environment which in itself contained so many counter-attractions to the regular and unremitting toil sought by the industrial employer.[41] Presbyterianism recognised the part it had to play in inculcating 'industrious habits' in the young but when the young refused to be helped additional pressures had to be brought to bear. By the 1840s presbyterianism, working through a variety of philanthropic institutions, increasingly tackled the problem of those who refused to be helped and who 'as a class had no love for school, for lessons, or for control of any description'.[42]

Education and the Disreputable Poor

Before discussing the various philanthropic institutions which were concerned with the education of the disreputable sections of the working class it must be realised that these bodies grew up in a piecemeal fashion and resulted from the failure to achieve this end by other means. 'Education' must be defined in its widest sense as a method of social control by which the whole society was regulated and shaped in an attempt to create an environment in which middle-class respectability could flourish at all levels in the social structure. Professor Pollard in an analysis of the methods adopted by early entrepreneurs to achieve factory discipline has described these as: 'the proverbial stick, the proverbial carrot, and . . . the attempt to create a new ethos of work, order and obedience'.[43] The method adopted by presbyterianism in Aberdeen followed a similar course. Those who conformed were rewarded; those who did not were punished or deprived; and on the wider front presbyterianism sought to remove institutional impediments to virtue and respectability and substitute socially acceptable alternatives.

Presbyterianism was better equipped than other religious bodies to tackle this problem. We have already seen how the kirk sessions were used as instruments of social control.[44] Acting together or through the presbytery, considerable pressure could be brought to bear on the magistracy who were often elders and always church members. The presbyterian churches pressed for the removal of such nuisances as low theatres, Sabbath drinking shops, brothels and other such attractions. Presbytery recommendations to the city magistrates often led to the 'immediate suppression of the nuisance'.[45] If the magistrates were unable or were slow to act other methods could prove equally effective. One such method was to purchase or lease the property containing the nuisance and then evict those concerned. Certain brothels, theatres, and drinking shops were dealt with in this way and even a periodical paper 'of the most immoral and degrading tendency' was thus silenced.[46]

It is important to remember also that the kirk sessions were vested with important quasi-legal and administrative functions which must have considerably strengthened their authority when imposing moral discipline. Admission to the Infirmary for medical or surgical treatment was obtained by means of a written testimony of a minister or kirk session member as to the worthiness of the applicant.[47] Certificates of poverty were issued by sessions to individuals who sought to pursue cases in court but lacked the necessary funds to do so. Similarly, sessions occasionally used their authority to bring to justice husbands who had deserted their families leaving them penniless.[48] Before 1845 the distribution of poor relief was controlled by the General Session who met to determine whether or not each claimant could be considered a 'proper object of charity' and to allocate relief accordingly.[49] Even after 1845 when the new Scottish Poor Law began to be introduced, power of distribution still lay largely in the hands of kirk session members who, in any case, continued to allocate by their individual recommendations funds raised for relief of the poor by sacramental collections.[50] Finally, for those working-class parents who did seek an education for their children the church was the main institution providing such a service.

The problem facing the churches, however, did not concern those who sought education for their children but those who 'refused to be helped' and resisted education and controls of any description. Whilst presbyterianism was able to some extent to act against institutional nuisances, and capable of applying various forms of constraint on individuals, increasingly Presbyterians became involved in attempts to create and evolve institutions to solve the problem of educating the children of the disreputable poor. The form and regulation of these institutions tended to mirror in microcosm the sanctions, gratifications, and deprivations, employed in regulating and shaping the wider society.

An early and important nineteenth-century example of the clear links between religion and industry can be seen in the Aberdeen Education Society which was established in 1815, in the hope that 'independent of the moral and religious feelings with which their [children's] minds would be impressed, habits of diligence, self-command, and reflection, would be acquired'[51] by children attending. Every leading mill-owner and industrialist in the city, as well as clergyman, was a director or office-bearer of the Society[52] which claimed in its report for 1825 that:[53]

> Almost immediately after the Boys' School came into operation, the Society had the satisfaction of being informed, that a very considerable amelioration, solely attributable to the habits of diligence and reflection acquired ... had taken place in the conduct of boys entering the various manufacturing establishments in town.

It was also maintained that 'out of the many thousands of the poorer classes who have been educated at the School, no single instance has occurred of any individuals being charged with crime'. On the contrary many had gained the approbation and confidence of their employers.[54]

Attendance at the Aberdeen Education Society's school was voluntary and this undoubtedly limited the constraints and sanctions which could be applied to ensure discipline and orderly behaviour. It would seem likely that the pupils attending this school did so because, although poor, their parents did seek an education for their children. Those who sought admission of their children to the Poor's Hospital, however, virtually abandoned any legal authority they had over them to the managers. No boys were admitted unless 'sound in constitution and free from any apparent disease'[55] and after admission:[56]

> their parents, relations, and all other persons, [were] expressly prohibited from visiting or calling for them; from meddling officiously . . . from buying them victuals, or any thing else; from decoying them to their houses, or harbouring them if they should come there.

A host of other regulations ensured that the boys admitted were more or less cut off from any contact with their former environment.

This attempt to isolate inmates from their former environmental associations was a feature of many similar institutions and was undoubtedly seen as a precondition for the inculcation of new behavioural norms suitable for future employment. At the female orphanage children were instructed 'so that they may be qualified for earning a livelihood as domestic servants'[57] and it was laid down in the regulations that:[58]

> Every girl, on leaving . . . shall be presented with a Bible, a Chest, and Clothes fit for a servant; and as a stimulus for good behaviour, if she obtain a good character from the Master or Mistresses, and from the clergyman of whose congregation she is a member, at the end of three years, she shall be rewarded in such manner as the Trustees resolve.

Similarly, at the House of Industry and Refuge where juvenile inmates had 'daily an opportunity of being taught the doctrines and practice of our Christian faith',[59] a new sewing mistress 'had the desired effect of securing the more steady application of the female inmates to their work, and of suppressing improper and idle conversation among them'.[60] The committee of the House were also pleased to report that they had disposed of twelve inmates by having them sent to Australia and America and that:[61]

> Another important mode of disposal is that of finding places of service in town and country, especially in the country for the

younger inmates. . . . In various instances the Superintendent has had the gratification to know that the parties disposed of, continue to give satisfaction to their employer.

The disposal of inmates was not easy, however, in times of high unemployment and it was during periods of economic recession that pressure for admittance to such institutions was greatest. The Female Penitentiary—an institution aimed at reforming girls who had 'adopted an immoral course of life'—found it especially difficult to place inmates in respectable employment. Although the inmates applied for admission and it was recognised that some as a result of early religious education had undergone 'great and protracted suffering . . . before the unhappy victims yielded' to the pressures of destitution, few could be placed in employment.[62] The aim was to make the Institution self-supporting by undertaking cut-price washing, glazing, starching, and sewing, but the pressure of work was such that many deserted, or were dismissed for improper conduct and returned to their former evil ways. Attempts were made to convince the inmates that 'though they had degraded themselves, they were not utterly beyond the reach of Christian sympathy',[63] but the policy of parading the girls individually before all twenty-three directors 'for examination on religious knowledge' seems to lack such a quality.[64] The voluntary confinement of the Female Penitentiary offered few rewards other than providing the basic necessities of food and shelter. The turnover of inmates was fairly high— the average residence being ninety-six days.[65]

Whilst the very existence of an institution such as the Female Penitentiary is to some extent a measure of the failure of the presbyterians to inculcate religious principles and industrious habits it is also indicative of their continuing struggle to promote such virtues. Although it is difficult to calculate the degree of success of these efforts it is certainly true that few, however disreputable, could avoid coming into contact with them. At the local Bridewell, industry, religion, and education were combined in a determined effort to reform 'the character and dispositions of the inmates', and incentives were offered to those who responded. Prisoners were required to work from 5 a.m. to 8 p.m. in summer, and 6 a.m. to 8 p.m. in winter with the necessary intervals for diet. A regular account was kept of the work done by each prisoner and:[66]

when his earnings exceed his maintenance, &c. one-third of the surplus is given to him at liberation, one-third at the end of three months on producing a certificate of his honesty and industry since dismissal, and the remainder after six months on a like certificate being produced.

Every prisoner who could read (and the majority had a degree of literacy)[67] was supplied with a Bible and visited by the chaplain 'who exhorts, catechises, and prays, with each separately' once a week.[68] Likewise a teacher attended the prison for three and a half hours each day 'to give instructions in reading, writing, and arithmetic to the prisoners who require them, each in his own cell'.[69] The prison governor was also required to report on their progress to the commissioners and it is clear that these reports were taken into consideration. Two young boys on trial in 1838 for the theft of 'small sums of money and a few trifling articles' were told by the judge, Lord Cockburn, that as they:[70]

> had learned to write in jail . . . it was not altogether absurd, considering their youth, to entertain hopes of their reformation and amendment. Instead, therefore, of proposing a sentence of transportation for fourteen years, as he would be authorised to do, he would propose one of seven.

The problem of dealing with young offenders such as these increasingly occupied the time of middle-class reformers from the 1840s onwards. There was a general realisation that the large number of vagrant children which roamed the streets were those who would in the future fill the prisons. The first attempts to deal with the problem were unsuccessful for various reasons. Parents were visited and tickets given entitling children to free education for a period of three months and these tickets were then renewed if the teachers reported that the attendance had been regular and the progress satisfactory:[71]

> The plan for a time seemed to succeed, and a great many poor children were enabled to attend school; but by and by objections were stated by the visitors, that in many cases offering a ticket to a starving child was like offering a stone instead of bread, and by teachers, that the ragged condition in which they appeared was injurious to their schools, and they declined to admit them.

It was to obviate these problems that the first industrial school was established in the city and one can detect in the development of the industrial school movement the whole pattern of fusing religion, education and industry, with basic gratification for those who conformed, and finally compulsion for those who remained obdurate. At the same time the initial philanthropic impulse soon became linked to a realisation of the longer-term need to protect private property.

The first industrial school was established in the loft of an old house in Chronicle Lane in October 1841. The most immediate problem was how to inveigle the vagrant children into the building. This was accomplished by means of the local police who gathered the boys from the streets and delivered them up:[72]

Doubtless the poor boys were greatly astonished, wondering for what offence they had been apprehended, and why they had not been taken at once to the police office. Their wonder must have increased when Professor Brown said 'Let us pray', and open-eyed and open-mouthed they listened when their fate was explained to them—that instead of being allowed to beg they were to be taught to read and write, and for their work they would get breakfast and dinner and supper, and would be allowed to go home at night. Delighted at these conditions, the poor waifs set themselves to tease a quantity of hair which had been procured.

A Female Industrial School was established in 1843 but the initial 'delight' of the waifs was fairly short-lived. The children were 'sharp, clever, half-starved, inured to hardship and harsh treatment of every kind at home and on the street'.[73] They disliked schooling of any sort and:[74]

The food was doubtless the immediate attraction; the value of it was understood by all, and there was no mode of getting it but by attending school.

It soon became evident, however, that for many the food was an insufficient attraction and that they 'preferred the liberty of begging and stealing on the street to the discipline and restraint of the school'.[75] A more stringent method of ensuring and compelling attendance had therefore to be devised. An old Police Act, long since a dead letter, was invoked. By this Act vagrants and common beggars had been apprehended and brought before the magistrates for examination and warned that if after the expiry of forty-eight hours they were again found idle and begging they would be committed to the Bridewell for up to sixty days and kept at hard labour. This Act was deemed sufficient for the magistrates to authorise the police to apprehend all juvenile beggars and convey them to the Industrial Schools and on 15 May 1845 this policy was begun. Poor waifs they may have been but:[76]

It has seldom happened that so many incorrigibles have been
brought together on the first day of opening a school. The first
act of duty required was to strip and get into a hot bath. They
stoutly resisted, but were told that till cleansed of their indurated
filth they should not get a morsel of the tempting wheaten bread
fully exposed to their view . . . so hunger got the better . . .
divesting themselves of their tattered garments they entered the
bath and were thoroughly cleansed. They greatly enjoyed the loaf-
bread and coffee, and, their hunger being appeased, became somewhat submissive to discipline, and when told in the evening,
before being dismissed, that they might all return next morning,
but whether they did so or not they would no longer be allowed
to beg, there was a general shout of 'We'll a' come back!' and
they all kept their word except three.

The problem of the hard-core incorrigibles who resolutely refused to
conform was not solved until the passing of the Reformatory School
Act by Parliament in 1854 whereby children found wandering or
begging could be detained at an industrial school until fifteen years of
age, or otherwise legally discharged.[77] In 1857 a reformatory school
was erected 'without the cost of one shilling on ornament' where the
children of the 'idle and disorderly class' who had acquired a 'criminal
taint' could be satisfactorily housed.[78]

It is important to note that the necessary finance for these schools
was from the start raised on voluntary contributions. If the initial
involvement was humanitarian the appeal for financial support from
the middle class was broadened on the clear basis of self-interest:[79]

Go to Chronicle Lane! Look carefully at these sharp little fellows,
and think of your own safety, if nothing else. Look at the fine rude
raw material here, ready to be manufactured for better, for worse.
In these hundred boys, as they are being trained, you have the
equivalent for one hundred patent locks, forty policemen, two
transports and one hangman.

It was argued at another level that financial contributions to the
Industrial Schools were a long-term investment and that ultimately,
by preventing juvenile vagrancy, pressure upon the poor's funds would
be greatly diminished.[80] The success of the school in inculcating new
behavioural norms was stressed and the public were urged to study the
ostensible changes in appearance of the children:[81]

Look round and notice how clean and neat they are. Their hands and faces have been well washed, and their hair carefully combed and dressed. Their general deportment is at once natural and modest; so much do they seem improved, that one is disposed to ask if they are indeed the debris of human society—the outcasts that haunted the streets extorting charity, imposing on the credulity of the benevolent . . . from a state of hopeless wretchedness and utter degradation they have been rendered blooming and obedient. They now take delight in serving and assisting each other, and the hardest work in the house is the most sought after.

Clean, tidy, obedient, hard-working, educated to their station in life, and having 'received careful religious instruction' the pupils found ready employment. The immediate results were more successful than could ever have been anticipated. It was claimed that 'during the first five years after the school was in full operation, *not one child who had been in attendance there* was committed to prison, or fell into the hands of the police for any offence' and a substantial number were placed 'in permanent situations, and from time to time reported to be self-sustaining and doing well'.[82] From 1850 to 1870 the average daily attendance climbed from 235 to 374 respectively.[83]

A significant feature in the financing of the first Industrial School was the part played by 'working men' who obtained subscriptions for the school and handed them over to the committee. About £250 was raised by their efforts about £150 of which had been subscribed by 'the richer classes'. When asked why they took such an interest in the school they replied:[84]

Formerly the poor neglected children earning a living by begging and stealing led ours astray, but since they have been taken into these schools they set an example which we would like our children to follow.

The support of influential sections of the working class must have contributed considerably towards the success of the Industrial Schools at their inception. Such support, however, must be seen as symptomatic of a general acceptance of the entire behavioural pattern associated with the urban middle class and an approval of the cultural imposition of these norms. The similarity of the cultural goals of the various philanthropic and other institutions, and the multiplicity of the institutions themselves, indicates a powerful propensity to impose these norms on the newly emergent working class. The large number of the institutions also suggests a low level of acceptance of the dominant bourgeois code of respectability. Consequently the alignment of craftsmen sections of the working class at that particular stage in the making of the working class from the new and raw, formerly agrarian labour force must be considered crucial. It is necessary to consider this ideological alignment, therefore, in some more detail.

Ideology and the Working Class

The prevalence of bourgeois ideology within the ranks of élite sections of the working class was linked not only to the all-pervasiveness of the ideology itself but to the fact that for these sections the ideology had an apparent relevance. Whilst it would require a definitive study of the social structure to clarify the issue, the evidence most readily available does suggest that the social gap between certain craftsmen sections of the working class and the lower middle class was not wide and the structure remained flexible enough to hold out the possibility at least for some to cross the divide between employer and employee. Although the numbers involved may have been relatively small in relation to the total, craftsmen such as masons, engineers, and printers were able to push themselves up into the ranks of the self-employed or small employers of labour. If such a move was not feasible for the majority in the craftsman situation the exceptions who succeeded held out the possibility for the others. It was regarded as 'too obvious to be contradicted' that the excessive competition and price-cutting among Aberdeen printers had been caused by the continual and increasing attempts of journeymen to push themselves upward into the ranks of master-printers.[85] Only a craftsman engineer could maintain, amidst the widespread misery and unemployment following the utter collapse of the Aberdeen textile industry, that 'from the lower classes large numbers are continually ascending and taking their place among the middle class'.[86]

Although a member of the emergent working class the better-paid, status-conscious 'labour aristocrat' was divorced from the new class both in terms of skill and ambition. He looked upwards rather than down to the 'great mass of our labouring population' who lived in squalor and depravity. When a compositor asked 'Is it not high time that all classes should unite, so that something may be done to cure those hideous evils that are festering and corrupting in the midst of us?'[87] he was pleading for a unity of middle class and 'respectable' working men to tackle a problem which particularly affected men such as himself. Whilst the middle class could escape from the overcrowding and squalor associated with the slums created by rapid population growth, the craftsman sections were often trapped amidst the thousands who 'never once cleansed their persons thoroughly with water since the period of childhood'.[88] It was only natural that such men feared the developing class-consciousness which they observed around them as a force which would make their acceptance by the middle class more difficult:[89]

> Instead of seeking to set class against class in deadly hostility and useless recrimination, it is better far to foster a kindly spirit, and endeavour . . . to unite the good men and true of every class. . . . If working men, instead of remaining ignorantly indifferent to their own welfare, would show an earnest desire *to elevate themselves* . . . their elevation, though undoubtedly a work of time, would be of comparatively easy attainment.

Elevation began with conformity which included church-going and for the vast majority meant moral improvement rather than social mobility. Conformity did bring the possibility of association, however, and the same type of working men who involved themselves in the initial activities at the Industrial School also participated in the early Total Abstinence and Temperance Societies.[90] The Mechanics' Institute —a society composed of 'working mechanics'—was another field of association. Occupational descriptions of members suggest that this society was a stronghold for sections of the labour aristocracy, but designations such as 'plumber', 'paper-maker', and 'iron-founder' were used to describe prominent members of the middle class and constitutionally the Institute was controlled by these men.[91] In fact it was the élite nature of the Mechanics' Institute which may have been one of the principal attractions for the skilled craftsman intent on making his way in the world:[92]

> In the lobby of that fine Market Street building you will not readily jostle against flax-dressers, weavers, shoe-makers, tailors, moleskin jackets, or clouted shoes. . . . Well shaved and clean chins, superfine coats, wellington boots, hands white and clean, are to be found there; but 'hewers of wood, and drawers of water', shuttle throwers, and hammer wielders, sweaty hands and brows, are not often to be met with under its useful ceiling.

The problem confronting these élite craftsmen sections of the work-ing class was that however much they attached themselves to the per-vasive bourgeois ideology their own position was never secure, and just as urbanisation brought sickness, squalor and degradation, so rapid industrialisation could bring redundancy and unemployment. The fear was always there that in a relatively short space of time they might be forced downwards to the widespread impoverishment which became increasingly prevalent in the 1840s. It was precisely from those élite groups confronted by this insecurity, or those already on the slippery slope of occupational redundancy, that the Chartist movement in Aberdeen derived its leadership. It was a leadership which ideologically reflected all the fears, aspirations, and contradictions, of insecure sections of the labour aristocracy which looked upwards for their political attitudes and downwards for their social support.

Although the Chartist leaders were drawn from the very groups which were specifically mentioned as not being seen in the Mechanics' Institute—flax-dressers, weavers, shoe-makers, and tailors—their political standpoint, whether moral or physical force, was bourgeois in principle and policy. The ideology of the Chartist leadership in Aberdeen has been analysed closely in a recent publication.[93] Although suspicious of middle-class support and middle-class motives the leader-ship failed to break from the framework of the bourgeois ideology, and the rank-and-file of the movement fell into the component parts of those seeking reform through 'practical Christianity', teetotalism, and working-class education. No clear distinction existed between the wings of the movement advocating moral and physical force, and news of vio-lence elsewhere or the desperate plight of the unemployed in the 1840s took the fire out of the activists' speeches. Collaboration was sought with the middle class, the magistrates, and the clergy in order that the distress and unemployment could be relieved and the leaders counselled the unemployed 'to peacefully await the benevolence of the authorities'.[94]

Whilst certain sections of the middle class feared the consequences of the unrest, the city sheriff was unperturbed and was always pre-pared to give the Chartists a sympathetic hearing, partly no doubt because he regarded vagrancy as a greater threat to law and order: '. . . the Chartists always conducted themselves in a quiet and orderly manner, and never for a moment offered the slightest opposition to the requirements of the Sheriff, who officially attended all their public meetings'.[95] Then again, if the Chartists' claims were considered extravagant, some of the leaders were worthy of respect. James

Thomson, precentor of the Chartist Church in Queen Street, had played a considerable part in the agitation for parliamentary reform before 1832 and according to one commentator had been 'at the beck of the Reform Committee'.[96] Moreover, the protests of the Chartists, amidst their extravagant claims for the working class, continually embodied grievances which found ready support from middle-class anti-landlordism, and dislike of aristocratic privileges and sinecures.[97] The inclusion of such grievances was not a matter of tactics; it represented the inability of the Chartist leadership to break from the middle-class dominated agitations of the past particularly over issues such as non-intrusion in the Church.

Even before the economic stability of the 1850s and the collapse of Chartism as a national movement after 1848 many prominent members of the local Chartist organisation were moving up the social ladder. Two gave up shoe-making and became newsagents and booksellers; the leading advocate of 'physical force' rose from employee to become manager of the local combworks; by the 1870s former Chartists were finding their way on to the Town Council.[98] The remarkable progress of these men was remarked upon by a local historian, an elder of Bonaccord Free Church:[99]

Among the prominent Chartists in Aberdeen were several men who afterwards rose to a good position in the town, and it was curious to note how circumstances alter the case for in nearly every such case, when the individual came to be possessed of capital and had . . . a stake in the country, his political views veered round to conservatism.

Chartism in the 1840s, however, represented the far left in politics and its emergence must be seen as indicative of the appearance for the first time of widespread class consciousness. However, certainly in Aberdeen, the leaders of this first mass movement of the working class were permeated with middle-class values. It seems reasonable to assume that those craftsmen sections which took little part in Chartist activities held similar values. It is also likely that this ideological alignment with the middle class was aided by a flexibility at certain points in the social structure which allowed skilled craftsmen to cross the social gap between journeyman and employer. Incentives to conform to the bourgeois code of respectability consequently differed at any point in the social structure. For the labour aristocrat conformity could lead to association with the middle class and acceptance by them and this was a precondition for social mobility. For the labourers and the great mass of working men who eked out a precarious existence in periods of high unemployment in the 1840s, conformity was a ritualistic response sharpened by economic necessity.

Conclusions and Further Considerations

As we have seen in earlier chapters, despite the relatively low degree of working-class participation in church affairs there was a wide-spread belief in church 'connection'. The reasons for this belief must largely be explained in terms of the content and form of education provided by the churches and associated philanthropic bodies, catering for the whole spectrum of the working class from the respectable to the disreputable, down to those whose children had developed 'criminal taints'. The great multiplicity of institutions involved in the process indicates that the problem was regarded as serious and extensive, and also that there was a powerful propensity on the part of the middle class to impose a normative pattern of behaviour on the new labour force. This imposition was assisted by the nature of the many quasi-legal and bureaucratic functions carried out by the churches, all of which demanded at least an outward conformity from those who sought assistance. The successful imposition was also furthered by the lack of any developed countervailing ideology on the part of the working class whose leaders tended to look upwards for their ideology and downwards for their social support.

The responses to such a social situation are to some extent predictable. Substantial sections of the emergent working class—many of them recent migrants from the countryside—found themselves confronted by a web of institutions seeking to impose values and norms having little immediate relevance to their former rural experience and life styles. Unable to identify with the existing denominations which often appeared large and remote, and yet retaining a belief in the propriety of church connection, they either lapsed into 'spiritual destitution' or sought an identity in a small peripheral religious group, often of a sectarian character. At the same time the existing denominations seeking to bridge the gap between church connection and church attendance, and to embrace the spiritually destitute, undertook a wide variety of missionary activities. These responses will be examined in the chapter following.

Notes

1 See ch. 2 and 6.
2 It was argued that for every individual who actually underwent conversion the process 'civilized' a hundred. See Thomas Chalmers, *On political economy in connection with the moral state and the moral prospects of society* (2nd ed., Glasgow, 1832), p. 426.
3 See ch. 1, pp. 5–6.
4 See ch. 8 on the activities of presbyterian and other missions.
5 Rev. A. L. Gordon, *An address to the inhabitants of Aberdeen on the necessity of establishing schools especially for the poorer classes* (Aberdeen, 1831), p. 18.
6 Even in the poorest part of the city a surprisingly high proportion of the children attended a school. In a census carried out in the Gallowgate area in 1854, 68 per cent of the 1,418 children under fourteen years of age were receiving some form of education. In the same year the average attendance, 'old and young', at the mission prayer meetings was between twenty and thirty-five, out of an estimated population of 5,092 (*First report of the General City Mission* [Aberdeen, 1854], pp. 7–8).
7 *Est. Gen. Sess.*, 12 January 1846. The one exception was the West Parish Church—the largest and wealthiest Established congregation at this time.
8 *Est. Presb.*, 5 May 1846.
9 *Est. South Assoc.*, half-yearly report, 16 October 1850, p. 34.
10 *Est. Greyf. Sess.*, 2 January 1854, 1 October 1855.
11 Ibid., 5 January 1857, 8 June 1863, 17 October 1864.
12 Ibid., 7 February 1859.
13 *Est. Greyf. Sess.*, 22 December 1840, attached sheet. Porthill School run by Greyfriars Free Church had accommodation for 400 children. John Knox Church also had a school.
14 Eight had session schools under the jurisdiction of the Free Presbytery. At least two other churches had session schools not directly under presbytery control. District schools were under the jurisdiction of the kirk session of the church concerned. Greyfriars and Bonaccord Free churches had schools with infant and junior departments (*Free Presb.*, 1 December 1846, 1 November 1849).
15 *Free South Sess.*, 5 November, 3 December 1844; 3 March, 24 March 1846.
16 *Free Presb.*, 20 March 1849; *Est. Presb.*, 5 February 1839; *Est. Greyf. Sess.*, 17 October 1864. The Established Presbytery do not appear to have concerned themselves regarding the appointment of teachers to district schools. (See appointment in Greyfriars parish, *Est. Greyf. Sess.*, 7 November 1853, 6 October 1856, 3 August 1857.)
17 Gordon, op. cit., p. 18.
18 *South Free Sess.*, 24 March 1846.
19 In the case of the district schools, when a paid teacher was provided, the fees were on a similar scale to that of Dr Bell's school in Frederick Street, where education was provided 'chiefly for the children of the labouring classes'—$1\frac{1}{2}d.$ per week including all materials (see *Post Office Directory*, 1861).
20 *Est. South Assoc.*, 9th annual report, 5 May 1853.

21 Thirteen by the Establishment (nine churches); twenty-seven by the Free (fifteen churches); and five by the U.P. (five churches): *Aberdeen Herald*, 3 May 1851; *Cornwall's New Aberdeen Directory*, 1853-4.

22 *Est. South Assoc.*, 7 May 1850.

23 *Free South Sess.*, 3 March 1846.

24 *The celebration of the centenary of Trinity Free Church* (Aberdeen, 1894), p. 34; *Free Trin. Teach.*, *passim*.

25 *Free Trin. Teach.*, 27 June 1866, April 1867.

26 See ch. 6, *passim*.

27 *Free West Sess.*, 23 October 1860.

28 *Free South Sess.*, 3 December 1844.

29 *Est. South Assoc.*, 26 February 1845.

30 At Marywell Street District School the pupils were 'composed of all denominations'. Of those who claimed to belong to a church, thirty-five were Free Church (twenty-one Trinity), ten Established, seven U.P., five Congregationalist. 'All denominations' does not appear to include Roman Catholics or Episcopalians (*Free Trin. Teach.*, 22 April 1867).

31 *Est. Presb.*, 8 December 1846.

32 Gordon, op. cit., p. 17. The Disruption did not lead to any alteration in attitudes either in the Establishment or those who went over to the Free Church. See *Report by the Endowment Committee to the General Assembly of the Church of Scotland*, 30 May 1851; *Est. Presb.*, 8 December 1846, 7 May 1850. The Free Presbytery recorded their praise of Gordon's unwearied efforts (*Free Presb.*, 25 September 1845).

33 Recommendation of committee anent the constitution of schools: *Free Presb.*, 20 March 1849.

34 *Free Presb.*, 16 April 1850.

35 *Est. Presb.*, 7 May 1850.

36 *Free Trin. Deac.*, 1 March 1848, 6 September 1849.

37 *Est. Greyf. Sess.*, 31 August 1836 (my italics).

38 Ibid., 22 December 1840, attached sheet (my italics).

39 *Est. Greyf. Sess.*, 17 October 1864; *Free Trin. Teach.*, *passim*.

40 A. S. Cook, *Pen sketches and reminiscences of sixty years* (Aberdeen, 1901), p. 188.

41 See ch. 1, pp. 5-10.

42 A. Thomson, *Preventive and reformative work in Aberdeen* (London, 1861), p. 4.

43 S. Pollard, 'Factory discipline in the Industrial Revolution', in *Economic History Review*, vol. xvi, no. 2 (1963).

44 See ch. 6, pp. 126-31.

45 *Est. Presb.*, 1 February 1842.

46 J. H. Wilson, *Brands plucked from the burning* (Aberdeen, 1883), p. 17; *First annual report of Aberdeen Lodging House Association* (1850), p. 7; *Est. Greyf. Sess.*, 22 December 1840, attached sheet. Individual churches also petitioned the magistrates, e.g. see *Charl. U.P. Man. Min.*, 17 March 1846, 4 January 1848; *Free West Sess.*, 14 January 1847; *Est. Greyf. Sess.*, 22 October 1849; *Free Greyf. Deac.*, 28 February 1856.

47 *Regulations of the Royal Infirmary of Aberdeen* (Aberdeen, 1838), p. 10.

48 For example, one kirk session wrote to London in order to stop the pension of an ex-soldier 'for behoof of the family' which he had deserted: *Est. Trin.*

Sess., 21 January 1839. There are numerous examples of kirk sessions undertaking similar duties. These are, of course, related to their role as administrators of poor relief.

49 *Est. Gen. Sess., passim.*

50 Prominent businessmen-elders acted as chairmen of the parochial board for at least the first fifteen years after its inception. See list of chairmen in J. A. Ross, *Record of municipal affairs in Aberdeen* (Aberdeen, 1889), p. 125.

51 *Annual report of the Aberdeen Education Society for promoting education on the system of mutual instruction* (Aberdeen, 1825), p. 6.

52 Ibid., p. 14.

53 Ibid., p. 7.

54 Ibid.

55 *Regulations of the Poor's Hospital of Aberdeen* (Aberdeen, 1826), p. 4.

56 Ibid., p. 5.

57 *Regulations of the Hospital in Aberdeen for orphan and female destitute children* (Aberdeen, 1850), p. 2.

58 Ibid., p. 8.

59 *Fifth report of the Committee of Directors of the Aberdeen House of Industry and Refuge, 1840-41* (Aberdeen, 1841), p. 7.

60 Ibid., p. 6.

61 Ibid., pp. 5-6.

62 Aberdeen Female Penitentiary, 26 Spital, *Seventh report* (Aberdeen, 1849), pp. 4-5.

63 Ibid., p. 8.

64 *Eighth report* (Aberdeen, 1850), p. 1. Of the twenty-three directors at least eighteen were elders and two were presbyterian ministers.

65 *Seventh report*, p. 5.

66 *NSA*, p. 80.

67 Although the categories are rather inadequately defined they give some indication of those who had undergone at least an intermittent schooling. In 1838 the number of those confined at the other city prison was 310 males of whom 29 could not read and 253 could read a little; 75 could not write and 209 could write with difficulty. In the female section out of 111 inmates 10 could not read and 90 could read a little; 59 could not write and 42 could write with difficulty. The remainder of each total of males and females could read and write easily. (*NSA*, p. 83.)

68 Ibid., p. 81.

69 Ibid.

70 Report of proceedings at circuit court, *Aberdeen Journal*, 25 April 1838.

71 W. Watson, *Pauperism, vagrancy, crime, and industrial education in Aberdeenshire, 1840-75* (Aberdeen, 1877), p. 43.

72 Description of the opening of the first Industrial School, Chronicle Lane, in A. Cormack, *Poor relief in Scotland* (Aberdeen, 1923), p. 98.

73 Thomson, op. cit., p. 3.

74 Ibid., p. 4.

75 Watson, op. cit., p. 44.

76 Ibid., p. 45. In *Preventive and reformative work in Aberdeen* (p. 8), Thomson gives the date as 19 May, and he also describes the water as 'cold' which seems more likely to be true. At the Poor's Hospital the regulations stated

'that all boys have their skins washed with soap and cold water every Saturday night, during the cold weather; and during the summer season they shall be bathed or washed with sea water on the open beach. . . ': *Regulations of the Poor's Hospital*, p. 12.

77 Watson, op. cit., p. 48. By this time the day school had been converted and the greater number of the children were not only clothed and fed by the school but were also lodged there.

78 Ibid., pp. 48-9.

79 *Aberdeen Herald*, September 1844; cited by Cormack, op. cit., p. 98.

80 Watson, *Should I subscribe to the Industrial School? or reasons for the education of pauper children* (Aberdeen, 1850), p. 12.

81 Ibid., pp. 5-6.

82 Thomson, op. cit., pp. 5-7.

83 Watson, *Pauperism, vagrancy, crime, and industrial education in Aberdeenshire, 1840-75*, p. 49.

84 Ibid., p. 45.

85 James Craighead, *Labour and capital: a lecture delivered to letterpress printers of the Aberdeen branch of the Scottish Typographical Association* (Aberdeen, 1858), p. 32.

86 James Tytler, *Essay on the elevation of the working classes* (Aberdeen, 1851), pp. 3-4.

87 James Gellan, *Essay on the elevation of the working classes* (Aberdeen, 1851), pp. 5-6.

88 Ibid., p. 10.

89 David Wright, *Essay on the elevation of the working classes* (Aberdeen, 1851), p. 7.

90 Cook, op. cit., pp. 5-6.

91 G. M. Fraser, *Aberdeen Mechanics' Institute* (Aberdeen, 1912), pp. 3 and 5. See also *Rules and regulations of Aberdeen Mechanics' Institute* (Aberdeen, 1824). In a *List of members . . . eligible for members of committee for 1845* (Aberdeen, n.d.), out of about 450 names not one could be described as working class.

92 A. Ramsay, *Essay on the elevation of the working classes* (Aberdeen, 1851), pp. 12 and 13.

93 S. McCalman, 'Chartism in Aberdeen', in *Journal of the Scottish Labour History Society*, no. 2, April 1970, pp. 5-24.

94 Ibid., p. 14.

95 M. Angus, *Sheriff Watson of Aberdeen* (Aberdeen, 1913), pp. 46, 47 and 53; Watson, *Pauperism, vagrancy, crime, and industrial education in Aberdeenshire, 1840-75*, p. 49.

96 James Bruce, *The Aberdeen pulpit and universities* (Aberdeen, 1840), p. 119.

97 McCalman, op. cit., pp. 6-7, 10-11.

98 Ibid., p. 8; Ross, *Municipal affairs*, p. 43.

99 W. Robbie, *Aberdeen; its traditions and history* (Aberdeen, 1893), p. 400.

Chapter 8

The Problem of Spiritual Destitution

*The only effectual remedy for the eradicating of all the evils
inherent in man or acquired by him, is a saving knowledge of
the true God.*★

Earlier we examined some of the factors which tended to inhibit
working-class participation and attendance at presbyterian churches.
The problem of why so few attended yet so many retained a belief in
church connection was analysed in the chapter immediately preceding
this. One important feature remains to be discussed within the context
of this work—the institutional responses which arose from a social
situation whereby working-class attendance remained low, but
religiosity—measured as a belief in connection—was high. These
responses, although often overlapping, approximate to internal and
external forces which resulted from, or acted upon, the social situation.
The internal forces emanated from the fragmentary nature of the
emergent working class and the difficulties encountered by certain
sections in adapting to the demands associated with urban life and
industrial employment. The response took the form of 'separatist'
churches derived from the mainstream denominations as well as an
outburst of small sectarian-type bodies often with a transient or
twilight existence. On the other hand the external forces acting upon
the social situation were planned efforts taking the form of missionary
efforts supported by the various denominations. However, whether
resulting from, or acting upon, the social situation, the responses which
we shall now examine were all of a religious nature—although they varied
considerably according to the source from which they were derived.

The three main sources to be examined are: the presbyterian missions,
the non-presbyterian missions,[1] and separatist churches and other
religious bodies. Each of these will now be considered under these
headings and thereafter cross-denominational comparisons will be
undertaken.

The Presbyterian Missions

Although considerable denominational animosity was prevalent—
especially between the Established and Free Presbyterians in the years

★ South Parish Parochial Association, *Eighth annual report*, 27 April 1852.

after 1843—there was a general Calvinist-based consensus among the presbyterian churches concerning the nature of spiritual conversion, how it would best be achieved, and what would be the resultant effects on society. The Free Presbytery were unanimous in the view that:[2]

> there is a fearful amount of spiritual destitution. . . . The masses of the Population thus devoid of the means of Religious Instruction are not only disregarding their own best interests, and in great danger of having soon to do with an unprovided for eternity—but also more or less spreading corruption crime and misery throughout the community at large and seriously endangering the peace and order and well-being of the society.

It followed that conversion of the individual was the obvious prelude to a total change in the nature of society itself. Any attempt to change society, or the individual, without achieving his spiritual conversion, was doomed to failure. Even those Free Church ministers, such as Simpson and Longmuir, who sympathised with the Temperance Movement would have been in fundamental agreement with the Established Church missionary of the South parish when he wrote:[3]

> The only effective preventive against intemperance, as well as against any other vice, is the influence of Christianity. Apart from it, every other remedy which man can propose, must prove abortive. It alone can reach the heart and influence the conduct. Make a man a Christian, and you make him temperate, careful and industrious. In short you make him useful to himself and a benefit to society. Christianity will fit him for performing the duties of life, prepare him for death, and make him happy through eternity.

Whilst it is obvious that this standpoint was not incompatible with that of any other religious body in the city, the real difference lies in the extent to which the Presbyterians concentrated their missionary efforts on the assumption that conversion must precede and take precedence over all other activities. Thus the Presbyterian missions tended not to provide facilities for community development but concentrated on being preaching stations which also offered elements of a religious education on a Sabbath or weekday evening basis. The purpose of the mission was to 'cream-off' converts who could then be admitted as members of a local congregation, or the congregation associated with the missionary effort. There was no question of communion or any other ordinances being dispensed as by right at the mission itself—a fact which as we shall see was to lead to serious conflicts between the Free Presbytery and the mission station.[4] Jurisdictional disputes were a feature of the Free Church missions and are not evident in those of the Establishment. The United Presbyterians do not appear to have operated mission stations to any extent, partly, no doubt, because their churches tended to have excess accommodation[5] and were generally sited in relatively poor areas and so might usefully have been used for centres for missionary operations without the necessity of preaching stations. Although all five U.P. ministers showed an interest in missionary work there is little evidence of denominational involvement.[6] However, if the message preached, and the mission organisation, were fundamentally similar in the Established and Free Churches other significant differences are apparent.

An immediate difference is apparent concerning choice of locality. Missions in the Established Church were operated within the parish unit—each church being responsible for the activities within the parish boundary. In the case of the Free Church, however, this was a vital difference. The Free Church abandoned the parish as an administrative unit in 1843 and it followed that there were administrative gaps in certain areas where no church accepted official jurisdiction, or in the case of Greyfriars where the Free Church had deserted the parish.[7] It was in an effort to solve this problem that the Free Church developed two types of mission. There were the district missions, which compared directly to the Established parish missions although these did not coincide with any former parish unit. Both parish and district missions, however, tended to concentrate on a destitute area nearby the church. The second type in the Free Church was the City Mission which operated a number of preaching stations in destitute areas of the city and was under the jurisdiction of the Free Presbytery. These stations were sited in areas of spiritual destitution thought too great for the local Free Church to tackle adequately, or where no Free Church existed—as in Greyfriars. As there was nothing really comparable as an institution in the Established Church with that of the Free Church City Mission this body will now be considered separately. Thereafter comparison will be made in the working of the parish and district missions in the two churches.

Free Church City Mission

This was the most ambitious and large-scale missionary project in the city and after its inception early in 1846 its financial and jurisdictional problems increasingly absorbed the time of the Free Presbytery. The ever-present problem was the question of control over the Mission's activities and occasionally this aspect became so serious that open conflict occurred and a schism resulted. The problem was exacerbated by the abandonment of the parish as unit of jurisdiction—a fact which gradually impressed itself upon the Presbytery and led them to agree unanimously in 1850 'that the church neither acted wisely nor properly after the Disruption in not continuing to take the super-intendence of the Parishes with which she had been connected previous to that event'.[8] From the start the Mission found itself involved in areas which, although obviously fields of spiritual destitution, were regarded as the province of a local church notwithstanding that the parish unit had been officially abandoned. Whilst it would seem that the local church had the most to gain from the activities of the City Mission—by way of 'creaming-off' converts—as we shall see often the reverse was the case. Perhaps it was recognition of the fact that the interests of the congregation did not lie in aiding the Mission that led certain churches not to respond to appeals from the Presbytery for financial support.[9]

In its first year of existence the Mission could scarcely claim to have made much impact. The average attendance at each of the eight preaching stations which it operated amounted to only twenty and overall only four converts were made.[10] Partly because of this failure the Presbytery decided to restrict the activities of the Mission to six stations, withdrawing from an area in St Clement's where they found the Mission was duplicating the efforts of the local Free Church minister 'who has been accustomed to hold meetings for addressing the adult population in that Locality', and from Justice Street where it was found that 'the aid of the missionary or the ministers in the Pres-bytery' was unnecessary.[11] At the same meeting, however, the Pres-bytery resisted a recommendation that the entire efforts of the Mission be confined to Gallowgate.[12] This area had, of course, been abandoned by Greyfriars Free Church when they moved to Crown Street after the Disruption.

Whilst it is clear that even at the outset there was a problem of the Mission 'stepping on the toes' of the ministers and congregational missionaries of local churches this difficulty remained relatively unimportant as long as the City Missionary was not dynamic or over-ambitious. In the case of the first City Missionary this problem certainly did not arise. McDouall, a probationer to the ministry, was appointed at a salary of £30 per annum only after considerable correspondence and discussion by the Presbytery concerning his refusal to visit those suffering from 'contagious diseases'.[13] McDouall could not be expected to operate all eight preaching stations without assistance; consequently the Presbytery sought to provide aid on a rota system from among its own ministers. Nevertheless, it was found impossible to open more than three of the stations for Sabbath services, and even this was accomplished only with difficulty and considerable reorganisation of the timetable:[14]

> Owing to the expressed unwillingness of some of the members to continue the amount of the supply required last year, viz. once in the 17 weeks, it will be necessary to alter the hour at the Jack's Brae Station from VII to VI½ p.m. to allow its being supplied by the missionary or those ministers who may exchange duty with him—the hour at the Gallowgate to be VI½ instead of VII which has been complained of by the parties as being too late.

Furthermore, to advance the work of the Mission it was decided to appoint two catechists who would assist McDouall and lessen the demands being made on the city ministers.[15] It is clear also that in the appointment of catechists the Presbytery was attempting to gain control over lay missionary movements which were beginning to play an important part in the activities of the preaching stations. Many of these lay workers knew the district in which they carried out their work and this must have been a great advantage over the ministers who attended infrequently and often irregularly. Indeed so irregular were some of the ministers in their attendance that it was decided in 1848 to appoint 'visitors' whose function was to attend the preaching stations:[16]

> as frequently as they could make it convenient, with the view of seeing if those who may have promised to attend have fulfilled this promise.

By this time there was a growing move to confine the efforts of the City Mission to the Gallowgate and McDouall was instructed to concentrate on this area and to maintain only a general supervision over the other stations.[17] Later, however, this supervision was transferred to the ministers of the local churches in the immediate vicinity.[18] It is evident that McDouall had other plans for his own career and had long since lost what interest he had had in the Mission. He was instructed by the Presbytery to cease immediately from activities which hindered his mission work as he had been:[19]

much too frequently employed for the supply of the Pulpits of Ministers who happened to stand in need of a probationer's service, to the injury of the mission.

The following year, in 1849, he finally obtained a charge in the south of Scotland and the Presbytery expressed its 'satisfaction at the prospect of Mr McDouall's obtaining a *permanent* appointment in the Church'.[20]

In his three years as City Missionary McDouall had accomplished little and it is clear that he had never regarded the post as anything other than temporary—he was a 'stickit minister' who had undertaken mission work as an alternative to teaching. However, his general lack of interest and supervision of the preaching stations had allowed some freedom of development which might have been crushed by a more dynamic City Missionary tied as he was to the official Presbytery view of how a successful mission ought to be operated. Within weeks after McDouall's departure the Presbytery found itself confronted with developments in their Jack's Brae preaching station which had previously gone ignored or largely unnoticed. Their struggle to control and later to crush these developments illustrates trends already remarked upon in an earlier chapter regarding the changing structure and ideology of the Free Church in the post-Disruption years.[21] The struggle, which was not finally resolved until 1863, also demonstrates the comparative failure of the Free Church in the mission field during those years. Furthermore, in order to show that this was not simply a 'personality conflict' this case study will be followed by one of the Gallowgate Mission where a rather similar situation was not resolved peacefully.

1 *The Case of 'Laing's Kirkie' (Jack's Brae)* Although the conflict between the Presbytery and the Jack's Brae station can to some extent be resolved around the personality of Alexander Laing, catechist and *de facto* missionary of the district, much more important issues were involved. Laing, a partner in a coachbuilding firm, was a fairly wealthy man. His interests in mission work were not confined to the Jack's Brae area although the fact he was born nearby, in Short Loanings, did give him an added interest and no doubt some advantage.[22] Jack's Brae was centred in an area of Gilcomston parish, then on the edge of the city, and was an enclave of working-class housing surrounded by what was rapidly becoming middle-class residential suburbs:[23]

The locality had a bad reputation, the more timid being afraid to go through it after dark. The residents did not expect quietness until a late hour upon paynights, as there was then a good deal of drinking. One who knew the district thoroughly estimates that only one out of twelve persons could read, and his descriptions of the conditions in which many of the families resided, disclose an amount of overcrowding which is almost incredible, and which rendered the observance of the most elementary rules of common decency an impossibility.

Nevertheless, despite the overcrowding and lack of sanitation of the area it did have certain advantages from the point of view of missionary activities. Unlike the sprawling areas in the east end of the city, the Jack's Brae district (known as Northfield) was relatively small and clearly delineated. Moreover, it was a district with a history of evangelical preaching and considerable working-class involvement. The nearby Gilcomston chapel-of-ease had been the scene of the preaching of Dr Kidd between 1801 and 1834 to large working-class audiences who enjoyed his eccentric ways, his use of the local dialect, his evangelical sermons, and his general unpopularity with his more staid conservative brethren in the ministry.[24] Kidd had been one of the first in the city to introduce Sabbath schools and he customarily distributed the entire collection at his evening service to the relief of the poor—despite attempts by the Oldmachar kirk session to prevent him preaching on the Sabbath evening. Kidd's popularity in the neighbourhood was partly the result of a love of the eccentric, but more particularly it resulted from an identification with the district in his conflict with his ecclesiastical superiors.[25] His successor, the Rev. James Bryce, never attained such popularity and his ordination in 1834 resulted in a congregational schism.[26]

Moreover, when Laing began his work in the area he built on the efforts of two other 'pious men'—John Ross, handloom weaver, and John Dalziel—who had conducted prayer meetings and ran a school in Northfield for some time prior to 1840.[27] Laing helped these men in their work and when the City Mission was created in 1846 some recognition was given to their work by supplying them with occasional preachers; 'although the assistance was not as regular as it might have been, it must have added interest to the meetings'.[28] However much 'the locality had a bad reputation' therefore, it possessed certain geographical advantages as a mission field, and had a tradition of working-class religiosity and self-help which had originated early in the nineteenth century. It had also a tradition of disregard for ecclesiastical authority. Rightly or wrongly the Free Presbytery firmly believed from the start that Laing was continuing this tradition.

The key to the Presbytery's concern about Laing's activities at the Jack's Brae station lay in the immediate situation in the Gilcomston area in 1849, when he first applied to be appointed a catechist at that station. Gilcomston Free Church congregation was declining in numbers for several reasons only one of which was related to the actions of Laing. When as we have seen in 1848 the preaching stations were placed under the jurisdiction of the local Free churches—in this case Gilcomston—Bryce was an old and sick man unable to provide for the needs of his own congregation. The Presbytery, therefore, were forced to make the proviso in his case that he should begin the work 'so soon as he feels himself able to overtake the duty'.[29] The decline of the Gilcomston Free congregation coincided with the rise of the Establishment's Gilcomston chapel-of-ease which in 1852 was disjoined from Oldmachar parish and allowed to form its own kirk session.[30] The Free Presbytery—already concerned by the low attendances at Greyfriars, Mariners' and Gaelic churches—all three were soon to be threatened by closure—could not afford another casualty.[31] In a sense, therefore, Laing began his work—not only in the wrong way from the official Presbytery standpoint—but in the wrong place, and at the wrong time. Had Laing's methods failed, or had he been successful in another mission field, or had he even worked in Northfield at a later or an earlier time, the Presbytery might well have ignored him. But Laing was not 'creaming-off' converts to consolidate a weakened Gilcomston; the evidence suggests that he was drawing support from a disillusioned Gilcomston congregation. The problem for the Presbytery was how best to tackle a man of Laing's energy and vigour. A man of the same dynamic quality which had created the Free Church was now threatening its overall strategy of carrying out the war against the Establishment.

The attempts by the Presbytery to deal with Laing are interesting as they reveal some of the forces which had begun to shackle the former vigour of the Free Church. Laing was a powerful evangelical preacher with a tireless energy[32] which must have been a serious embarrassment to the half-hearted efforts of the Presbytery ministers who undertook occasional work at the Jack's Brae station on a rota system. As long as supervision of the stations was minimal Laing could go his own way, but with the transfer of the stations to the jurisdiction of the local churches, and the removal of McDouall, it was necessary for Laing to obtain some sort of official recognition. In February 1849 Laing applied to the Presbytery seeking appointment as catechist at the Jack's Brae station. The Presbytery provisionally sanctioned his appointment but allotted him to the outlying Fintray station in Aberdeenshire.[33] This was not enough to quell Laing, however, and he would appear to have undertaken work in both stations. The Presbytery then cited Laing to appear before them and explain 'the mode in which he proposed to discharge the duties of catechist'.[34] Laing failed to satisfy his inquisitors, who decided to set up a committee to enquire into the matter of the duties of catechists; but this committee found that 'the law of the church anent catechists admits of considerable latitude'.[35] A second committee was instructed to draw up 'definite regulations' on the subject and it was decided that 'catechists be assigned to a specific area and on ceasing to be connected with that district are no longer officiate except by the sanction of Presbytery'. Moreover, each catechist was 'to be associated with a particular minister who shall direct his services'.[36] Laing was required to appear personally and satisfy the Presbytery regarding the state of his theology and Bible knowledge—which he did[37]—although there is no record of any other catechist being called upon to do this. These attempts to harass Laing were accompanied by a reluctance on the part of the Presbytery to supply the Fintray station with the cash grant which had been allocated for the purpose of running the station. Despite appeals from the station the cash had not been forwarded as late as May 1850.[38]

The real struggle between the Presbytery and Laing, however, was only beginning. In 1850 Laing decided to concentrate his efforts in the Northfield area and petitioned the Presbytery to assist him by providing evening preachers at a chapel he was to build at his own expense in that district.[39] The Presbytery submitted the matter to a committee for consideration, but the report was delayed for so long that Laing withdrew his application and proceeded without the Presbytery's official approval.[40] The Presbytery thereupon decided to continue the Jack's Brae station as the official mission disregarding the presence of Laing's Northfield Mission (affectionately known as 'Laing's Kirkie') which stood nearby.[41] Laing's personal popularity in the district was such, however, that the official mission remained empty and within three months the Presbytery had second thoughts and closed the Jack's Brae station.[42]

Despite repeated snubs over the next few years, Laing continually petitioned the Presbytery to give their support to the Northfield Mission. In 1853 a committee was set up to report on the matter and it finally proposed that the only solution was for the control of the mission to be transferred to the kirk session of Gilcomston who would regulate its affairs with regard to 'the time and manner of conducting public worship and the time and manner of teaching the Sabbath and week-day schools and generally take cognizance of all the institutions connected with this station'. It was also proposed that if at any later date the mission was raised to a regular charge the Presbytery would purchase the buildings at a fair valuation. Laing thereupon completely out-manoeuvred the Presbytery by agreeing to all these proposals without any qualification.[43] The Presbytery, however, decided that further time was required to consider the situation. Two months later they dismissed the agreed proposals and absolutely refused to countenance the providing of half-yearly communion at the mission although a petition from 300 members of the mission had sought the Sacrament. A saving clause, introduced by a small group on the Presbytery, that it must be:

> distinctly understood that the object of the labours carried on there shall be the reclaiming of the spiritually destitute population and not the providing of ordinance for those who are already members of the Free church . . .

failed to find sufficient support from a suspicious Presbytery.[44] The Free Presbytery in ten years had not moved an inch from their original stance regarding the nature of missions and missionary endeavour which was essentially to 'cream-off' converts. No mission was to be allowed to develop ideas of becoming an autonomous church which might compete for members with those already in existence.

The conflict between Laing and the Presbytery lessened after 1854 when a successor was called to Gilcomston Free to take the place of Bryce who had finally retired. The new minister—Dr Macgilvray—'a fluent and eloquent speaker, with true Celtic fire and fervour', soon put new life into the 'somewhat disorganised congregation' and 'attracted immense audiences to the church'.[45] By 1859 occasional communion services were being conducted at the Northfield Mission although the Presbytery were still reluctant to negotiate a final settlement with Laing regarding the future of the station and insisted that if the Presbytery did acquire the property Laing must immediately 'retire from the management of the Station'.[46] It was not until 1862 that the issue was finally resolved when Laing retired and gifted the property to the East Free Church who then undertook supervision of the Northfield district, the Presbytery giving its approval to this solution.[47] Yet at the very time that the longstanding problem of 'Laing's Kirkie' was finally resolved to its satisfaction the Presbytery found itself confronted by a much more serious crisis in its own Gallowgate Mission.
2 *The Case of the Gallowgate Mission* Whilst Laing had carried on his

work at Northfield the Gallowgate had increasingly become central to the involvement of the City Mission in the work of converting the spiritually destitute—each church gradually assuming responsibility for the local preaching stations.[48] There had been high hopes that the Grey-friars Free congregation which finally decided to abandon the Crown Street church in 1853 would return to the Gallowgate. The City Mission committee were jubilant at this possibility and stated that 'they would do all that lay in their power' to carry such a proposal into effect.[49] Neither the minister—Rev. John Thomson—nor his con-gregation were in favour of such a step and it was not until the follow-ing year that the church building was virtually sold over their heads and they were forced to settle on a site in George Street.[50] It is clear that the move to the new site did not lead to an increase in the size of the congregation. The church was ill-equipped and poorly designed to undertake missionary activities and Thomson—'a man of courtly instincts, gentlemanly and dignified in bearing'—belonged to 'the old school of ministers with but little interest or sympathy towards the newer movements which were then beginning to develop'.[51] Ultim-ately the congregation declined to the point at which the church had to be closed as a regular charge. Some of the reasons for this continued decline were to be found in the activities taking place in the Gallowgate.

The City Mission committee's decision to concentrate efforts in the Gallowgate was implemented in 1853, but it was not until the following year that a man of sufficient calibre was found to undertake the work. When Rev. Thomas Brown began work at the Gallowgate Territorial Mission he found a roll of only twelve members but, unlike Thomson, Brown 'possessed in considerable measure the gifts of an organising home missionary, as well as the zeal of an evangelist', and his labours were rewarded by an 'almost phenomenal' success.[52] By 1855 the Presbytery approved Brown's application for the dispensation of communion sacraments at the mission—the only dissentient being Thomson.[53] There was no sign of the storm that was to come. Brown had successfully involved his own and other congregations in the work which he pursued energetically:[54]

Two catechists . . . were engaged as regular assistants; a staff of 30 ladies visited from house to house; 12 prayer meetings were held weekly; the Sunday Schools were staffed by 30 teachers, with 400 scholars; about 30 poor children were educated in the day schools from the Funds of the Mission; and a Penny Savings Bank was instituted, and soon had 500 depositors.

In 1856 the first signs of a spirit of independence began to manifest themselves in the Gallowgate congregation, which objected to the Presbytery's decision to dispense the communion sacraments in the mission at a time different from the regular charges.[55] Thereafter regular petitions were presented to the Presbytery from the congregation asking that Brown be allowed to dispense the communion sacraments and that the mission be erected into a regular charge.[56] Certain delays and changes in the plans for the construction of a new mission church building for the Gallowgate would appear to have heightened the tension[57] and the completion of the new church in 1861 appeared only to make the congregation more impatient for their independence. Although the Presbytery finally decided to recommend that the General Assembly give 'favourable consideration' to the Gallowgate congregation's request there was also a move afoot by a sub-committee to have Brown dismissed from his post at the Mission, this being 'probably the best means of increasing its prosperity'.[58] Brown must have got to hear of this move for a few days after this sub-committee had reported a congregational meeting was called at which a decision was taken to secede and apply for recognition from the U.P. Church.[59] Brown resigned from his post as missionary, disjoined himself from the Free Church, and carried most of his congregation numbering 300 over to form a new United Presbyterian congregation.[60]

The Presbytery were shocked by the action of the Gallowgate seceders. Their response to the continual petitions had been condescending, treating the petitioners rather like the 'impudent young boys' which they themselves had once been considered. The strategy of drafting in senior, often retired, elders from other city sessions as a stabilising influence had merely exacerbated the problem.[61] It was, no doubt, a stunned Presbytery which heard Brown explain that:[62]

> I used my influence to restrain the people from leaving the communion of the Free Church, until there was no hope of their desire for sanction as a congregation being granted.

Many of those present must have been haunted by the spectre of the Disruption which had occurred twenty years before almost to the day. To the credit of the Presbytery they turned aside an effort to inaugurate a witch hunt against Brown and learned from the event itself. Three years later the remnants of the Gallowgate congregation were allowed to form their own kirk session and were sanctioned as a separate charge, although the congregation was still only half the size it had been under Brown.[63]

In both of these cases—'Laing's Kirkie' and the Gallowgate Mission—the Presbytery's attitude hindered rather than helped the effective development of missionary activities. However, the struggle over jurisdiction concealed other more crucial factors concerning the general strategy of the Free Church in its conflict with the Establishment. The demands made by the Sustentation Fund Committee in Edinburgh were a heavy burden on many congregations as we have seen.[64] The threat of possible closure was never far away from the smaller and poorer churches and it was these very churches which tended to be sited in the areas of greatest spiritual destitution. An energetic missionary, who was active in visiting the neighbourhood, could soon build up a following and attract members from other congregations which often could ill afford to lose them. Indeed, far from 'creaming-off' converts from the mission it seems more likely that these missions attracted existing members from neighbouring churches which were failing to satisfy all of their members' needs. When the Presbytery placed these missions under the management of the kirk sessions of two city churches[65] it was a retreat from the concept of a 'city' mission and the associated jurisdictional problems, and a return to something nearer the parish system which the Free Church had too hastily abandoned in 1843. Throughout the period of tension between the Free Presbytery and the Northfield and Gallowgate Missions both Established and Free Church congregations operated missions or employed missionaries. This range of missionary activity will now be considered.

The Parish and District Missions

Following the Disruption the Establishment was too hard-pressed financially to embark on a policy of expansion even if the will had been there to do so. Greyfriars, North, and Trinity churches were so weak congregationally that closure for a time seemed imminent and this in fact eventually occurred in the case of Trinity.[66] The chapels-of-ease were also undergoing a series of financial crises which left their future in considerable doubt.[67] As far as the Establishment was concerned, therefore, missionary activities were left to those churches which were able and willing to undertake the work. It followed that choice of field was largely determined not by the needs of an area but by the simple fact that certain parish churches had survived the Disruption more successfully than others. It was these churches who were best able to tackle the problem of the spiritually destitute in their midst. However, kirk sessions tended to adopt differing roles in such matters. Thus it was the elders of the West Church who were most active on the Presbytery in their attempts to save churches threatened by closure and also to raise cash for the running of the chapels-of-ease.[68] The South Church on the other hand was the first to organise extensive missionary efforts on a parish basis. Only two years after the Disruption the minister and kirk session re-instituted the Parochial Association which had fallen into abeyance in 1843.[69] A missionary was appointed the following year.[70] In Greyfriars Church the appointment of a parish missionary was not seriously discussed until 1866 and the following year the matter was again shelved because the kirk session regarded it as more important to defray the debts on the schools.[71]

However, one should not read too much into the fact that certain kirk sessions were prepared to raise the cash for a missionary and others were not. In some cases the relatively small annual contribution required for the support of a missionary amounted to a convenient means of placating conscience and resigning personal responsibility. When the parish minister found an unbridgeable gap between himself and the spiritually destitute the function of the missionary was to establish psychological and physical contact with the unredeemed. Some ministers found this gap wider than others. In Greyfriars Church after the immediate convulsions of the Disruption had passed the parish found itself with two successive ministers who undertook extensive visitation and appeared to take a personal interest in the distribution of poor relief to the most needy.[72] Temperament was a vital feature of successful mission work. One of the Greyfriars ministers—Rev. James Smith—was described as 'a couthie, plain man, paying little heed to conventionalities in regard to dress, determined in his way, and able to fight his own battle in the Presbytery, even against its leaders'.[73] Smith offended his fellow ministers by allowing lay preachers to use his pulpit and he fought a running battle with his own kirk session over this and other matters considered unconventional.[74] Unpaid and apparently unsupervised lay missionary work was also undertaken in the parish.[75] However, if one ought to be careful in ascribing lack of interest to a church which had no parish missionary, it is certainly the case that had Smith obtained the help and co-operation of his kirk session his efforts might have been more rewarding.

In the South Church where as we have seen above a missionary was appointed as early as 1846 there was considerable sessional and congregational involvement in his activities. The missionaries appointed in the period under study were not licentiates of the Church although they were carefully examined with regard to their scriptural knowledge.[76] The terms of appointment required the missionary to place, at a salary of £40 per annum:[77]

> his whole time at the disposal of the Minister and Session for missionary purposes within the parish—and that he assist in one or other of the Sabbath Schools connected with the church.

An important distinction emerges as to the function of the missionary in the Established Church as compared to that of the district missionary in the Free Church (see below). The purpose of the parish missionary was visitation of the entire parish and, with the assistance of a team of lady visitors from the congregation:[78]

> to ascertain from personal enquiry the condition of the poorer classes . . . as to Church attendance and the Education of their children, and in finding neglect or indifference on either of these points to impress upon the Parties the importance and advantage of attending to them,—as well as to remove any obstacles which the Parties might urge as preventing them doing so.

Thus it followed that if any of those visited claimed they were too poor to pay for seats then gratis sittings were to be procured for them. Likewise in the event of want of proper clothing being given as the reason for non-attendance either of the parents at church, or the children at school, then clothing would be obtained for them.[79] Generally, however, such efforts were unsuccessful: 'many of them have appeared once or twice to take possession of their seats and have been no more seen', others 'have never yet appeared'.[80] Nevertheless, the significant point was that missionary endeavour was regarded as a means of bringing the spiritually destitute into the parish church, and not into a preaching station or district mission as a preparation for 'creaming-off' ultimately into the parent church. Although this policy successfully avoided the recurring problems of jurisdiction which plagued the City Mission, it was rooted in the paternalism of the Establishment and not on any concept of egalitarianism. Any equality was not of this world but of the next. It was the duty of the congregation to strive to save the unreclaimed population of the parish so that they might be brought 'under the means of grace, may be rescued from eternal death, and with *us* rise from the grave. . . .'[81] The working people who did not attend church were ignorant and obdurate, lamented the minister:[82]

> They never mention the name of the Supreme Being, but to blaspheme it; their Sabbaths are the days of their idleness or

pleasure; their hard won earnings are squandered in riot and dissipations; and all the decencies of life are scorned and set aside; vices the most odious are shamefully indulged in and palliated; and crimes are frequently perpetrated which bring them to open disgrace, and criminal punishment. Such is the demoralised state of those who lived in the vital neglect of the worship of God, and ordinances of religion; and it is evidently the duty of all who live under the influence of Christianity, to do all in their power for the reformation of this self-degraded population.

The equation of spiritual destitution with economic poverty may have lessened the pangs of middle-class conscience but it heightened the problems of the parish missionary. Believing as he did that the 'saving knowledge of the true God' was the only answer to destitution, he was led to doubt that those who attended ordinances but remained destitute were in fact truly converted although 'we are bound in all charity to believe that their profession is sincere'.[83] The problem of aligning a genuine humanitarianism with the implications of theological position led the energetic and sincere parish missionary to feel somewhat ill-at-ease among the destitute converts and more able to converse with one of the few declared infidels.[84] When sin and spiritual destitution coincided with economic poverty, and this was common, he was eager to describe the details of the case in his report. Concerning a family guilty of Sabbath desecration he wrote:[85]

> Look at the size of ill dwelling—which is not more than two yards by three. There is nothing in the bed but a little straw, nothing in the room but a stool and chair. The parents are young. . . . They had a month ago three children. . . . Now they have only one— and that one is lying at present in the Infirmary—ill with hooping cough. And here I cannot refrain from telling you what has been done for this family. We have visited them. The Parochial Board has assisted them. The Session gave them—upon application when the boy died—ten shillings. The minister on seeing the distress and misery of this family sent them medical advice and gave them something to relieve their wants. . . .

The parish abounded with such cases where you 'will not find a bible yet you will witness scenes of the greatest poverty—vice and sin'.[86] In reading the many cases in which poverty was identified with sin[87] and spiritual destitution it is clear that he, and his readers, were able to gain confirmation of their own election. Occasionally, however, there were doubtful cases where spiritual destitution did not coincide with the poverty he expected to find. One day when he called at a house in the course of his regular visitation he was surprised to discover that:[88]

> there was everything in abundance—a table spread and loaded with food in great variety—no expense seemed spared to make the company comfortable and happy—An excellent fire blazed on the hearth. The gas burned in all its brilliance—you no doubt will be surprised when I tell you that this was the dwelling of a broom-maker. Now we do not find fault with the broom-maker's feast— nor have we any desire to mar his happiness—but we cannot but blame his extravagance which leaves him on the morrow naked and poor.

Certainly in the years after 1848 few working-class families could afford the 'extravagance' of the broom-maker's feast. The closure of the textile mills led to a dramatic increase in theft and prostitution and there was a sharp rise in the numbers seeking poor relief.[89] The South parish missionary and his voluntary workers responded with a further distribution of 'clothes and Soup-kitchen tickets among the most deserving and destitute' and set up a 'stocking manufactory . . . for the purpose of giving work to unemployed and aged females'. It was also urged that there must be a more free and plentiful distribution of religious tracts. Despite these efforts it was admitted that 'some there were, who devoid of every Christian principle and right feeling, murmured and were discontented'.[90]

Whatever one might think of the attitude, or the methods, of the missionaries it cannot be denied that considerable time and energy was spent in the field. In the course of a year the whole parish was visited: 'every dwelling house has been entered where an entrance could be obtained and this was only prevented by the family being from home'.[91] Certain areas were visited on four or more occasions and as it was found that those in the greatest spiritual destitution were 'residing contiguously to one another' prayer and scripture readings were held in these localities.[92] Nevertheless, it was only 'with the greatest difficulty that some are made to attend—so deeply rooted is enmity to God'.[93] The missionary was also dismayed to find that meetings, which were 'generally well attended', were *not* in fact attended by:[94]

> the parties for whom they were established. Those who are most regular in their attendance at a Prayer Meeting are those who statedly worship God in his sanctuary—so that the only way by

which these unfortunate and miserable individuals . . . can be approached, seems to be, by entering their own houses and conversing with them privately about those things which relate to the salvation of their Souls.

Thus the feature observed in the Northfield and Gallowgate stations of missionaries attracting hearers from other congregations was also present in the South parish. However, the continuance of the parish unit and the absence of permanent mission buildings did not allow the problem to escalate into one concerning jurisdiction. What is also clear is that the parish missionary was well aware that the 'only way' to reach the spiritually destitute was to visit and converse with them in their homes. To carry out such painstaking work required a great deal of time, considerable motivation on the part of the missionary, and a fair degree of active support and encouragement from members of the kirk session. If the South Church Parochial Association was not rewarded with a great deal of success by way of converts it was not because of the absence of any one of these three factors.

This was certainly not the case in many of the Free churches. The failure of a large number of kirk session members to carry out their obligations concerning visitation of the congregation has been discussed in an earlier chapter.[95] Too often it would seem missionaries found themselves substituting for elders and even ministers to the neglect of the mission field. James Aiken, district missionary of the Free West Church, was required to interview sinners undergoing church discipline, and to undertake the visitation of eighty-five sittings within the congregation.[96] It was perhaps because of the gradual encroachment of congregational work on the time of the missionary that rules were drawn up for Aiken's successor, who was required to:[97]

devote three hours per day, for six days in the week either— First—In co-operation with College Street Mission Committee in their labours in that district, or—Second—*In the visitation of the sick of the congregation.*

If the appointed missionary was a licentiate of the Church the demands on his time were likely to be all the greater. John Crombie, a probationer, was appointed missionary in Trinity Free Church in the belief:[98]

that he would not only prove a laborious and efficient missionary in the district that might be assigned to him, but that his services might in various ways be rendered of great importance to the Congregation by his preaching occasionally for the Minister, when he required to be absent, visiting the sick when called upon to do so, teaching in the Sabbath school or otherwise. . . .

So popular were Crombie's occasional sermons that it was decided by the kirk session to inform other congregations requiring his services 'that it would be necessary for them to give the usual allowance on each occasion that he preaches to them'.[99] Crombie, like McDouall of the City Mission, regarded mission work as a temporary necessity prior to finding a permanent charge in the Church.[100] In such circumstances there must have been a tendency to neglect the mission field for the pulpit in an effort to gain a reputation as a preacher. Moreover, the often rapid turnover of missionaries could scarcely have advanced the cause of seeking to embrace the spiritually destitute. In Greyfriars Free Church no less than four missionaries tendered their resignations in a period of twelve months—perhaps because they were being required to undertake most of the work of the regular charge for a salary of £30.[101] This particularly high turnover was obviously related to the general state of the congregation which as we have seen had never re-established itself after the move from Crown Street. Nevertheless, district mission-aries in the Free Church were generally in an insecure situation and could be removed at the will of the kirk session. Aiken of the Free West was forced to resign soon after it was found that there was 'a considerable deficiency' in the congregational funds available for the payment of his salary.[102] One of his successors—he was employed at two-thirds of the salary paid to Aiken—resigned when it was thought that the mission building was about to be sold to the Railway Company, but although the sale did not take place until nearly three years after-wards, the post was allowed to remain vacant.[103]

Perhaps because of the greater job insecurity of the district missionary, who could be dismissed more easily than the City Missionary, and certainly because of their considerable lack of time and commitment, there is no evidence of the district missions run by Free Church con-gregations seeking to break from the parent body and develop along their own lines. When a request was made by the College Street Mission committee for the Sacrament of the Lord's Supper to be dispensed at the station, the Free West kirk session considered the matter and stated categorically that if communion was dispensed it must be recognised by all concerned that the station was not to be considered 'either now or at any future time, other than as a Missionary

Station, or as an appendage of the Free West Church'.[104] However, the session were ready to believe:[105]

> that there were not a few of the people of the district who have, doubtless, received good from the Mission's labours, and who would be found on examination, to be such persons as might well be received into Communion with the Church.

Thereafter, two or three members from the mission were admitted on recommendation to take communion with the Free West congregation.[106]

Nevertheless, disputes did occur—again largely as a result of the abandonment of the parish unit—although these were not concerned with missions seeking autonomy. The Lower Denburn was the scene of missionary activity for several congregations of the Free Church and, lacking clearly defined mission districts, overlaps in the various projects were inevitable. Trinity Free congregation, active in the provision of district schools, found their efforts, or perhaps their methods, offended those already established in the Lower Denburn. Bonaccord Free Church had a fairly large school in Marywell Street which was run by two paid teachers who provided 'the most useful branches of common education to the children of the working classes at the lowest possible charge'.[107] Trinity sought and received permission to use the basement of the school for teaching Sabbath scholars, but finding this accommodation insufficient, attempted to purchase or rent part of the Bonaccord School. Finding the Bonaccord session could not help them they proceeded to open their own gratis district school nearby in the same street. Thereupon Bonaccord Free Church demanded payment for the basement school-room which Trinity had occupied 'in the evenings for several years past'.[108] When the Free West Church sold their Denburn Mission to the Railway Company, Trinity took over the working of the area which the Free West had 'recently vacated'.[109] This provoked an almost immediate crisis over the Dee Village School where the teacher resigned 'considering that her services were not needed now that Trinity Church had taken the superintendence'. Her resignation might have caused bother in finding a replacement but for the fact (as the Trinity clerk recorded) that all her pupils 'left with her so that she will not be so much missed on this account'.[110] About the same time the Trinity District School in Marywell Street found itself embroiled in a struggle with nearby St John's Episcopal Church which had 'been tempting many of the children about the district with clothes, etc. to go to their school'. The Trinity teachers were instructed 'that every effort be made to reclaim the three lost scholars and that every means be taken to prevent others from being led away'. Later one girl was reclaimed.[111]

The Presbyterians—A Concise Summary

What emerges from the above examination of the Established and Free Church missions is that the presbyterian view of spiritual conversion preceding all other changes in the individual largely confined their efforts to station preaching and exhorting during visitation. The close association in the mind between spiritual conversion and economic improvement would appear to have led to some doubt regarding the sincerity of the converts when the latter did not follow the former. As far as the parish and district missions were concerned the main difference would appear to be that in the Establishment the aim was to bring the spiritually destitute into the parish church, whilst in the Free Church the aim was to bring them into the preaching station and thereafter 'cream-off' converts into the communion of the parent church. Whilst the latter method may have been less socially 'democratic' it perhaps was more successful in the long run. There was clearly a reluctance on the part of many to take up seats in the Establishment although gratis sittings and suitable clothes had been provided.

The evidence available, however, suggests that visitation was more likely to be undertaken by the parish missionary than his Free Church counterpart. Although this occasionally was the fault of the missionary it is clear that institutional factors often made it difficult for him to find time to carry out this duty. Nevertheless, the extent of voluntary effort put in by Laing at Northfield far exceeded the paid efforts of any district missionary.

Concerning scale of involvement the Free Church effort far surpassed that of the Establishment. This partly resulted from a genuine desire to make up for the deficiencies resulting from the abandonment of the parish unit, and partly must be seen as an aspect of the Free Church's 'war against the Establishment'. Although jurisdictional conflicts and schism were a feature of the City Mission it might be argued that the Mission succeeded *despite* the Presbytery, who tended to regard it as an extension of its general strategy of weakening the Establishment by building up its own numerical strength. Certainly both 'Laing's Kirkie' and the Gallowgate Mission successfully built up local support.

An important feature, however, emerging from Laing's and Brown's efforts, as well as those of the South parish missionary, was the tendency of the Presbyterian methods not to reach the spiritually destitute by preaching but to attract instead those who already were members or attended other churches. This might in part be explained by the nature of the hellfire preaching which to some may have been an 'acquired taste', or it may have resulted more directly from the methods and organisation of the mission itself. These factors must be kept in mind when examining the non-Presbyterian efforts to reach the spiritually destitute, where the message and mission organisation differed radically from the Presbyterian efforts.

Non-Presbyterian Missions

The sectarian attitude adopted by Trinity Free kirk session towards their Episcopal neighbours who were attracting children to attend school by offering clothes is indicative of a general attitude of the Presbyterian churches towards the non-Calvinist denominations. As one would expect their opposition was most rabid in the case of the Roman Catholics, who were scrutinised with an *uncritical* eye for any hint of resurgency—the slightest of pretexts resulting in a virtual barrage of hellfire and dire warnings from the Presbyterian pulpits. News or reports of any real or imagined 'aggression of the Bishop of Rome' took precedence over all other matters on the Presbyteries and in 1851 a proposal to petition the Queen and both Houses of Parliament calling for the repeal of the Catholic Emancipation Act was only narrowly defeated on the Free Presbytery.[112] Later a proposal to set up Anti-Popish Missions was discussed but does not appear to have been acted upon.[113]

Much of the Presbyterian wrath fell upon the head of the local priest, Charles Gordon, whose popularity was seen as a threat to presbyterianism, and every opportunity was taken to discredit him and hinder his work.[114] Despite the general alarm there is no evidence of Gordon leading any Roman Catholic revival. Indeed, given the harsh Calvinist environment, he must have been fully occupied maintaining his flock rather than challenging the presbyterian order. On the other hand the time spent debating supposed Roman Catholic conspiracies may well have hindered presbyterian mission work.[115]

Such upsurges in anti-Catholic feeling must to some extent have diverted the attention of the Presbyterians away from the Episcopal Church which was only one step removed from 'popish heresy'.

However, as was noted earlier,[116] the Episcopal churches were inward-looking in attitude, concerned only with their own congregations, and it was not until later in the century that any extensive missionary activities got under way. The beginning of this involvement can be seen in the above-mentioned concern of Trinity Free session over the tempting of children. One of the first actions of the Rev. John Comper after his appointment at St John's in 1861 was to set up a day school for children of the district.[117] Thereafter as we shall now see he increasingly turned his attention to mission work in slum districts, particularly the Gallowgate.

The Gallowgate Episcopal Mission

Although the efforts of Comper extend far beyond the period under study, consideration must be given to the work inaugurated in the 1860s because it was different in organisation from any prior denominational mission and it would appear to have been successful. Moreover, it was carried out in the Gallowgate, where an Episcopal church—St Paul's—was already situated, without any apparent conflict over jurisdiction. The absence of such conflict may be partly explained by the nature of the incumbent of St Paul's—Rev. Frederick Bouverie. Bouverie had little or no inclination to undertake missionary activities. Indeed, if his own pastoral addresses are to be believed, he had little or no contact with working-class members as he categorically refused to see anyone in the evenings except 'in an extraordinary case of sickness and distress'.[118] Moreover, he was afflicted with a peculiar infirmity which made it impossible for him to identify working-class members of his flock:[119]

It is the custom of the poorer people here, those belonging to the working classes, to expect the first acknowledgment to come from the Minister, and so it seems they look at him and wait for him to bow first, when, if he fails to do this, they assume that he is unwilling to speak to them. This is simply a mistake, the Minister is most ready to conform to any custom; but when the working class members of his flock are assured that he never *does* pass them intentionally, he hopes that in consideration of his infirmity in not being able to see as far as other people, they will, rather than let him pass, address him first; when they will always find him most glad to have an opportunity of shaking hands with them, as those who have kindly made the attempt can testify.

Consequently, when Comper began his work in the Gallowgate there was little likelihood of Bouverie or his congregation being adversely affected. His methods were startlingly novel. For the first time since the Reformation he brought Sisters into the work of the Scottish Episcopal Church, and despite initial prejudice and opposition the experiment proved successful. The Sisters lived in the Gallowgate among the poor that they sought to tend and as well as visiting they ran mission services, night schools, Sunday and day schools, and soon 'a large bare room' was fitted up as a chapel at which 'a surpliced choir gathered from the slums took a prominent part'.[120] By 1870 Comper resigned his incumbency at St John's and dedicated all his time to the Gallowgate Episcopal Mission, where many guilds, classes, schools, special services were held and the Sisters of Mercy became renowned for their 'gentle and sympathetic dealing' with the sick and the poor. In 1879 the Mission was consecrated as St Margaret's Episcopal Church, but Comper's work was just beginning. He went on to open a number of similar missions in some of which 'no one could be admitted who came in a hat or bonnet'.[121] Comper and his Sisters of Mercy accomplished in the Gallowgate by kindness and persuasion what the Presbyterians had failed to do by hellfire and fear. He built a large and flourishing working-class congregation.

The Albion Street Mission

Of all the other non-presbyterian denominations only one—the Congregationalists—were active and successful in the mission field. However, by far their most notable success was that achieved by James R. Wilson at the Bool Road or Albion Street Mission. Wilson was a journalist who later became editor of the *North of Scotland Gazette* and in some respects his career in the mission field is comparable to that of Laing at the Northfield Mission. At the outset Wilson was not attached officially to any denomination and it was only after his work was marked by success that he was ordained Congregational minister in 1847.[122] It is possible that Wilson's progress from journalist to minister may have influenced the attitude of the Free Church towards Laing's rather similar activities at Northfield where, as we have seen, they continually sought to confine his energies and regulate his teaching as a catechist. Wilson, however dedicated a missionary, was more of a careerist than Laing, and partly as a result of his own publications on the subject of 'ragged churches' he was appointed Home Mission Secretary of the Congregational Union of England and Wales.[123]

Without in any way denigrating Wilson's efforts at the Albion Street Mission it is necessary to add a cautionary note that much of the 'folk myth' of the Bool Road project has been derived from Wilson's own writing. Nevertheless, Wilson's 'ragged kirk' was a pioneering effort of a sort which must have influenced Comper's later activities in the Gallowgate.

Wilson began his missionary work about 1846 in a small room 'at a rental of sixpence a week' in an area of the North parish regarded as:[124]

> the very centre of slum-land, and the abode of all manner of evil characters. Albion Street in those days was the scene of one of the most notorious 'penny gaffs' in Scotland, popularly known as the Bool Road Penny Rattler, and frequented by the most disreputable classes. The district had acquired the unenviable reputation for fostering the lowest forms of vice, and the unchecked ruffianism of its inhabitants was so pronounced that it was regarded as unsafe for any respectable citizen to venture unprotected within its confines. Into the very heart of this hot-bed of crime Mr Wilson bravely ventured in his reforming zeal.

Wilson however, although he ventured alone, was not without friends and in the course of the next few months successfully gained the support of the Lord Provost, Sheriff Watson, Mr Barclay—the superintendent of police—and Queen Victoria.[125] Wilson, a practical man, decided to remove the countervailing attractions of the 'penny gaff' and after buying out the site erected a chapel in its place.[126] If Wilson is to be believed the chapel proved an immediate success, drawing crowds who 'formed part of a population, set down by common consent as the most depraved and vicious in the community, and who had long been looked upon by every denomination of Christians as irreclaimable'.[127] At first no regular congregation was formed—those who were reclaimed being urged to join existing churches. However, it soon came to be felt 'that it was not possible in this way to reap the results of the many-sided efforts of the mission and consolidate the work' and in 1847 the mission was erected to a Congregational church with Wilson as its minister.[128]

The most interesting feature of the Albion Street Mission are its 'many-sided efforts' which, unlike the Presbyterian emphasis on conversion as a prelude to association, sought to involve the church in the affairs of the community and thus convert the individual by association. As well as running gospel, prayer, and tract meetings, schools were operated which also provided special classes for adults who wanted to learn to read and write. A Bible Society, a Music Society, a Temperance Society, a Penny Savings Bank, a Library, a Reading Room, and so on, were all set up and run by the mission members who were interested.[129] From the start Wilson insisted that all involved in these activities should contribute financially towards them and not expect them to be supported by middle-class philanthropy. The subscriptions made to the Bible Society suggest that he was successful in promoting what he called 'the philosophy of self-reliance'. Of the £14 5s. 11d. subscribed in the first year of its operation there were 4 shillings, 40 sixpences, 1,440 pennies, and 3,426 halfpennies.[130] It seems reasonable to assume that much of the money which had previously been spent at the 'penny gaff' was now drawn into the mission. Though Wilson might not himself have seen it in that way, the mission had replaced the 'penny gaff' as a centre for communal activities.

Wilson was a first-class 'public relations' man. By inviting many prominent people to visit or to give 'popular lectures' he drew forth favourable comment on the success of the mission as a 'civilising' influence in the neighbourhood. The superintendent of police wrote that:[131]

> the moral character of the district has been very much improved. Numerous instances are known at this office in which persons who were habitually given to intemperance, and debauchery, and crime have been reclaimed.

The Earl of Carlisle also visited the Mission and praised its efforts which he saw as substituting:[132]

> order for disorder, industry for idleness, cleanliness for filth, decorum for rudeness, temperance for intemperance, and above all, Godliness for indifference to all that is good and holy.

Certainly changes had occurred in the neighbourhood. There was a heightening community consciousness which had led to co-operative efforts to resist the threat of diseases such as cholera by 'assisting each other to cleanse their houses' and practising 'salutary ablutions' in the neighbourhood.[133] Changes were also occurring in the congregation which were to have long-term consequences. Wilson noted how much the members had 'improved in their domestic circumstances—men who for years had nothing better than fustian clothing being now to be seen with good black coats'.[134] Developments such as these must have brought their own problems and after Wilson left in 1859 it would appear that the congregation was ceasing to maintain its tradition of being a 'ragged kirk'. In 1878 a large section of the congregation 'hived-off' with the minister to build a new church outside the district at a cost of £7,000, and thereafter the remnant congregation at Albion Street declined steadily in numbers of whom 'not a few fell back into their old habits'.[135] Notwithstanding the problems associated with a 'ragged kirk' whose congregation had prospered, full credit must be given to Wilson's experiment at Albion Street. It was not until Comper and his Sisters began their work in the Gallowgate in the 1860s that so novel an approach can be seen to the problem of spiritual destitution among the working class.

What is clear from the efforts of both Comper and Wilson is that those sections of the population which the Presbyterians were unable to reach, could be attracted into mission churches by different methods. Certainly the Presbyterians' insistence on the wearing of respectable clothing at their services was a serious impediment, but the problem ran much deeper than this. At Albion Street and later in Comper's missions in the Gallowgate area men and women were able to identify with a congregation and contribute in their own ways towards its operation— a privilege denied them in the Presbyterian churches.[136] It was in large part this same desire for identification and participation which acted as a primary force in the religious bodies now to be examined. Although none of these groups could strictly be described as missions, they all successfully involved in their activities sections of the population which otherwise would probably have remained outside the fold of any denomination or church.

'Separatist' Churches and Other Religious Bodies

Of the groups now to be considered few had congregations of more than fifty and by the middle of the century many were being dispersed or drawn into mainstream churches. Their significance lies in the fact that they represented groups of individuals who found it impossible to identify themselves with the larger churches or denominations and yet retained a high level of religiosity. They were those who found, in the fragmentary nature of the emergent working-class culture, that simple tenuous 'connection' was insufficient for their religious needs. These groups fall broadly into two sections, namely 'separatist' churches, and what might loosely be defined as 'sectarian' bodies.[137]

Of the two sections the latter were certainly the more colourful although all were comprised of sects of relative unimportance in numerical terms. Their meetings were held in the east end of the city in rented rooms or in the house of their leader. The Bereans met in a converted attic in the Denburn—the room being so low that the preacher occasionally knocked his head against the ceiling. The 'garret-kirk' drew an audience of about twenty-five persons.[138] The Glasites were an older and more respectable body numbering about thirty, who met in St Andrew Street and were known as the 'Broth kirk' because soup was served at each service.[139] The Southcotians also met in converted rooms in the same street as well as holding open-air meetings at street corners, where they harangued the respectable. Their strange manners and dress, however, drew the unwelcome attentions of the mob. Although said to be on the increase in 1830 they would appear to have disappeared by the middle of the century.[140] The Irvingites, like the Southcotians and the Glasites, also followed the teachings of a national leader. They made their appearance in Aberdeen in the early 1830s and at once began their work of warning the existing generation of its defections and preparing the people for the second Advent of Christ.[141] The Primitive Christians made their appearance about the same time as the Irvingites. A tiny sect, the Primitive Christians acknowledged 'no authority but that of Christ our living head' and held that the sole source for the judgment of *all* matters was the Holy Scriptures 'according to their plain and obvious meaning'.[142] Although all of these sectarian groups were small they are significant as a social rather than a religious phenomenon; it seems highly probable that many similar groups existed at this time but are lost, perhaps forever, to the social historian. They were thrown up by a society whose members were being subjected to rapid technological change and consequent social dislocation. Unable to identify themselves with the churches of the established denominations, members of these bodies felt they had a place in the small primary group atmosphere of a sect often with an exclusive code of theological beliefs which give meaning to an otherwise normless urban existence. However, few of these groups survived the rapid falling-off in migration in the 1840s and the emergence of a fully fledged industrial labour force in the decade following.[143]

The 'separatist' churches on the other hand, although characterised by a high degree of group identification, were perhaps better able to survive the social transition as members were associated by nature of occupation, language, or place of origin, rather than theological position. Examples of place of origin determining religious attachment can be seen in the first Congregational and Anti-Burgher churches to be founded in the city. The first Congregational Church (George Street) had close associations with families in the Rhynie and Lumsden districts of Aberdeenshire, and at least half of the office-bearers elected between 1820 and 1832 would appear to be first generation migrants.[144] The first Anti-Burger Church was founded by seven migrants who began as a praying society in the city but continued to walk back to their former Aberdeenshire church to take communion. The rural kirk session (at Craigdam) assisted the migrants in founding the new church.[145] The Mariners' and Gaelic churches (both Established and later Free Presbyterian) provide examples of occupational and language association. As the name implies, the Mariners' Church catered specifically for seamen. The church was situated in the harbour area and a full-rigged sailing ship was suspended from the interior ceiling.[146] The church began as a seamen's mission run by shipmasters and shipowners who exhorted their fellow masters to remind seamen of their duty:[147]

> to avail themselves of the services in the Seamen's Chapel. A habit of neglecting the ordinances of God, cannot be too early checked, nor too severely reprobated. They who despise the authority of God, can have little respect for the authority of man. . . . We are satisfied that the more religious our Sailors become, the better Sailors they will be.

The Gaelic Chapel began with the same religious-cum-social function in mind. As we have already seen Gaelic-speaking highlanders began to migrate into the city in increasing numbers towards the end of the eighteenth century in search of employment and 'it was soon found necessary to institute special means for supplying them with religious ordinances'.[148]

With the exception of the first Congregational Church, which by the mid-nineteenth century had grown into a large and prosperous congregation, all the other 'separatist' churches and sectarian groups were either small, struggling congregations, or had been assimilated into larger bodies, or had disappeared.[149] The one congregation which remains to be discussed appears comparatively large and successful in 1851.[150] The lifetime of this church—the United Christian Church—was the lifetime of its minister, the Rev. Hugh Hart, who provides another example of how it was possible to build up a working-class congregation by methods not dissimilar to that of Laing, Brown, Comper, or Wilson, and yet peculiarly different.

Hart came to Aberdeen in 1823 to minister to the remnants of a former dissenting Presbyterian congregation in the harbour area. He speedily built up the congregation which had been made up of sea-farers and weavers by 'a large infusion of factory girls'.[151] From the start he ran into trouble with the Presbyterian ministers who shunned him, partly on the grounds that his divinity qualifications were regarded as inferior, and partly because he advocated a unity of all Christian religions[152] (although no doubt such a position was simply regarded as proof of his inferior training). His success in attracting a working-class following whose contributions were sufficient to support him as well as pay for the running of the church must have rubbed salt in presbyterian wounds, for the ministers of the Establishment embarked on series of pulpit exposures of Hart's theological position as well as ridiculing in pamphlet form his dress, mannerisms, and sermons.[153] Hart did not enter seriously into the debate although his pulpit reply, if somewhat pathetic, was also sociologically significant:[154]

> I suppose they do not consider poor Hart respectable enough. . . . If I had a fine house and fine clothes to cut a dash with, and if I were to break and cheat half the world, I should be *respectable* then.

Hart's rejection by polite and respectable middle-class society must have raised his standing in the eyes of his working-class congregation, many of whom may have identified his rejection with their own. The sympathy between Hart and his congregation can be seen during the threat of cholera when it was said he abandoned his sermon and dis-cussed instead the use of certain patent medicines and when the con-gregation later moved to a new hall it was a band of factory girls who scrubbed it out at Hart's invitation, on the Saturday evening.[155] It was not just the fact that Hart's economic well-being was tied up with the congregation—his stipend being raised by collections—that made him identify with them in his sermons:[156]

> Mr Hart remembered in particular that class in the community of whom . . . his congregation mainly consisted. 'Bless the working classes', was his formula in praying for them, 'and give them adequate remuneration for their labour'.

The congregation did not survive his death in 1862 when the church building was sold and its members dispersed. What Hart had demon-strated was that a working-class congregation could be assembled without recourse to threats of hellfire or the temptations of free hand-outs of clothes, shoes, and occasional relief.

Whilst the disappearance of a religious group was often related to the death or removal of a leading member, by far the most important single reason for their general decline was the process of structural assimilation by which minor social groups lost their distinctiveness and were absorbed into the total culture of an urban society. Perhaps the best example of this process at work can be seen in the case of the Gaelic Church which had some guarantee of continuity of existence, being a congregation within the Free Church, and yet gradually lost its peculiar distinctiveness:[157]

> For some years after the church was built the services were conducted entirely in the Gaelic language, with an optional English service in the evening; but as the families of the congregation grew up, the need of a regular English service was greatly felt. At first the Gaelic service was superseded by one in English, and later another change took place by which provision was made for two services in English and one in Gaelic. Notwithstanding these modifications, it was known that many of the general public were still under the impression that the services were entirely in Gaelic, and doubtless the congregation suffered in consequence. It was therefore to obviate this difficulty and dispel any idea that the congregation was exclusively for those proficient in the Gaelic language to alter the name of the church to that of St Columba.

On the other hand if structural assimilation of formerly distinctive occupational or language groups, or groups associated by common rural origins, weakened the foundations upon which certain congregations had been built, it could be seen as a force widening the basis of support for the mainstream denominational churches. Consideration of these factors, however, would extend beyond the chronological and thematic confines of this work.

Missions and the Working Class: Some Conclusions

In examining the efforts of the various denominations and churches to embrace the spiritually destitute (and this term can be equated to the mass of the emergent working class) and the extent of their success, certain common characteristics emerge which assume some importance. The most notable of these would appear to be the apparent success of individuals of diverse religious affiliation in building up working-class congregations. Just as Laing—an unpaid Presbyterian lay-preacher—succeeded at Northfield, so did Brown—a paid and probationary Presbyterian minister—succeed in the Gallowgate. Likewise Wilson, who was a journalist, lay preacher, and finally a Congregational minister, built up a working-class congregation in Albion Street. Comper, an Episcopal priest with strong English high-church leanings, achieved remarkable results in the Gallowgate. Finally Hart, whose divinity orders were sneered at by the Presbyterians, successfully collected and retained the support of a working-class congregation throughout his ministry in the city.

One might be tempted to draw a conclusion from this record which amounted simply to believing that the working class were little concerned about theological matters and that the apparent success of these men was based on certain shared characteristics. All five men were hardworking, energetic, and were considered to varying degrees to be fine preachers. All had the capacity to organise effort and the initiative to involve others in their work. It follows naturally from this analysis that if there had been more men of their capabilities there would have been fewer spiritually destitute.

However, such an analysis, although perhaps containing an element of truth, is a gross over-simplification avoiding as it does any real estimation of the success of their efforts. It also fails to grapple with the more difficult but essential problem of defining spiritual conversion both in general terms and from the specific viewpoint of the church with which they were associated. When one examines the efforts of these men more critically one is compelled to ask just how far they did build their congregations from the formerly spiritually destitute, and what general criteria can be used to judge their success when it would appear that they had done so.

In the case of the Presbyterians—Laing and Brown—the first question is particularly relevant. Although their conflict with the Free Presbytery was ostensibly over the problems of jurisdiction and control over the development of the preaching stations, the issues ran much deeper than this. If these two missionaries had been drawing the unattached spiritually destitute into the stations in Northfield and the Gallowgate the Presbytery would not have shown the concern that it did. As it was, however, both men were evangelical preachers in the best Free Church tradition, and their energy and enterprise was attracting disillusioned members of neighbouring Free Church congregations whose ministers lacked their former fervour. Although some of those so attracted may have been lapsed members of these congregations it was nevertheless clear that their very success constituted a threat to the overall strategy of the Free Church—already perturbed by declining attendance in certain of their city charges. The success of Laing—a lay preacher—must have been particularly galling, especially perhaps when it came to mind that Wilson had been ordained a Congregational minister at Albion Street. However, notwithstanding the obvious abilities of both Laing and Brown, it seems clear that neither were embracing the spiritual destitution of the sort that the Presbytery intended.

In the case of Wilson completely different issues arise. Although he was fond of pointing out in his own printed 'case studies' of men and women who had been reclaimed,[158] that many were relapsed church members, it seems clear that he did attract the spiritually destitute into his church. The problem of assessing Wilson's success to some degree involves a consideration of whether what he achieved was some form of 'social' rather than spiritual conversion. Wilson was always ready to emphasise the social improvements resulting from his efforts at Albion Street and it is highly likely that the community-oriented form of mission, which he ran, did have a much wider social impact than anything which even the most optimistic Presbyterian could hope to achieve from a preaching station. Clearly Wilson brought many into his church who would never have been reached by Presbyterian methods. Nevertheless, the problem remained unsolved as to what happened to 'ragged churches' after the initial stage had been passed and demonstrative respectability—such a strong element in presbyterian congregations—began to make itself felt. In such circumstances, whereby the newly-found respectable were continually confronted by the evidence of their own former disreputability, secession may have been the only long-term solution.

The same problems of continuity arise in the efforts of Hart and Comper. Hart, a charismatic figure, successfully identified himself with his working-class congregation by invoking a rudimentary class consciousness amongst its members. However effective this may have been for Hart, it was insufficient to maintain the congregation intact after his death.[159] In the case of Comper critical assessment is impossible within the confines of this work as his activities extended far beyond the period under study. Nevertheless, the evidence of his earlier work does tend to suggest that he was more successful in maintaining continuity of both effort and congregation. The work of the Sisters became a permanent feature and has continued down to the present day. Comper, himself, was well aware of the dangers of demonstrative respectability and, as we have seen, he attempted to stop any tendency towards this at his meetings.[160] It is possible that Comper may have been made aware of such dangers by studying the earlier efforts of the Congregationalists in this field.

However, the importance of the work of Wilson, Comper, or even Hart, lies beyond any critical appraisal of their success in building working-class congregations from those considered spiritually destitute. By any measure, all three men succeeded, where the Presbyterians by and large failed. And yet if the total efforts of these men were combined they amounted to only a fraction of the Presbyterian contribution in the mission field. The relative success of these three men, therefore, provides a significant starting-point in understanding some of the ideological and institutional problems which hampered the Presbyterian efforts.

The most immediate and important feature which arises from comparison is that the Presbyterians did not approach the problem of embracing the spiritually destitute from the simple pragmatism of Wilson and Comper. The Presbyterians saw the problem essentially as being answerable from the standpoint of theological principle. We have already seen that in the field of educational provision, religion was regarded as the base for the teaching of any curriculum.[161] Although the Presbyterians were in the forefront of those who saw the importance of religion as a stabilising force in society, they saw social control as emanating from, and not preceding, the act of spiritual conversion. Any attempts to cure the ills of society were doomed to failure unless accompanied by the conversion of the individual to the true Christian faith based on Calvin's precepts. When this was accomplished the individual's whole character and well-being would be permanently changed.

Consequently, Presbyterian efforts were concentrated on preaching, visitation, and exhortation, in the sincere and humanitarian belief that the spiritually destitute—the damned—must be warned of their danger without delay. Sympathy they could be shown; but it must be the compassion of those saved, for those who were damned unless they repented the evil of their ways. Once the spiritually destitute individual had been made to see the danger of his mode of life, and showed evidence of conversion, he could be admitted to full communion in the Church. Until this occurred he must be encouraged to attend church and see the error of his ways by the example of others.

Whilst the Establishment and the Free Church diverged to some extent on whether this was to be accomplished by exhortation (and the provision of the necessary clothes), or through the medium of a preaching station, both held that the spiritually destitute must be drawn into the existing parish and Free churches. The reasons for this policy would appear to be largely dictated by practical problems resulting from the Disruption. There was certainly adequate accommodation in most of the Established churches in the city, and the Free Church following the strategy in the years after 1843 of destroying the residuary Establishment could scarcely allow the development of further charges (fifteen to the Establishment's nine) which might prove a financial burden on her stretched resources. Just as the Establishment had sought to control the activities of their impatient and 'impudent' *quoad sacra* churches in the years before 1843, the Free Presbytery found itself struggling to contain and discipline similar elements within its own ranks (Laing and Brown) whose desire for autonomy disturbed policy commitments. Indeed the desire for involvement in the running of their own mission station—which was successfully organised by Wilson into a variety of community activities at the Albion Street Mission— was continually thwarted by the Free Presbytery who saw such requests (perhaps rightly) as the prelude to demands for complete autonomy.

It was a policy which in the long run was doomed to failure. Just as the Established churches found a marked reluctance among the spiritually destitute to fill the gratis sittings provided for them, so the Free Church process of 'creaming-off' was both impractical and in a sense inconsistent. If 'creaming-off' had been successful what the Free Church would have been maintaining was no less than 'ragged preaching stations' although they condemned 'ragged churches'. It was a position maintained by the Presbyterians up to the time that Comper was achieving his successes in the Gallowgate, that 'Ragged and Mission Churches are Class Churches . . . opposed to that spirit of Christianity, which teaches that in the sight of God all men are equal'.[162] And yet it must have been manifestly clear in mid-nineteenth-century Aberdeen, to the 'thoughtless sinner' and the 'obdurate infidel', that all men were certainly not equal in the sight of middle-class dominated presbyterianism.

Notes

1 Presbyterian and non-Presbyterian approximate to Calvinist and non-Calvinist theological positions. However, the Congregationalists

are considered under the latter heading although with the exception of one church (St Paul Street) which was a member of the Evangelical Union, they held by Calvin's doctrine of the elect. The Baptists were also Calvinists but were not denominationally active in the mission field and were numerically weak. Consequently they have not been considered.

2 *Free Presb.*, 15 April 1851.
3 *Est. South Assoc.*, annual report, 2 May 1849.
4 See pp. 177-8.
5 See ch. 2, p. 39.
6 All were members of the General City Mission which was an all-Calvinist inter-denominational body founded in 1853. See *Annual report of General City Mission* (1854).
7 See ch. 3, p. 60.
8 *Free Presb.*, 7 May 1850.
9 Ibid., 28 March, 11 July, 26 September, 5 December 1848.
10 J. H. Wilson, *City Missions and how to work them* (Aberdeen, 1849), p. 17.
11 *Free Presb.*, 11 January 1847.
12 Ibid.
13 Ibid., 6 and 13 January, 3 February 1846.
14 Ibid., 5 January 1847.
15 Ibid. (six county ministers were also drafted into the scheme).
16 Ibid., 4 January 1848.
17 Ibid.
18 Ibid., 5 December 1848.
19 Ibid., 4 January 1848.
20 Ibid., 20 March 1849 (my italics).
21 See ch. 5, *passim*.
22 J. Whyntie, *The early history of Rutherford Church* (Aberdeen, 1895), p. 5.
23 Ibid.
24 A. Gammie, *The churches of Aberdeen* (Aberdeen, 1909), pp. 18-19. See also Stark's *Life of Dr Kidd*, and Martin's *Eminent divines in Aberdeen and the north* (Aberdeen, 1888).
25 In certain respects he can be compared to the Rev. Hugh Hart of the United Christian Church. See pp. 195-7.
26 The seceding section founded Holburn chapel-of-ease. (See Gammie, op. cit., pp. 19, 28.)
27 Whyntie, op. cit., p. 3.
28 Ibid., p. 4. (It is possible that this comment was derived from a conversation with Laing whom Whyntie knew. He was also conversant with members of Ross's family.)
29 *Free Presb.*, 5 December 1848.
30 See ch. 4, p. 69.
31 See ch. 5, pp. 110, 112-13.
32 At Northfield Mission 'when he was obliged to be absent he had to secure two or three substitutes, as no single person cared to undertake the whole work. If anyone did undertake it he was careful not to do so a second time': Whyntie, op. cit., p. 7.
33 *Free Presb.*, 6 February 1849. His petition to be appointed catechist was

supported and 'signed by most of the residents' of the area: Whyntie, op. cit., p. 6.

34 *Free Presb.*, 24 April, 12 January 1849.

35 Ibid., 3 July 1849.

36 Ibid., 4 September 1849. (Detailed instructions were also provided concerning the manner in which a catechist ought to conduct his religious services.)

37 Ibid., 4 September 1849.

38 Ibid., 20 November 1849, 7 May 1850.

39 *Free Presb.*, 3 September 1850. (Earlier at the same meeting the Presbytery decided to go ahead with the building of a mission chapel in 'a destitute district of the city' not then decided upon. However, they were still looking for a site in 1853. See *Free Presb.*, 4 January 1853.)

40 Ibid., 5 November 1850. Laing designed and built the chapel and schools costing £700 at his own expense. See Whyntie, op. cit., p. 6.

41 *Free Presb.*, 10 December 1850.

42 Whyntie, op. cit., p. 7; *Free Presb.*, 4 February 1851.

43 *Free Presb.*, 25 November 1851, 5 November 1852, 29 March 1853.

44 Ibid., 3 May 1853.

45 Gammie, op. cit., p. 127. ('He became famous as an antagonist of Roman Catholicism, and his great Anti-Popery discourses, in which he let himself go in bursts of passion, made something of a sensation, and he became the talk of the town.' Ibid., p. 127.)

46 *Free Presb.*, 4 January 1859.

47 Whyntie, op. cit., p. 9; *Free Presb.*, 31 March 1863.

48 As noted earlier this policy had been decided at a meeting of the Free Presbytery on 5 December 1848. (See p. 6.)

49 *Free Presb.*, 6 December 1853.

50 *Free Greyf. Deac.*, 1 May 1854. (The office-bearers were instructed to give 'an early entry to the purchasers. Please get this arranged.' Thereafter a petty squabble developed over whether the window blinds and other minor fixtures had been included in the sale: ibid., 3 July 1854.)

51 Gammie, op. cit., pp. 132-3.

52 Ibid., p. 123.

53 *Free Presb.*, 16 August 1855.

54 Gammie, loc. cit.

55 *Free Presb.*, 5 February, 2 September 1856.

56 Ibid., 2 December 1856, 3 February 1857, 1 February and 1 March 1859, 7 February 1860, 21 February 1861, 4 February 1862.

57 Ibid., 3 May and 7 August 1860.

58 They made this recommendation on 20 January 1863. (*Free Presb.*, 3 February 1863.)

59 Gammie, loc. cit.

60 *Free Presb.*, 3 February, 16 February, 3 and 31 March 1863.

61 Ibid., 1 December 1857, 25 September 1860, 30 September 1862.

62 Ibid., 5 May 1863.

63 Gammie, op. cit., p. 124; *Free Presb.*, 6 February, 6 March, 19 June 1866.

64 See ch. 5, pp. 111-13.

65 When Laing relinquished Northfield it had been placed under East Free

kirk session. After the secession from Gallowgate the mission was placed under the jurisdiction of South Free Church. (Gammie, loc. cit.; *Free Presb.*, 6 February 1866.)

66 See ch. 3, p. 60.

67 *Est. Presb.*, 20 February, 18 April, 3 May, 4 and 19 June, 18 September, 9 October 1844; 31 March, 26 April 1845.

68 Ten years later the expenses incurred by certain of these elders acting for the Presbytery had not been repaid: *Est. Presb.*, 3 February, 30 March, 28 September, 7 December 1852; 7 February, 29 March, 3 May, 27 September 1853.

69 *Est. South Assoc.*, 26 February 1845.

70 *Est. South Sess.*, 17 February 1846.

71 *Est. Greyf. Sess.*, 2 June 1866, 7 January 1867.

72 Their names were David McTaggart and James Smith. Both took an intense interest in the affairs of the parish and the various philanthropic bodies associated with it. McTaggart continually made personal recommendations regarding the distribution of poor relief, no doubt on the basis of contacts made during his visitation. Smith was actively concerned with the need for improved educational facilities in the parish and repeatedly pressed for new and larger accommodation. (See *Est. Greyf. Sess.*, 1848-62, *passim.*)

73 Gammie, op. cit., p. 24.

74 *Est. Presb.*, 17 February, 29 March, 27 September 1859.

75 For example, the session authorised the payment of rent for a room in the Gallowgate which had been used for missionary purposes: *Est. Greyf. Sess.*, 2 October 1865.

76 *Est. South Sess.*, 17 February 1846.

77 *Est. South Assoc.*, 13 December 1849.

78 Ibid., 22 October 1845.

79 Ibid.

80 Ibid., quarterly report, 19 January 1848.

81 *Est. South Assoc.*, 20 November 1846 (my italics). From a printed leaflet written by the minister entitled 'An address to the South Church Congregation' (p. 1), attached to minutes of aforementioned date.

82 Ibid., p. 2.

83 *Est. South Assoc.*, eighth annual report, 27 April 1852; half-yearly report, 18 October 1849.

84 Whilst visiting an 'open and avowed infidel in the parish' (there were two of them in 1853—see 'Statement of the Object and Operations' attached to minute book) he conversed with him as he papered his room, giving him advice on the subject which he 'thankfully took and instantly put into practice': *Est. South Assoc.*, 7 May 1850.

85 *Est. South Assoc.*, ninth annual report, 5 May 1853.

86 Ibid.

87 It was admitted in 1848 that there were causes prevalent 'altogether beyond the control of human agency' and that these were more active than at any other period of the city's history. (*Est. South Assoc.*, quarterly report, 18 October 1848.)

88 Ibid., seventh annual report, 17 April 1851.

89 See W. Watson, *Pauperism, vagrancy, crime and industrial education in Aber-deenshire* (Aberdeen, 1877).

90 *Est. South Assoc.*, annual report, 2 May 1849. (It was later pointed out that 'no stockings can be had so good and so cheap as those procured from this Department. Hence there is a double blessing annexed to this scheme: "It blesseth him that gives and he that gets".' Ibid., ninth annual report, 5 May 1853.)

91 Ibid., quarterly report, 20 October 1847.

92 Ibid., half-yearly report, 18 October 1848.

93 Ibid., eighth annual report, 27 April 1852.

94 Ibid., half-yearly report, 18 October 1849.

95 See ch. 6, pp. 135-7.

96 *Free West Sess.*, 25 October 1853, 23 January 1855.

97 Ibid., 20 February 1857.

98 *Free Trin. Sess.*, 15 June 1849.

99 Ibid., 16 July 1849.

100 Crombie had been a member of the congregation and at the instigation of the minister was granted £10 annually towards his expenses at Divinity College. When the award was first made on the basis that he was 'a young man whom we think possessed of the qualifications' an unknown hand added a query to the 'we'! The minister also got him appointed as mission-ary during his probationary period—half the costs of his salary coming from the Home Mission Committee in Edinburgh. See *Free Trin. Deac.*, 6 January, 8 September 1845; *Free Trin. Sess.*, 15 June 1849; *Free Presb.*, 3 July 1849.

101 *Free Greyf. Deac.*, 2 May, 2 August, 25 October 1865; 21 June 1866.

102 *Free West Sess.*, 7 January, 22 December 1865. Aiken's salary had been £60 per annum.

103 Ibid., 30 April 1862, 7 January 1865.

104 Ibid., 18 June 1860.

105 Ibid.

106 For example, see *Free West Sess.*, 23 September 1861, 29 September 1862.

107 W. Robbie, *Bonaccord Free Church; a retrospect, 1828-82* (Aberdeen, 1887), p. 23.

108 *Free Trin. Deac.*, March 1848; 1 March, 6 September 1849; 27 February, 1 May 1850.

109 *Free Trin. Sess.*, 24 January 1866.

110 *Free Trin. Teach.*, 22 April 1867.

111 Ibid., 16 August 1866.

112 It was defeated by only three votes. See *Free Presb.*, 3 December 1850, 7 December 1851.

113 Ibid., 2 March 1852.

114 See ch. 2, p. 38 and n. 40.

115 For example a great deal of effort was put into devising a series of lecture courses pointing out the dangers of Roman Catholic aggression. (*Free Presb.*, 10 December 1850.)

116 See ch. 2, pp. 38-9.

117 Gammie, op. cit., p. 296.

118 *Fourth pastoral address* (Aberdeen, 1863), p. xiv.

119 Ibid., p. xix. The number of working-class members must have been very small. The average number of communicants was only ninety-two. (Ibid., p. xvii.)

120 Gammie, op. cit., p. 298.

121 Ibid., p. 299.

122 Ibid., p. 238.

123 Ibid. For examples of Wilson's publications see *City missions and how to work them* (London, 1849), *Ragged Kirks and how to fill them* (Aberdeen, 1849), *Our moral wastes and how to reclaim them* (London, 1859), *Brands plucked from the burning* (Aberdeen, 1883).

124 Gammie, op. cit., p. 238.

125 Ibid., p. 239.

126 Ibid., p. 238.

127 Wilson, *City missions and how to work them*, p. 6.

128 Gammie, loc. cit.

129 Wilson, op. cit., p. 9.

130 Ibid., p. 8.

131 Ibid., p. 11.

132 Wilson, *Our moral wastes and how to reclaim them*, p. 20.

133 Ibid., p. 19.

134 Wilson, *City missions and how to work them*, p. 10.

135 No attempt was made to incorporate the old name in the new church which was called Trinity Congregational and was sited in Shiprow. It was claimed at the time that the Albion Street Church was too small to house the congregation (800 sittings). The new church had accommodation for 1,000. About 500 had seceded from the Albion Street congregation (Gammie, op. cit., pp. 238-40, 261).

136 See ch. 6, *passim*.

137 Not all the groups could be defined precisely as 'sectarian'. For a stimulating analysis of this problem see volume edited by B. Wilson, *Patterns of sectarianism* (London, 1967), pp. 22-45.

138 Gammie, op. cit., p. 386.

139 J. Bruce, *The Aberdeen pulpit and universities* (Aberdeen, 1844), pp. 145-6. They are well known enough to be included in the National Census, see Appendix B.

140 Bruce, op. cit., p. 145; *Aberdeen Journal*, 3 March 1830.

141 Gammie, op. cit., pp. 339-40; Bruce, op. cit., p. 145.

142 *A brief sketch of the principles on which the Primitive Christian Church is formed* (Aberdeen, n.d. but identifiable as the 1830s), p. 7.

143 As we have seen the Glasites did. The Bereans and the Southcotians would seem to have dispersed. The Irvingites had joined the English Episcopal congregation (Gammie, op. cit., p. 339). The Primitive Christians may have formed what was called later the Church of Christ (Gammie, op. cit., pp. 348-9) although there is no definite evidence to show that they were the same group.

144 G. King, *Brief historical sketch of the Congregational Church in George Street* (Aberdeen, 1870), pp. 20, 64. See also J. Bulloch, *Centenary memorials of the first Congregational Church in Aberdeen* (Aberdeen, 1898).

145 Gammie, op. cit., p. 88.

146 Ibid., p. 180.

147 Twenty of the twenty-nine members of the controlling committee can be positively identified as shipmasters and shipowners: *The seventh annual report of the Bethel Seamen's Friend Society of Aberdeen* (Aberdeen, 1829), pp. 8-10.

148 See ch. 1, p. 17. The church was erected by subscription in 1795—a principal subscriber being Alexander Hadden, textile manufacturer and one of the biggest employers of labour in the city: Gammie, op. cit., pp. 187-8.

149 See n. 144. The first Anti-Burger Church after a series of crippling schisms survived as Belmont Street U.P. Church (see Gammie, op. cit., p. 89; ch. 2, p. 33). The Gaelic and Mariners' churches were saved from closure in 1850 on the basis that they were special cases. (See ch. 5, p. 113.)

150 See Appendix D, United Christians ('Isolated congregation').

151 Gammie, op. cit., p. 377.

152 James Riddell, *Aberdeen and its folk* (Aberdeen, 1868), p. 74. For an example of his theological views, see H. Hart, *Diversity of theological subjects scripturally stated . . . amicably to compose religious differences and to assist in repairing breaches occasioned by schism* (Aberdeen, 1830).

153 Gammie, op. cit., p. 377; Bruce, op. cit., pp. 125, 140-2, 147.

154 Riddell, op. cit., p. 78.

155 Bruce, op. cit., pp. 150-4; Gammie, op. cit., pp. 377-8.

156 Riddell, op. cit., pp. 74, 76.

157 Gammie, op. cit., pp. 190-1. (The Mariners' Church changed its name to Commerce Street Free Church about 1883. 'The time had passed when the seafaring community wished a church of their own. They even preferred to attend one of a less distinctive name, while it was well-nigh an impossibility to get any of the other classes to become associated with a Mariners' Church.' Gammie, op. cit., p. 161.)

158 For example, see *Our moral wastes and how to reclaim them* and *Brands plucked from the burning*.

159 Some of the congregation may have joined the John Street Congregational Church which bought the United Christian Church building after Hart's death in 1862. However, as the new John Street congregation numbered only forty it seems unlikely that many of Hart's congregation had joined. (Gammie, op. cit., p. 249.)

160 See p. 190.

161 See ch. 7, *passim*.

162 A. S. Cook, *Home mission work in towns* (Aberdeen, 1886), p. 10.

In Conclusion

> No individual power could have reared this Free Church. It is the
> result of a confluence of circumstances.*

Whilst Lord Cockburn—author of the above statement—was describing the diverse origins of the Free Church nationally, his observation is
equally applicable with regard to the situation in Aberdeen. Furthermore, the same 'confluence of circumstances' which reared the Free
Church to a large extent explains its subsequent development.

Not all of the forces or circumstances, however, which were to
mould and determine the nature of the new Church, were inherent in
the Free Church itself. An important determinant was the fundamental
weakness of the Establishment which failed on the one hand to coerce
and intimidate those who challenged its authority, and on the other to
make sufficient conciliatory gestures in order to blunt and weaken the
force of the challenge. This failure is to a considerable degree explicable
in terms of certain contradictions which were becoming increasingly
apparent within the ranks of the old ruling oligarchy. These contradictions were of a structural and ideological nature. The old eighteenth-
century alliance between the landed and merchant families on which the
prosperity of the city had been built was breaking down. The contraction of industry away from its former domestic and rural basis
into the city factories, and the changes in agricultural technology leading to greatly increased production, created a divergence of interest
amounting to a rural/urban dichotomy. The urban sections of the old
landed-merchant families sought to promote free trade which, rightly
or wrongly, the landed sections saw as endangering their future
economic prosperity, and rightly saw as a long-term threat to their
social position in the community. On the issue of patronage in the
Church, however, the urban sections, who would have lost nothing if
reforms had been forthcoming, were not prepared to widen the developing schism between themselves and the landed gentry. Consequently,
the urban families of the old merchant-landed oligarchy found themselves promoting a newspaper in order to advocate the ending of
restrictions on trade—these having placed agriculture in a privileged
position—and at the same time defending the privileges of the landed
sections with regard to patronage in the Church. Had these families

* Henry Cockburn, *Journal, 1831-54* (Edinburgh, 1874), p. 39.

been able to make the break complete between themselves and the landed sections at this point, it seems a fair assumption that they could have taken over, or controlled and accommodated, many of the non-intrusionists. Instead they half-heartedly defended patronage on the grounds of the illegality of the demands of the non-intrusionists and allowed Adam and the *Aberdeen Herald* to ridicule, taunt, and ultimately drive into secession, clergymen who might well have been courted by conciliation and compromise.

The failure of the ruling oligarchy of city families to treat the demands of the non-intrusionists with some sympathy and apparent consideration, was not just the result of a lack of political foresight—although they would seem to have misjudged the extent of support the 'nons' enjoyed. Their antipathy towards non-intrusion must certainly have been based on dislike and distrust of many of those most vociferous in support of its cause—men of increasing wealth but often of obscure origins; men who having been denied accommodation by their social superiors increasingly sought confrontation with them. It is in this positive response by these men towards what was on the whole a negative attitude of the ruling oligarchy, that one detects an important circumstance which was to provide in Aberdeen the great initial impetus of the seceders, and was to shape the subsequent development of the Free Church in the post-Disruption years.

The differences between the old dynasty of ruling families and the newcomers ran deeper than the question of non-intrusion and contrasting social origins. The emergent middle class, who were to provide the dynamic elements of the new Church, were characterised by a high degree of social mobility based on a readiness to switch occupations and to diversify business interests. Thus it was not uncommon among the elders of the Free Church to find a stockbroker who had been a butcher in the east end, or a wholesale tea and coffee dealer who had formerly been a druggist, or a fancy and photographic goods warehouseman who had begun as an east-end hairdresser. Moreover, in their climb up the social ladder these same men might well have made and unmade several business partnerships, and occupied any number of business premises. But if their aggressive entrepreneurship in the field of business contrasted vividly with the staid respectability of their counterparts in the Establishment, so were their life styles sharply differentiated. Whilst the adherents of the Establishment clung to the older residential areas of the city around the Castle Street, Adelphi, east end of Union Street, the Upperkirkgate and Netherkirkgate, venturing as far as Belmont Street, the new men of the Free Church crossed over to the areas west of the Denburn often occupying several houses in a relatively short space of time in the new residential areas of Bonaccord Street, Crown Street, Dee Street, Union Place, Holburn Street, Carden Place and Rubislaw district. These men alone had the dynamism, enterprise, and wealth to raise stipends, build churches, and generally ensure the success of the Free Church which was clearly demonstrated by the census of religion in 1851.

However, in the making of the success they left their own peculiar stamp on its economic organisation. Urged on to fight a war against the residuary Establishment they fought it with all their economic expertise, treating each church, every congregation, and ultimately each individual member as part of a business enterprise. Contributions to national schemes such as the Sustentation Fund tended to become a measure of religiosity, the criterion for election to eldership, and to some extent for membership of the Church. The 'new shoots' of the Free Church, many of them insecure in the middle class of which they had only recently become part, saw the success of the new Church as a measure of their own ability. The desire to destroy the residuary Establishment led to the creation of a Free Church which in all ways was to be superior to the Church from which they had seceded. In the final analysis the Establishment survived despite, or perhaps simply because of, the success of the Free Church. In seeking comparability with the Establishment the Free Church became not the new Establishment, but *another* Establishment with all the financial disadvantages attached to maintaining such a position. The 'new shoots' having demonstrated their ability, lost the great motivating drive, and with this loss of motivation passed away the vigour which had characterised the Free Church at its inception. Thus the ultimate decline of the Free Church, rather paradoxically, was rooted in the circumstances at its inception and the social base of its original dynamism.

Notwithstanding its outstanding success as a denomination, the Free Church must be considered a failure in certain important respects. In its war against the Establishment it would seem likely that the first casualties were its working-class members who were driven out by the middle-class nature of the new Church and its inquisitorial financial organisation, coinciding as it did with a period of grave economic recession in the city. It was a loss which the Free Church failed to make good although considerable time and money was spent in attempting to do so. The widespread religiosity of the working class, measured in terms of their belief in church 'connection', which was largely the result of historical circumstances and the efforts of the churches in the field of social control—notably in educational provision—was never fully exploited by any of the Presbyterian churches. Whilst this may be partly explained by the Calvinist view of conversion, in the case of the Free Church the difficulty ran deeper than this, involving the overall strategy of the Church in its struggle with the Establishment, and the more subtle ideological changes which had occurred within its own organisation. It was now necessary to discipline the 'impudent boys' who were threatening the structure of an 'establishment' not so dissimilar from the one they themselves had disrupted in the previous decade. Whilst the Free Church, denominationally, was unable to embrace the spiritually destitute working class, it feared that the efforts of others might be successful. Consequently considerable time and effort was expended in exposing the doctrinal errors of men like Hugh Hart, in issuing dire warnings of the dangers of Popery, in condemning the concept of 'ragged churches', and in winning back children who had fallen to the temptations of the Episcopal Church.

Of all the 'confluence of circumstances' which went into the making of the Free Church in Aberdeen, the most vital in the understanding of its subsequent development was the nature of the social support it received in 1843. It was the 'new shoots' who were to direct the new Church along its initial dynamic course, shape its organisation, make it a success as a denomination, and having achieved their own ambition, and proved their ability, leave it with unsolved problems such as its role as a twin to the Established Church. Writing in 1844, and still fearful of the social consequences which she saw as resulting from the Disruption, one lady defender of the Establishment rather hopefully declared:*

> The Secession which has taken place will not weaken the Establishment, for this is not the first Dissent from the Church of Scotland, nor will it probably be the last.

She was, of course, wrong both in her fears and in her prediction. What she had witnessed was not the disintegration of society but a phenomenon that reflected social forces which ultimately would lead to its stabilisation. She was in fact observing the arrival of the new urban-based bourgeoisie.

---

* *Observations on the relative positions . . . by a lady* (Aberdeen, 1844), p. 9.

Appendix

A   Scottish Churches *c.* 1733–*c.* 1860

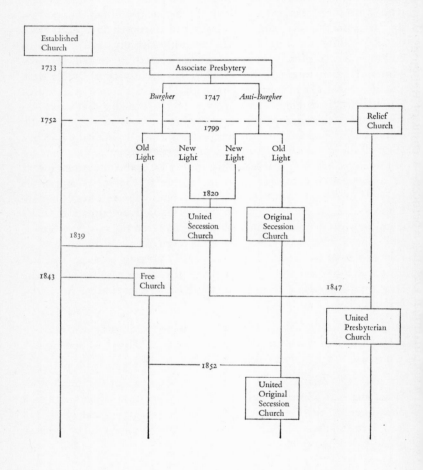

Table 5 (Denominational Details) ABERDEEN—Census of Religious Worship, 1851*

Religious denomination	Number of places of worship	Number of sittings			Number of attendants at public worship on Sunday 30 March 1851 (including Sunday Scholars)		
		Free	Appropriated	Total	Morning	Afternoon	Evening
Total	43	6576	25367	34543	18569	16883	6084
Protestant churches:							
Established Church	7	963	5172	7735	3215	3613	1813
Original Secession Church	1	227	223	450	212	212	—
United Presbyterian Church	5	2231	1740	3971	1351	1595	450
Free Church	15	1497	11766	13913	9426	8533	735
Episcopal Church	2	—	1925	1925	1350	980	1100
Independents or Congregationalists	6	1228	2971	4199	1545	1605	1380
Baptists	2	280	—	280	76	—	—
Unitarians	1	—	—	—	160	—	64
Wesleyan Methodists	1	—	820	820	354	—	292
Glasites or Sandemanians	1	100	—	100	30	45	—
Isolated congregations	1	—	—	350	150	—	250
Other Christian churches:							
Roman Catholics	1	50	750	800	700	300	—
Latter-Day Saints or Mormons	—	—	—	—	—	—	—

* It has not been found possible in all cases to give the statistics for the exact Burgh; since, where Burghs are not conterminate with parishes, the figures do not show which of the places of worship are within and which outside the limits of the Burgh. In such cases, the figures have been taken for the parochial limits; and the additional population thus included is shown in the heading. ABERDEEN. The number of sittings is not returned for one of the above forty-three places of worship. It belongs to the Unitarians. Returns are altogether wanting for twelve [sic] other places of worship. Of these, two belong to the Established Church; one to the United Presbyterian Church; one to the Free Church; one to the Episcopal Church; two to the Independents; three to the Baptists; two to isolated congregations; and one to the Society of Friends.

C(i) Percentage of Sittings Occupied at Each Service

Service	Churches open	Sittings available	Attendance	% occupied
Morning	43	34543	18569	53·7
Afternoon	34	31397	16833	53·6
Evening	15	11469	6084	53·0

C(ii) Percentage of Sittings Occupied by Each Denomination at the Morning Service

	% sittings occupied	% appropriated sittings occupied
Established	41·6	62·2
Original Secession	47·1	95·1
United Presbyterian	34·0	77·6
Free Church	67·7	80·1
Congregational	36·8	52·0
Episcopal★	70·1	—
Baptists†	27·1	—
Unitarians‡	—	—
Methodists★	43·8	—
Glasites†	30·0	—
Isol. cong.‡	42·8	—
Roman Catholics	87·5	93·3
(Average)	(53·7)	(73·2)

★ All appropriated.   † None appropriated.   ‡ No information.

D Estimated Attendance at Aberdeen Churches, 30 March 1851

Denomination	Morn.	Af./Ev.*	Nons.*	Total	% population	% attendance	% Presbyterian
Established	3215	1356	750	5321	7·26	18·72	27·55
Original Secession	212	—	—	212	0·03	0·07	1·10
United Presbyterian	1351	511	100	1962	2·67	6·90	10·16
Free Presbyterian	9426	2315	80	11821	16·14	41·58	60·16
Total Presbyterian				19316	26·37	67·95	100·00
Episcopal (Scotch and English)	1350	1540	905	3795	5·18	13·35	
Congregational (C.U. and E.U.)	1545	1492	150	3187	4·35	11·21	
Methodist (Wesleyan)	354	146	—	500	0·07	1·75	
Baptist (Scotch and English)	76	—	80	156	0·02	0·05	
Unitarians	160	32	—	192	0·03	0·06	
Glasites	30	22	—	52	—	0·02	
United Christians (isol. cong.)	150	125	—	275	0·04	0·10	
Quakers, Christadelphians and Church of Christ	—	100	100	200	0·01	0·03	
Roman Catholics	700	150	—	850	1·16	2·99	
Total non-Presbyterian				9207	12·43	32·04	

Total attendance: 28,423
Percentage population: 38·59

* *Estimates*: Seventy-five per cent allowed for double attendance in Presbyterian churches with the exception of the O.S. congregation. Fifty per cent allowed in all other denominations. (See ch. 2, pp. 42-4.) On non-returns see chapter 2, 'The Conduct of the Census'. The Established Church figures are derived from attendance figures listed in *Register of General Session*, vol. 50, 12 January 1846.

E(i)   Secession of Elders in Six Parishes

Kirk session	No. of elders	High status elders	Remaining	Seceding	Unknown
West	24 ⎱	20 ⎱	14 ⎱	8 ⎱	2 ⎱
South	13 ⎰ 54	11 ⎰ 41	6 ⎰ 25	7 ⎰ 23	0 ⎰ 6
East	17 ⎰	10 ⎰	5 ⎰	8 ⎰	4 ⎰
St Clement's	16 ⎱	7 ⎱	4 ⎱	9 ⎱	3 ⎱
North	9 ⎰ 36	3 ⎰ 17	1 ⎰ 6	7 ⎰ 24	1 ⎰ 6
Greyfriars	11 ⎰	7 ⎰	1 ⎰	8 ⎰	2 ⎰
Totals	90	58	31	47	12

E(ii)   Secession and Seniority of Elders in Six Parishes

Kirk session	Senior*			Junior		
	Rem.	Sec.	Unk.	Rem.	Sec.	Unk.
West	8 ⎱	2 ⎱	2	6 ⎱	6 ⎱	0
South	5 ⎰ 16	1 ⎰ 6	0	1 ⎰ 9	6 ⎰ 17	0
East	3 ⎰	3 ⎰	2	2 ⎰	5 ⎰	2
St Clement's	3 ⎱	3 ⎱	2	1 ⎱	6 ⎱	1
North	1 ⎰ 5	2 ⎰ 9	1	0 ⎰ 1	5 ⎰ 16	0
Greyfriars	1 ⎰	4 ⎰	0	0 ⎰	5 ⎰	1
Totals	21	15	7	10	33	4
Percentage	48·8	34·9	16·3	21·3	70·2	8·5

* The problem of finding the best criterion of seniority is not difficult after 1843 because one can refer simply to pre-Disruption or post-Disruption elders. Before the Disruption the difficulty is to affix a date which takes into account the issues being debated in the society at large, whilst also considering the peculiarities of the various sessions. As elections were held at the discretion of the minister and the existing session, and because the decision to increase the number of elders was related to the age of the existing session, natural wastage by death, illness and resignation, it is not helpful to fix a precise date (say 1838-9) and consider those elected before that date as senior, and those after as junior. Long periods might pass without election. The East parish had no elections after 1836, whilst Greyfriars had an election in 1840 and 1842. Then again sessions occasionally simply co-opted a man ordained by another Established church if he joined the congregation. The creation of *quoad sacra* parishes after 1834 is a further complication as some elders (e.g. South parish) withdrew to serve on these new sessions. There is also the practical problem of not being able to establish the exact date at which an elder was elected in certain sessions. The problem has been resolved, therefore, in an arbitrary way. Elders were listed by the kirk sessions according to seniority (i.e. length of service)—each new elder being placed at the bottom of the list and those leaving by resignation, etc. being struck off. Accordingly, the first half of the list of elders of any session has been considered senior; the bottom half junior.

E(iii) Secession and Seniority—Status Distribution of Elders in Six Parishes

Kirk session	Remaining						Seceding						Uncertain					
	Senior			Junior			Senior			Junior			Senior			Junior		
	Status			*Status*			*Status*			*Status*			*Status*			*Status*		
	High	Unk.	Low	High	Unk.	Low	High	Unk.	Low	High	Unk.	Low	High	Unk.	Low	High	Unk.	Low
West	8	—	—	4	—	1	1	1	—	6	—	—	1	—	1	—	—	—
South	5	—	—	1	—	—	1	—	—	4	—	2	—	—	—	—	—	—
East	3	—	—	1	—	1	3	—	—	1	2	2	1	—	1	1	—	1
St Clement's	1	—	2	1	—	—	2	—	1	1	2	3	1	1	1	1	—	—
North	—	1	—	—	—	—	1	—	1	3	—	2	—	1	—	—	—	—
Greyfriars	1	—	—	—	—	—	2	—	2	3	—	2	—	—	—	—	—	1
Totals	18	1	2	7	—	2	10	1	4	18	4	11	3	1	3	2	—	2

F   Status Classification

The biographical details of the elders were compiled by extracting the names of kirk session members from the *Aberdeen Almanac*, and tracing these names in the Post Office directories. Extensive reference was also made to the Presbytery and kirk session records. Occasionally it was found necessary to refer to property valuation although the absence of an official Valuation Roll before 1855 is a drawback.

Classification Code

A   Professional group (university graduates): 1 advocates 2 professors, lecturers—generally also practising medicine 3 principals, rectors, headmasters of important educational establishments.

B   Commercial group: 1 bankers, bank managers and agents 2 cashiers, principal clerks, accountants, insurance company managers, and brokers, company treasurers.

C   Large merchant-manufacturer group: 1 suppliers of capital goods, timber, etc., construction companies, ironfounders, textile manufacturers, wholesalers and importers, tobacco manufacturers 2 suppliers of consumer goods and services catering for middle class, silversmiths, silk mercers 3 suppliers of food and wines, grocers, vintners, etc. 4 commission merchants, ship agents.

D   Retired-rentier group: 1 shipowners 2 landlords, those retired and living on income from rented property, shares, or capital; including Members of Parliament.

E   'Public servants' (I): 1 doctors, druggists 2 local government officials, building inspectors, architects 3 shipmasters, marine and civil engineers.

F   'Public servants' (II): 1 teachers, 'stickit ministers' 2 clerks, writers.

G   Small merchant-tradesmen group: 1 shopkeepers 2 self-employed tradesmen, agents living in premises 3 foremen, overseers 4 retired tradesmen and shopkeepers.

H   Artisans and others: 1 employed artisans 2 semi- and unskilled, fishermen, ropemakers, etc.

O   *Uncertain:* individual cannot positively be identified.

X   *Unknown:* name of individual known, but no trace of occupation or place of residence, either in *Post Office Directory* or elsewhere.

High status: Groups A, B, C, D.
Low status: Groups E, F, G.

Group H is the one group containing working-class occupations although these may be present in Group X and to a lesser extent in Group O.

The fundamental difference between Group O and Group X is that in the latter case the individual's name alone is known and no other details can be gathered; whilst in the former Group O there is a difficulty over positive identification, generally because of name similarities—e.g. 'Smith'.

G(i)   Status of Elders in Established Churches, 1851

Established Church	No.	Found	Status High	Low
West	19	19	17	2
South	12	12	8	4
East	14	13	8	5
North	4	3	2	1
Greyfriars	12	12	8	4
St Clement's	3	3	2	1
Totals	64	62	45	17

Percentage:
   High status, 70·31.
   Low status, 26·56.

G(ii)   Status of Elders in Equivalent Free Churches, 1851

| | | | Status | |
Free Church	No.	Found	High	Low
West	12	12	10	2
South	20	20	15	5
East	12	12	8	4
North	7	7	5	2
Greyfriars	(3)	(3)	(1)	(2)
St Clement's	13	11	5	6
(Trinity)	(11)	(11)	(10)	(1)
'A' Total	67	65	44	21
'B' (including Trinity and excluding Grey-friars)	75	73	53	20

Percentages:
 'A' 65·67—31·34.
 'B' 70·66—26·66.

G(iii)   Status of Elders in Free Churches (Former Q.S. Churches), 1851

| | | | | Status range | | | |
Church	No.	Found	High	Low	H	O	X
Bonaccord	12	10	3	6	1	2	0
Melville	6	6	0	6	0	0	0
Union	12	6	2	4	0	2	4
Holburn	9	9	2	7	0	0	0
John Knox	9	5	1	4	0	2	2
Gilcomston	15	11	0	11	0	4	0
Gaelic (Spring Garden)	3	0	0	0	0	2	1
Mariners'	8	2	0	2	0	4	2
Totals	74	49	8	40	1	16	9

Biographical Notes

Ministers of the Disruption Period

ALLAN, JOHN. Born 1798 at Belhelvie, Aberdeenshire. Eldest son of a farmer. Educated University of Glasgow, and Marischal College. Ordained Union chapel-of-ease in 1832. Seceded and joined Free Church in 1843. Resigned in 1846 owing to a throat condition and married in the same year. Died 1885.

BRYCE, JAMES. Born 1792. Son of a Renfrew farmer. Educated University of Glasgow. Licensed Presbytery of Stirling 1819. Schoolmaster until 1824. Admitted Gilcomston 1835. Seceded and joined Free Church 1843. Minister of Gilcomston Free Church until 1854 when he resigned because of ill-health. Died 1861.

DAVIDSON, ALEXANDER DYCE. Born 1807. Son of wright superintendent of Devanha Brewery. Educated Grammar School and Marischal College 1825. Tutor in family of James Blaikie. Licensed 1830 by Presbytery of Aberdeen. Ordained South Church in 1832. Admitted to West parish in 1836. Seceded and joined Free Church in 1843. Minister of Free West Church until his death in 1872. Awarded D.D. by Marischal College in 1854. Davidson married daughter of James Blaikie.

DEWAR, DANIEL. Professor of Moral Philosophy and minister of Greyfriars chapel-of-ease in 1814. Translated to Tron Church, Glasgow, 1819, where he served until his appointment as principal of Marischal College in 1832. He was the last principal prior to the union of the two colleges—Marischal and King's—to form University of Aberdeen in the 1860s. Dewar was 'the foremost and most fearless speaker among the evangelical party' (J. Martin, *Eminent divines in Aberdeen and the north* (Aberdeen, 1888), p. 225), but was the most notorious of the fence-sitters after the Disruption. He attended the public meeting held by the seceders in Holburn Church (*Banner*, 13 May 1845) but in the months following he did not commit himself openly to either side and as late as November 1843 the Established Presbytery were still seeking a declaration on his position (see ch. 5, p. 101). Martin explains his prevarication as resulting from 'a love of lucre'—a fear of losing his university position (op. cit., p. 225) but in this he was no worse than other Free churchmen such as Macrobin and Bentley. His prominence amongst the non-intrusionists must have made continued prevarication impossible and he remained in the Establishment. Thereafter he was regarded with contempt by both sides and he never preached in any city church after 1843. When MacIntosh of the East Church invited Dewar to preach at an evening service the entire kirk session threatened to resign unless the invitation was withdrawn. (A. Gammie, *The churches of Aberdeen* (Aberdeen, 1909), p. 23. See also James McCosh, *The wheat and the chaff gathered into bundles* (Dundee, 1843), p. 83.)

DEWAR, THOMAS. Born 1809. Son of a merchant. Educated University of Edinburgh. Ordained to charge in Edinburgh in 1839. South Parish Church, 28 September 1843 until his death in 1873.

FOOTE, JAMES. Born 1781. Son of a Fettercairn minister. Educated Marischal College. Licensed Presbytery of Perth. Elected by the town council in 1824. Minister of East parish 1828-43 when he seceded and became minister of East Free Church until his death in 1856. He received a D.D. from Marischal College in 1850. He was said to be an accomplished musician and excelled as a violinist.

FORSYTH, JAMES. Born 1797 at Kirkintilloch. Educated University of Glasgow. Licensed Presbytery of Glasgow 1819. West Church, 10 November 1843 until appointment of assistant in 1869. Died 1879.

GORDON, ABERCROMBIE L. Born 1803. Son of a minister at Banff. Educated King's College 1817-21. Elected by town council 1826. First minister of Greyfriars parish in 1828. Seceded and joined Free Church but left Aberdeen soon after completion of new Greyfriars Free Church in Crown Street. He later became minister of Presbyterian Church, London. He died in 1873. Gordon wrote many pamphlets on the need to provide education for the working class, and had been active in this field when minister of Greyfriars parish.

LONGMUIR, JOHN. Son of a sailor. Educated Aberdeen Grammar School and Marischal College. Ordained minister of Mariners' Church 1840. Seceded in 1843 and became minister of Mariners' Free Church until 1881. He died in 1883. Longmuir was 'an unflinching advocate of total abstinence' (Gammie, op. cit., p. 180), and published numerous works on the subject. He also edited a dictionary and other learned publications of a historical, antiquarian, and theological nature.

MACINTOSH, SIMON. Born 1815. Educated King's College, graduating 1835. Licensed Presbytery of Lochcarron 1840. Presented to Daviot, Inverness, but was not settled 'being unacceptable to the people'. Ordained to third charge Inverness 1842. East parish, 27 September 1843. He was widely held to be the best evangelical preacher of his time in the city. He died in 1853.

MACKENZIE, HUGH. Born Beauly in 1787. Graduated M.A. at King's College in 1811. Licensed Presbytery of Dingwall 1820. Lochtayside 1822. Gaelic Chapel 1823. Seceded in 1843 and became minister of Gaelic Free Church until his death in 1859.

MCTAGGART, DAVID. Born Angus in 1804. Educated at King's College, Aberdeen, graduating in 1827. Held charge in Ireland. McTaggart was minister of Greyfriars parish from 1848 until 1857, and followed the short pastorates of Archibald Stewart (April 1844-June 1845) and Professor Pirie (September 1846-October 1847). He built up a flourishing congregation. He died in 1881.

MILNE, DAVID. Born 1808. Son of brewer. Educated King's College, graduating 1832. Ordained assistant at Cluny in September 1843. Admitted to Gilcomston chapel-of-ease 19 June 1845, and served until appointment of assistant in 1876. He died in 1879. According to Gammie (op. cit., pp. 19-20) it was Milne's diligence which restored Gilcomston to the high point in numbers it had reached prior to the Disruption.

MITCHELL, JOHN. Born about 1825 at Arbuthnott, Kincardine. Graduated King's College 1846. Ordained to Holburn chapel-of-ease in 1850. Translated to St Fergus in 1855. Died 1895. Mitchell's ordination at Holburn followed a lengthy period when the charge was vacant, and the short pastorate of Rev. Alexander Ross.

MITCHELL, WILLIAM LAMB. Born Glamis *c.* 1804. Son of farmer. Graduated St Andrew's 1829. Licensed Meigle 1832. Assistant in Dundee charge. Ordained Holburn (Q.S.) Church in 1838. Seceded in 1843 and became minister of Holburn Free Church until he retired in 1875. Died in 1880.

MURRAY, JOHN. Born 1784. Son of a farmer at Insch. Educated Aberdeen Grammar School, Marischal College, and University of Edinburgh. Tutor to landed family in Peeblesshire. Assistant at Dundee. Minister of Trinity chapel-of-ease in 1816. Elected by town council 1824. First minister of North Church in 1828. Seceded in 1843 and became minister of North Free Church until his death in 1861.

NEWLANDS, JAMES. Born Banff about 1811. Educated King's College, graduating in 1831. Schoolmaster at Foveran. Licensed by Presbytery of Turriff. Ordained St Clement's parish, 28 September 1843. He was deposed by the Presbytery on 2 June 1849 for intemperance and fornication after a lengthy hearing of the evidence of forty-eight witnesses. The accusation alone occupied twenty-four pages of the Presbytery minutes (*Est. Presb.*, 20 October 1848).

PARKER, GAVIN. Born in Port Glasgow, son of a 'craftsman'. Educated at Glasgow University. First minister of Bonaccord chapel-of-ease in 1828 which resulted from a schism at Trinity when Simpson was elected. Seceded in 1843 and became minister of Bonaccord Free Church until his death in 1845.

PRIMROSE, WILLIAM. Born Kincardine-on-Forth 1783. Youngest son of farmer. Educated University of Glasgow and Original Burgher Synod Hall. Licensed Presbytery of Perth 1805. Ordained Original Secession Church, Aberdeen, in 1806. Congregation joined Establishment in 1839. Seceded and became minister of Melville Free Church until his death in 1866.

SIMPSON, DAVID. Born Findhorn 1795. Son of shoemaker. Educated Marischal College, graduating 1812. Admitted Trinity chapel-of-ease 1825. Seceded in 1843 and became minister of Trinity Free Church until his death in 1864.

SKENE, CHARLES. Born 1799. Son of farmer. Schoolmaster at Skene for a time. Licensed Presbytery of Aberdeen 1826. Ordained John Knox chapel-of-ease on 21 December 1843. Resigned 1877 and died the following year.

SMITH, JAMES. Son of flax-dresser. Educated King's College, graduating 1836. Ordained minister of Presbyterian congregation in Ireland in 1837. Missionary at Galashiels 1846 and admitted minister there in 1856. Translated to Greyfriars parish in 1857 following McTaggart's ministry (see above). Translated to Ellon in 1862 and died in 1871.

SPENCE, ALEXANDER. Born 1804. Son of a minister at Glenbucket. Educated Marischal College. Licensed Aberdeen Presbytery 1822. Ordained minister of St Clement's parish in 1838. Seceded in 1843 and became minister of St Clement's Free Church until his death in 1890, although he had retired from active duty twelve years earlier. He was the last surviving Disruption minister; and the first Free Church minister to be elected patron of the Incorporated Trades in 1879. He received a D.D. in 1866.

STEPHEN, JOHN. Born New Deer, 1800. Apprenticed to uncle who was a cooper in Aberdeen. Educated Marischal College, graduating 1821. Licensed Presbytery of Aberdeen 1835. Ordained to John Knox (Q.S.) Church in 1835. Seceded in 1843 and became minister of John Knox Free Church until his death in 1881.

STEWART, JAMES. Born 1813. Son of farmer. Educated University of Glasgow. Tutor to landed family. Licensed Presbytery of Glasgow 1836. Ordained 1838. Translated to South parish in 1842. Seceded in 1843 and became minister of South Free Church until his death in 1846.

TWEEDIE, WILLIAM KING. Born Ayr 1803. Educated Glasgow and St Andrews Universities. Licensed by Presbytery of Arbroath 1828. Ordained Presbyterian Church, London Wall, 1832. Translated to South parish in 1836; Tolbooth, Edinburgh, 1842. (Seceded in 1843.)

WILSON, JOHN. Born 1793. Son of merchant, Ayr. Educated University of Glasgow, Assistant at Ayr Academy and later at Madras College, Fife. Ordained Methil 1839. Minister of the North parish from 27 September until his death in 1873.

Elders Serving on Kirk Sessions, 1831-51

ABERNETHY, JAMES (South parish, South Free). Firm of J. Abernethy & Co., founders, engineers, and machine makers, Ferryhill. By 1861 they also undertook blacksmith and boilermaking work. Family had close associations with South parish, but all would appear to have seceded at the Disruption. James Abernethy became an elder in South Free and was still serving in 1851. John and Robert Abernethy became deacons in South Free Church. (See THOMAS LAURIE.)   (C1)*

AIKEN, JAMES (Free West). Missionary at the Denburn Mission, College Street. He was elected to serve on the session in June 1844 although he is not listed in J. Ogilvie Skea's *The Free West* (Aberdeen, 1963). It is probable that he was a retired shipmaster living with his son, a ship and insurance broker, Gilcomston Cottage. He was still a member of session in 1851.   (D2)

AIR, JOHN (Holburn Free). A cart- and plough-wright, 5 Skene Row; he lived in Whitehouse Street. He would appear to have died or left city by 1861.   (G2)

ALLAN, ALEXANDER (North parish). Cannot be positively identified regarding occupation, nor can he be traced after 1843 concerning denominational allegiance. He was ordained c. 1831.   (O)

ALLAN, GEORGE (St Clement's Free). A writer in 1842; he lived in Links Street and would appear to be the son of a shipmaster of the same name. He was admitted to the Society of Advocates in 1844 and thereafter lived in his premises in 1 Marischal Street. He was agent for the Dissenters' Fire and Life Assurance Company and the Mariners' General Assurance Company. By 1850 he lived at Bloomfield, Holburn Street; by 1861 he lived at 33 Albyn Place. He represented the Free Church congregation in their attempt to prevent an interdict on the erection of St Clement's Free Church temporary wooden building. He was ordained in 1843 and was still serving in 1851.   (A1)

* Status classification, see p. 218 for details.

ALLARDYCE, WILLIAM (East parish). Wine merchant and provision preserver, office: 40 Union Street. He lived at Tullos in 1831, 1 Crown Place in 1841 and 1851. By 1851 he also had a factory at Clayhills and had formed partnership with William Jopp (Allardyce and Jopp, wine merchants to the Queen, stock and share brokers, 13 Marischal Street). Allardyce was an elder in 1831 but had ceased serving on session before 1842. He served on town council 1833-6. (C1)

BAIN, WILLIAM (West parish). Manager of the City of Glasgow Bank; he lived at Victoria Court, Castle Street. He was ordained between 1847 and 1851. (B1)

BARRON, JOHN (South parish, Trinity parish, Trinity Free). Watch and clockmaker, 11 Netherkirkgate. In 1831 he lived next door at No. 13 with an advocate (Soc. of Adv. 1834) who was probably his son—Lambert Barron. John and Lambert moved to 83 Crown Street before 1851 on John's retirement from business. John died in 1852. An elder in the South parish, John Barron was a member of Trinity parish's first session in 1834. He seceded in 1843 and became an elder in Trinity Free Church's first session. He was narrowly elected to the city council in 1833 (6 votes); served for one year. (G2-D2)

BEATTIE, WILLIAM (East parish, East Free). Cannot be positively identified. An elder of East parish c. 1836—in 1843 he seceded but was not a member of East Free Session by 1851. (O)

BENTLEY, JAMES (South parish, Trinity parish). Professor of Oriental Languages, King's College; he lived at 134 King Street. Bentley was an elder in the South parish and was a member of Trinity parish's first session in 1834. He seceded in 1843 but did not officially become an elder in Trinity Free Church although his death is recorded in the session minutes in 1846. (A2)

BERRY, JAMES (Gilcomston Free). He cannot be positively identified. (O)

BIRNIE, GEORGE (South parish). A foreign merchant in 1837, living at 20 Golden Square, he had retired before 1841 and lived at Johnstone Place, Rubislaw Road. He was ordained elder of South parish in 1833 and was still serving in 1851. (D2)

BIRNIE, WILLIAM (North Free). In 1831 he was a painter and glazier with premises in King Street and a house at 25 Frederick Street. Before 1841 he had moved premises and house to 40 and 36 King Street. By 1851 he also undertook paper-hanging and had moved his premises to 81 King Street and lived at 24 James Street. Ordained after the Disruption, he was still serving in 1851. (G2)

BISSET, JOHN (North parish, North Free). In 1831—a tea, wine and spirit dealer at 39 Queen Street with a house at Concert Court, Broad Street. Before 1837 he had moved house and premises to 35 and 37 Queen Street. By 1851 he had formed partnership (J. & W. Bisset) as wholesale grocers at the same premises. He had by 1846 moved house to 122 Crown Street. By 1861 he had opened an additional wholesale warehouse at Exchange Street. He was ordained elder of North parish between 1837 and 1842, seceded at the Disruption and became elder in North Free. (See WILLIAM BISSET.) (G1-C1)

BISSET, PETER (John Knox Free). Builder, 8 Porthill, Gallowgate, in 1846. He moved to 110 Loch Street in 1851. (G2)

BISSET, WILLIAM (John Knox Free). Wholesale grocer (J. & W. Bisset), 37 Queen

Street. He lived at 124 Crown Street in 1846 but moved to 34 Skene Terrace by 1861. (See JOHN BISSET.) (C1)

BLACK, JAMES (West parish). Stock and share agent of 7 Adelphi Court and later Crown Court, Union Street, he lived at Willowbank. By 1850 he had formed a company described as 'stock, share and produce brokers, and forwarding agents to H.R.H. the Duchess of Kent' at 23 King Street, and had moved house to 1 Wellington Place. He was ordained between 1847 and 1851. (See JAMES BURGESS.) (B2)

BLACK, WILLIAM (West parish). Wine merchant (William Black & Sons, Concert Court, Broad Street). Devanha Brewery was owned by a William Black who would appear to be the same person. He lived at 173 Union Street and was an elder from c. 1831 to 1836. (C3)

BLAIKIE, JAMES (West parish). An advocate; member of the Blaikie family (see THOMAS BLAIKIE) who were prominent in business life in the city. James Blaikie was in partnership with Patrick Bannerman of the equally well-known Bannerman family. House: Craigiebuckler. He was an elder in the West parish c. 1831 until his death in 1836. He was lord provost of the city 1833-6. (A1)

BLAIKIE, THOMAS (West parish). Born 1801; he was a partner in father's business— John Blaikie and Sons, and partner-founder in his own firm Blaikie Brothers, iron founders. Blaikie was lord provost 1839-46 and played a leading part in obtaining the Harbour Act of 1843, and the improvements which were carried out at a cost of £155,000. He was active in the various railway schemes and in 1846 put forward sweeping proposals concerning city improvements which were rejected, whereupon he retired from the council. He later served another term 1853-5. Blaikie does not appear to have been an active member of the West parish session which is not surprising considering his other interests. He was an elder prior to the Disruption when he remained loyal to the Establishment—but he had retired from the session before 1851. He was knighted shortly before his death in 1861. In 1831 he lived next door to his father's premises in Littlejohn Street but before 1841 he moved to a house at 32 Bonaccord Terrace. (C1)

BRANDS, GEORGE (St Clement's parish). Fisherman, living at Footdee. An elder in 1831 he remained loyal to the Establishment in 1843 but had ceased serving on session before 1851. (H2)

BREBNER, JAMES (West parish). Advocate (admitted to Society, 1828). Advocates' buildings; agent for Argus Life Assurance Co., London, and Farmers' and General Fire and Life Assurance and Loan and Annuity Company, London. He lived at 44 Marischal Street 1831-41 but before 1851 he had moved to Albyn Place. He was ordained between 1847 and 1851. (A1)

BRECHIN, HENRY (John Knox Free). He was a foreman in moulder's shop of J. McKinnon & Co., ironfounders, and lived at 11 Canal Street in 1861. He served on town council 1871-9 and was active in temperance work. (C3)

BROWN, ALEX (West parish, Free West). An elder in the West parish c. 1831 until the Disruption, Brown seceded and became an elder in the Free West Church until his death in 1848. He was probably a bookseller living in Castle Street, but cannot be positively identified. (O)

BROWN, JAMES (Bonaccord Free). Son of a Free Church minister, his own occupation cannot be positively identified. He was an elder from 1851 to 1858.　(O)

BROWN, R. J. (Greyfriars parish, Greyfriars Free). Professor of Greek, Marischal College; lived at 3 Adelphi Court in 1831; Doctor of Divinity by 1841 and lived at 19 Golden Square, where he continued to live after his retirement some time before 1861. Brown was an elder in Greyfriars parish *c.* 1831 until the Disruption when he seceded and thereafter he stood by Greyfriars Free Church through its many financial and other problems. He was the only Disruption elder in Greyfriars Free Church by 1851.　(A2)

BROWN, ROBERT (South parish, South Free). A wine merchant with R. Moir, 23 Adelphi. By 1851 he had become a partner in firm—Moir and Brown. He lived at 23 Castle Street in 1841; 14 Adelphi in 1851. Brown was an elder of the South parish *c.* 1831 until 1843 when he seceded and became an elder in South Free Church. He was still a member of session in 1851.　(C3)

BROWN, THOMAS (St Clement's parish). An engineer with W. Simpson & Co., Footdee; he lived at 17 Prince Regent Street. Ordained after the Disruption he was no longer a member of Session in 1851 and probably resigned at the time of the Newlands case. (See ALEXANDER DAVIDSON, GEORGE SPARK and ROBERT THOMSON.)　(E2)

BROWN, WILLIAM (North parish, Free West). Inland revenue collector, distributor of stamps, and collector of land and assessed taxes for the counties of Aberdeen and Kincardine. He lived at Broadford Cottage in 1842, but had moved to 52 Union Place by 1851. Brown was an elder in the North parish *c.* 1831-43. He seceded at the Disruption and was ordained elder in the Free West in 1844 and remained so until his death in 1861.　(E2)

BRYCE, JAMES (South Free). In 1842 he was a writer at 20 King Street (probably Alex. Stronach, advocate). He lived with his widowed mother at 5 Black's Buildings. Bryce was admitted to the Society of Advocates in 1845 and thereafter opened premises at 49 Broad Street and moved house to 18 St Mary's Place. By 1850 he had moved his premises to 36 Union Street and had an estate at Westbank, Fonthill. Ordained in 1845 he was still a member of session in 1851.　(A1)

BURGESS, JAMES (West parish). Manager, later partner, in James Black & Co. He lived at 29 Union Street in 1835, 2 Adelphi in 1842-7 and 73 Crown Street 1850. He was ordained between 1847 and 1851. (See JAMES BLACK.)　(B2)

BURNESS, ALEXANDER (Greyfriars parish, West parish). Wholesale grocer and provision merchant, 7 Adelphi Court, Union Street. He lived in Crown Street. He had retired by 1841 and had houses in Crown Street and Prospect Place. Burness was ordained elder of Greyfriars parish *c.* 1831, but ceased to serve on the session before 1842. He was elected to the West parish session between 1847 and 1851.　(D2)

BUYERS, PETER (St Clement's Free). Grocer, ship's chandler, and spirit dealer, 32 Quay; also receiving post office. In 1841 he lived at 18 James Street. By 1851 he had removed to 40 Constitution Street and before 1861 he had moved to 31 Quay. Charles Runcy (St Clement's parish) shared building at 32 Quay. Buyers was ordained after the Disruption and was still serving on session in 1851.　(G1)

CADENHEAD, ALEXANDER (West parish). Advocate admitted to Society of Advocates 1809. (A. & J. Cadenhead, city fiscals, Hunter Row.) In 1831 he lived near premises at 22 Adelphi Court but had moved to an estate at Seafield by 1841. By 1851 he had a house at 5 Bonaccord Square. His son George—also an advocate—later succeeded him in partnership with Alexander Simpson, jun. (Simpson and Cadenhead, Hunter Row.) He was a member of West parish session from *c.* 1831 until after 1851. (See ALEXANDER SIMPSON and JOHN WHYTE.)   (A1)

CALDER, JAMES (West parish). Cannot be positively identified. Ordained elder of St Nicholas parish on 25 February 1773, he had ceased serving by 1836.   (O)

CAMERON, JOHN (East parish, Union parish). Cannot be positively identified. An elder in the East Church, he transferred to Union in 1834 at the formation of first kirk session. He was still an elder in 1843 but his denominational allegiance is uncertain thereafter.   (O)

CAMERON, WILLIAM (Bonaccord Free). A shoemaker, he lived at 10 Skene Street. He was ordained elder in 1851.   (G2)

CAMPBELL, ALEXANDER (Mariners' Church). 1843. He seceded and became an elder in Mariners' Free. He was still an elder in 1851, but his occupation and residence cannot be traced.   (X)

CATTO, ROBERT (Greyfriars parish, Free West). Of the firm of Robert Catto & Son, merchants and shipowners, 47 Marischal Street. He lived at Belvidere. Family and business connections with Robert Catto & Co., wine merchants, 14 King Street; Catto & Co., block, pump, and mast-makers, York Street, and possibly with John Catto & Son, merchants and insurance brokers, 88 King Street. Catto was elder on Greyfriars session from *c.* 1831; seceded from Greyfriars parish in 1843 and was ordained elder in Free West in 1844. He was still serving on session in 1851. (See JAMES MCLAREN and GEORGE THOMSON.)   (C1)

CHALMERS, ALEXANDER W. (Gilcomston Free). He was governor of Bridewell in Rose Street in 1831 and by 1841 had become General Governor of Aberdeen Prisons. He lived at the West Prison in Rose Street.   (E2)

CHALMERS, DAVID (West parish). Proprietor, *Aberdeen Journal*, Adelphi Court. He lived at 13 Adelphi and had an estate at Westburn by 1841. He served on the town council 1839-48. He was ordained *c.* 1836 and was still serving in 1851.   (C2)

CHALMERS, WILLIAM (Greyfriars parish). A grocer with premises at 36 (house, 34) Gallowgate, in 1837, he had retired from business by 1842 but continued to live at same address. Chalmers was an elder in Greyfriars parish *c.* 1831-43. He is not listed as having demitted from the Establishment in 1843 although his allegiance thereafter is not claimed by the Establishment. There is no trace at all of his denominational allegiance after 1843. In June 1844 a man by the name of 'William Chalmers, King Street' declined to serve as an elder in the Free West, but it seems unlikely that this was the same person.   (G1-G4)

CHREE, JOHN (West parish). Tinsmith (Hugh Gordon & Co., manufacturers of copper and brass, dealers in foreign and British iron, 89 Broad Street); he lived at Kingsland Place, Broadford. Chree was an elder of West parish from 1828. He had ceased serving on session before 1842.   (G3)

CLARK, THOMAS (Trinity parish). Clothier and haberdasher, 18 Broad Street, he lived at Bonaccord Street. He was co-opted to the session in 1835 and died in 1839.

CLARK, WILLIAM (Bonaccord, Established and Free). Ironmonger, 16 Union Street. He lived at Westburn in 1830 and moved to 12 Union Terrace before 1841. By 1851 he had a residence at Bloomfield, but on his retirement from business before 1860 he returned to his house in Union Terrace. Clark was an elder from 1835 to 1871. (C2)

COBBAN, JAMES (Greyfriars parish, Greyfriars Free). Builder, Jopp's Lane in 1831, by 1837 he lived at 132 George Street and continued to occupy premises at Jopp's Lane. Cobban was an elder of Greyfriars parish from c. 1831 to 1843 when he seceded and went over to the Greyfriars Free Church. He had ceased being a member of the kirk session before 1851. (G2)

COBBAN, WILLIAM (Union Free). He cannot be traced. (X)

COCHRAN, FRANCIS JAMES (East parish). Advocate 1831, and collector of the Oldmachar Poor assessment, agent for Insurance Company of Scotland, and Standard Life Insurance Co., and clerk of the Shipmasters' Society, 137 Union Street. He lived in Crown Street. By 1851 Cochran had formed a partnership with Robert Smith (Smith and Cochran). By 1861 he also acted as collector of the county rates at 1 Huntly Street. He had moved house to Crown Terrace. Ordained after 1843 he was still serving in 1851. (A1)

COLLIE, JAMES (Greyfriars parish). Advocate, 1841, 64 Union Street. By 1851 he had moved house to 153 Crown Street and was agent for London Union Assurance Society. Before 1861 he formed a partnership with George Collie with premises at 38 Castle Street where he then lived. Country residence: Waulchhill. Ordained 1850, formerly elder of St Matthew's, Glasgow. (A1)

COLLIE, ROBERT (Union Established and Free). A hairdresser with premises at 62 Shiprow, he lived at Marywell Cottage, College Street. He had retired by 1861 and lived at 64 Shiprow. Collie seceded in 1843 and was an elder in Union Free until after 1851. (G2)

COLLIE, ROBERT (Trinity Free). In 1831 Collie had a hairdressing business at 36 Green where he lived. By 1835 he had moved his premises to 37 and his house to 55 Green. In 1841 he lived at 53 Green. Before 1844 he converted his premises at 37 Green to a wholesale and retail hardware and fancy warehouse and had moved to a house in Affleck Street. By 1861 he had new premises at 1 Belmont Street. His son ran a photographic warehouse at the same address. Ordained after 1843, he resigned from Trinity Free session in 1866. (C2)

CONNON, WILLIAM (Greyfriars parish, Greyfriars Free). In 1831 Connon lived at 5 Drum's Lane with his partner William Davidson (W. Davidson & Co., grocers, wine and spirit merchants, 44 Broad Street). He lived at Canal Road (1837); Constitution Street (1842) and Albyn Place by 1851. When Connon was ordained elder in Greyfriars parish in 1840, along with John McLaren and John Philips, certain members of the congregation lodged a protest with regard to the form of election (co-option). Connon served on the session until 1843 when he seceded. He did not remain long in Greyfriars Free Church and in June 1844 he was unsuccessful in the election of elders for the Free West. He declined to accept office as deacon. (C3)

COPLAND, WILLIAM (East parish). A retired turner living in Shiprow, he served as an elder *c*. 1831 until some time before 1842. (G4)

COSSENS, JAMES (Melville Free). A wright, he lived at Kingsland Place, Broadford, in 1831; 14 St Andrew Street in 1836; 36 St Andrew Street in 1841; by 1846 he had moved to Castle Brae. (G2)

COUTTS, GEORGE (John Knox Free). A wright, living at 88 John Street. By 1861 he described himself as a cabinetmaker. (G2)

COUTTS, WILLIAM (Melville Free). Cannot positively be identified, but one of three men all of whom fell into G2 category. (G2)

COWIE, ALEXANDER (East parish, Union parish). Brewer, 5 Virginia Street with a house at 88 Chapel Street. By 1851 'Cowie & Co.' occupied these premises although Cowie himself would appear to have died or retired from business. An elder in East Church *c*. 1831, he transferred to Union parish when first kirk session was formed. His allegiance in 1843 is uncertain. (C1)

CRANE, JOHN (Union Free). He cannot be traced. (X)

DAVIDSON, ALEXANDER (St Clement's parish). A shipmaster living in Virginia Street (1831), Mill Street (1842), Davidson became an engineer with W. Simpson & Co. *c*. 1846 and moved house to 55 Wellington Street. He retired before 1861 and probably had an estate at Desswood. Davidson became an elder of St Clement's parish after the Disruption but had ceased serving on session about the time of the notorious Newlands case. (See THOMAS BROWN, ROBERT THOMSON and GEORGE SPARK.) (E3)

DAVIDSON, ALEXANDER (Gilcomston Free). His occupation and residence cannot be positively identified. (O)

DAVIDSON, ANDREW (Holburn Free). A shipmaster before 1836, he had retired by 1841 and thereafter described himself as a shipowner. He lived at 56 Wellington Street but would appear to have died or left the city by 1861. (D2)

DAVIDSON, DUNCAN (West parish). Advocate (1794), 239 Union Street, with an office at 1 Bonaccord Street. Davidson was still a member of the Society of Advocates in 1851 but appears to have retired some time before that date to live at his Tillychetly estate. He was an elder of West parish *c*. 1831 but had ceased serving on session by 1836. (A1)

DAVIDSON, ROBERT (Greyfriars parish). In 1831 a yeast-brewer living at 5 Drum's Lane. By 1841 he described himself as a 'manufacturing chemist' and lived at Canal Road with William Davidson, partner of William Connon (Greyfriars). Davidson was an elder *c*. 1831 but had ceased serving on session before 1836. (G2)

DINGWALL, ALEXANDER (West parish). Wholesale grocer with premises at 38 Netherkirkgate and a house at Spring Garden. Thomas Blaikie (West) married his daughter in November 1828 and Dingwall was probably a member of the Dingwall Fordyce family (East). Alexander Dingwall was an elder in West parish *c*. 1831 but appears to have died before 1842. (C2)

DINGWALL, KENNETH (Gaelic Chapel, Spring Garden parish). In 1843 he seceded and became elder in Gaelic Free. He cannot be traced although he was still an elder in 1851. (X)

DON, WILLIAM (Union Free). A precentor in Union Church until 1840, he became overseer at Broadford Works about 1841. After 1843 he became an elder in the Free Church. He lived at 78 Gerard Street in 1836, but before 1841 he moved to 68 Catherine Street. He later moved to 256 George Street (c. 1851) and returned to 70 Catherine Street before 1861. (G2)

DUGUID, PETER (East parish). Agent for Bank of Scotland, Bank of Scotland Court, 35 Castle Street. Duguid was an elder of East parish c. 1831 but had ceased serving on session before 1842. (B1)

DUGUID, WILLIAM (Greyfriars parish). Ordained 1850. An ironmonger with premises at 37-9, and a house at 41, St Nicholas Street. He had retired by 1841 and lived at 30 Broad Street and at Richmondhill. (D2)

DUNCAN, M. (John Knox Free). Cannot be traced. (X)

DUNN, JOHN (South parish). Merchant tailor with premises at 6, and house at 4, St Nicholas Lane. He had a son who became an advocate in 1839 and lived at same address until after 1841. Dunn was no longer at this address in 1851—business was being continued under the name of Peter Middleton. He was ordained to South parish session before 1842 but had ceased being an elder by 1847. Evidence seems to suggest that he had died or left the city. (C2)

DUTHIE, ALEXANDER (West parish). Merchant and shipowner, he lived at Broadford. Family had connections in shipbuilding—A. Duthie & Co., Footdee. Duthie was an elder in West parish c. 1831 but was no longer serving on session by 1842. (C1)

DUTHIE, GEORGE (Union Free). He cannot be traced. (X)

EDDIE, ALEXANDER (St Clement's parish). Baker with premises at 6, and a house at 8, Commerce Street. He became an elder after 1843 and was still a member of session in 1851. (G1)

EDMOND, FRANCIS (West parish, Free West). Advocate (1829). Ordained in West parish after 1836, he seceded and became an elder in Free West until his resignation in 1876. Francis Edmond was one of the most eminent Free churchmen in the city during the years following the Disruption. He negotiated the purchase of the sites for the West, East, and South Free Churches and supervised the building contracts, etc. He also played a prominent part in Presbytery affairs. Francis Edmond was in partnership with his brother James until about the time of the Disruption. James remained in the Establishment. Francis Edmond lived at 165 Union Street before 1851 but afterwards moved to Albyn Place. (See JAMES EDMOND.) (A1)

EDMOND, JAMES (West parish). Advocate (1821). In 1831 he had premises at 47 King Street and lived in West Craibstone Street. Before 1841 he was in partnership with his younger brother Francis Edmond at 64 Union Street. He then lived at 48 Skene Terrace. The partnership with Francis would appear to have been severed about the time of the Disruption when the brothers also went separate denominational ways, although by 1861 they were occupying premises adjacent to one another at 22, 23 Adelphi. James Edmond was by this date living at an estate called Carden's Haugh. Edmond was ordained in West parish between 1832 and 1835. He remained loyal to the Establishment in 1843 and in the decade following was probably the most prominent elder in the Established Presbytery. It was the efforts of Edmond and several others which saved the chapels-of-ease from extinction. Edmond also assisted on Greyfriars and North sessions in the years after 1843, and their recovery was largely set under way by his efforts. (See FRANCIS EDMOND.) (A1)

EMSLIE, WILLIAM (Melville Free). Cannot be positively identified, but one of two men both of whom fall into G1 category. (G1)

FAIRWEATHER, DAVID (East parish). Cabinetmaker, 182 George Street. Son of cabinetmaker of same name, who had shop at 156 George Street in 1831. By 1851 Fairweather described himself as a 'mahogany, rosewood, and general timber merchant' with timber yards at 182 George Street and Inches. He had moved to 69 Dee Street. An elder c. 1831 he was still serving on session in 1851. (G2-C1)

FALCONER, GILBERT (East parish). Cannot be identified. An elder in East parish c. 1831, he had ceased serving on the session before 1836. (X)

FARQUHAR, GEORGE (Union Free). He had been a wine, tea, and spirit dealer with premises and house in Upperkirkgate. About 1841 he became a mealseller with a house and premises at 39 Castle Street. (G1)

FARQUHAR, NATHANIEL (South Free). Advocate (1829) of Chalmers and Farquhar, Union Street. In 1831 he lived in Farquhar Court, 17 Upperkirkgate. By 1837 he lived at 24 Marischal Street and between 1840 and 1846 at 75 Bonaccord Street. He had moved to 33 Union Place by 1851 and to 13 Rubislaw Terrace by 1861. His son lived at this address and was a clerk with Thomson, Catto and Buchanan. Ordained after 1843, he was still serving in 1851. (See GEO. THOMSON and ROBERT CATTO.) (A1)

FENTON, ROBERT (Greyfriars Free). Bookbinder, 50 Gordon Street. Ordained after the Disruption, he was one of the three remaining elders in Greyfriars Free in 1851. (See R. J. BROWN and ALEXANDER SCOTT.) (G2)

FERGUSON, JAMES (South parish). Advocate (1816). He had offices at Upperkirkgate 1831, McCombie's Court 1841, Belmont Street 1851, 85 Union Street 1861. He lived at Cooperstone Place. Ordained elder of the South parish in 1833, he remained an elder until after 1851. (A1)

FIDDES, ALEXANDER (St Clement's parish). Collector of customs, 16 Quay. His denominational allegiance in 1843 is uncertain. He was ordained between 1831 and 1835. (E2)

FINDLAY, JOHN A. (Melville Free). A druggist, at 43 Castle Street. He lived in Brebner's Court. (G3)

FORBES, ROBERT (West parish). Teacher at Grammar School. He lived at 74 Hutcheon Street. Forbes was an elder in the West parish c. 1831 until the Disruption. Thereafter he cannot be traced and his denominational allegiance is unknown. (See JAMES MELVIN.) (F1)

FORDYCE, ALEXANDER DINGWALL (1) (East parish). Merchant living at Millburn Cottage. An elder in East parish c. 1831, he had ceased serving on the session before 1836 and would appear to have died before that date. (See ALEXANDER DINGWALL FORDYCE (2), ARTHUR DINGWALL FORDYCE and ARTHUR DINGWALL FORDYCE, jun.) (C1)

FORDYCE, ALEXANDER DINGWALL (2) (East Free). Another important member of the Dingwall Fordyce family. A captain in the Royal Navy, he served as a town councillor 1842-4, and was elected Member of Parliament for the city in 1847-52. He inherited the Brucklay estate and lived at Crown Street in 1841 and Albyn Place from 1845. Ordained elder in East Free Church following the Disruption, he was still serving on session in 1851. (See ALEXANDER DINGWALL FORDYCE, ARTHUR DINGWALL FORDYCE and ARTHUR DINGWALL FORDYCE, jun.) (D2)

FORDYCE, ARTHUR DINGWALL (West parish). Head of an important family with landed, legal, commercial and parliamentary interests. He lived at Arthurseat— the family mansion in Ferryhill—and had an estate at Culsh. Fordyce was an elder of the West parish c. 1831 until his death in 1834. (See ALEXANDER DINGWALL FORDYCE, ALEXANDER DINGWALL FORDYCE (2) and ARTHUR DINGWALL FORDYCE, jun.) (D1)

FORDYCE, ARTHUR DINGWALL, jun. (East parish, East Free). Advocate (1821). Office at 49 Schoolhill, he lived at 4 Dee Street. He appears to have inherited the estates of Culsh, Arthurseat, and Brucklay before 1840. He lived at 240 Union Street in 1841. Fordyce was an elder in East parish c. 1831 until the Disruption, when he seceded. He had ceased serving on East Free session before 1851. (See ALEXANDER DINGWALL FORDYCE, ALEXANDER DINGWALL FORDYCE (2) and ARTHUR DINGWALL FORDYCE.) (A1)

FRASER, JAMES (East Free). Grocer, wine and spirit dealer, 197 Union Street. Houses (1831) 10 Gordon Street. (1837) 73 Bonaccord Street. (1841) Rubislaw Den. (1842) Albyn Place. (1845) Upper Park, Deeside. (1846) 9 Bonaccord Street. (1850) 54 Dee Street. By 1840 a company had been formed—James Fraser & Co.— and by that date the firm also acted as receiving office for the Post Office. Ordained after 1843, he was still serving in 1851. (C3)

FRASER, JAMES (South parish, Trinity parish, Trinity Free). Boot- and shoe-maker with premises at 6 Drum's Lane and living next door in 1831. By 1841 he had brought his son into business and had opened premises in Exchange Court, Union Street. Fraser was an elder in the South parish and became an elder in Trinity parish's first session in 1834. He seceded and became an elder in Trinity Free until his death in 1850. Immediately after his death his son moved house to Bonaccord Street. (G1)

FRASER, JAMES (Bonaccord Free). Overseer at the Commercial Co., The Quay. He lived in Marywell Street. President of the Sons of Temperance, he was active in temperance work among the shore labourers. He conducted three meetings weekly, 'the members were rough in manner and uncouth in speech'. He did a considerable amount of good work among those 'whom it was difficult to teach'. His own 'plain, homely speech, to refined and sensitive ears, was considered vulgar and common place . . .' (W. Robbie, *Bonaccord Free Church; a retrospect* (Aberdeen, 1887), p. 188). He was an elder from 1851 to 1879. (G3)

FRASER, JOHN (John Knox Free). Cannot be positively identified regarding occupation and residence. (O)

FULLERTON, GEORGE (South parish, South Free). Baker, 45 St Nicholas Street with a house at 47 St Nicholas Street. He was ordained an elder of South parish in 1833 and seceded in 1843 and joined South Free Church. Before 1851 he had vacated his premises in St Nicholas Street and these were occupied by another baker. He was not a member of South Free session in 1851. (G1)

FYFE, JOHN (Gilcomston Free). He cannot be positively identified. (O)

GALEN, JOHN (East parish). M.D. 10 Union Terrace. By 1851 he lived at East Craibstone Street. He appears to have been a member of old merchant family of Galen who lived in Galen's Court, Guestrow. He was ordained after 1843 and was still serving in 1851. (E1)

GARDEN, JAMES (East Free). Advocate (1842). Formed partnership with James Murray about 1843—Murray and Garden, 50 Schoolhill. Garden lived at 204 Gallowgate (home of Robert Garden) in 1841-5 but moved to Barkmill Cottage about 1846. By 1850 he lived at 145 Crown Street. Ordained after 1843, he was still serving in 1851. (See ROBERT GARDEN and JOHN MURRAY.) (A1)

GARDEN, ROBERT (Greyfriars parish). Grocer, tea, wine and spirit dealer, 204 Gallowgate. James Garden, advocate and elder of the East Free Church, lived at same address. Robert Garden was an elder of Greyfriars parish c. 1831 but had ceased serving on the session before 1836. (See JAMES GARDEN.) (G1)

GIBB, ALEXANDER (East Free). Civil engineer (John Gibb & Son, civil engineers, contractors, and stone merchants, Waterloo Quay). He lived in King Street in 1842 but by 1850 had moved to Willowbank. Ordained elder in 1843, he was still serving on session in 1851. He also served on town council 1844-7, 1852-8, 1860-3. (C1)

GIBBON, JOHN (East parish). Clothier and haberdasher (John and William Gibbon, 54 Union Street), he lived at 3 Kidd Lane. An elder in 1831, he had ceased serving on session by 1836. His house at 3 Kidd Lane was occupied by a 'Miss Norrie' in 1842. (She may have been a relative of JOSEPH NORRIE.) (G1)

GIBSON, THOMAS B. (Gilcomston Free). In 1846 he was a grocer with W. Milne & Son, but before 1851 he had moved to J. Lumsden & Co. He then lived at: 26 Summer Street and 24 Union Row (1846), 13 Huntly Street (1850). By 1861 he was partner in firm of Lumsden & Gibson, grocers and wine merchants, 123 Union Street, and lived at 124 Crown Street. (G2-C2)

GILDAWIE, ALEXANDER (North parish). Late farmer, Gateside, 6 Carmelite Street. He was probably related to the family of same name living in Causewayend. He was inducted to session sometime before 1847 and was still serving on session in 1851. (D2)

GILL, DAVID (South parish). Painter and glazier, 53 Loch Street in 1831; before 1842 had formed partnership—Farquhar & Gill, 2 Drum's Lane and 24 Upperkirkgate, with his house at 12 Upperkirkgate. By 1851 he had moved to a house at 6 Caroline Place. The firm had also expanded its activities to plumbing and gasfitting. Gill was an elder of South parish c. 1831 until after the Disruption, when he remained loyal to the Establishment. He was no longer a member of the session by 1847. (G2–C2)

GORDON, THOMAS (South Free). A grocer, wine and spirit merchant, he was involved in a series of partnerships. In 1841: Hunter & Gordon, 175 Union Street; 1851: T. & G. Gordon at same address; 1861: an amalgamation with Charles Smith to form Gordon & Smith at 203 Union Street. He lived at his father's house, Gordon's Court, Gordon Street, between 1831 and 1841 but before 1851 moved to Berryden Cottage and by 1861 to Berryden House. He served on the town council 1866-8. Gordon family were communicants in South parish before Disruption. Ordained elder after Disruption, he was still serving on session in 1851. (C3)

GORDON, WILLIAM (South Free). Advocate (1825). In 1831 he had a house and premises at 89 Union Street. By 1841 he had moved to 14 Adelphi where he was agent for Scottish Equitable Life, and York and London Fire, Life, and Annuity Offices. Between 1846 and 1851 he formed partnership with William Hunter (Hunter & Gordon) and by the latter date he had bought mansion at Raeden. He would appear to be of the same family as Thomas Gordon, who also formed partnership with the Hunter family in the grocery trade. Ordained after the Disruption, he was still on the session in 1851. (See WILLIAM HUNTER, THOMAS GORDON.) (A1)

GORDON, WILLIAM (Gaelic Chapel, Spring Garden parish). In 1843 he seceded and joined Gaelic Free. Occupation and residence cannot be positively ascertained. He was still an elder in 1851. (O)

GOULD, JOHN (Mariners' Free) in 1851. He cannot be traced. (X)

GRANT, DAVID R. L. (Bonaccord, Established and Free). A merchant with Brebner & Grant, 56 St Nicholas Street. Before 1851 firm had been known as Brebner & Ragg. Grant had prior connections with the Ragg family possibly by marriage. It has not been possible to establish the precise nature of the business although when known as Brebner & Ragg they had acted also as commission agents. Grant lived in Marine Terrace and was an elder from 1834 to 1884. (See ROBERT RAGG.) (C2)

GRANT, GEORGE (Trinity Free). Advocate (1835), National Bank Court, 42 Castle Street prior to 1843; by 1851 he had moved to 10 King Street; by 1861 to 30 King Street. Ordained elder after Disruption, he was still alive in 1894 when it was reported at centenary celebrations that his step was 'as elastic as any man of thirty'. (A1)

GRANT, JOHN (Mariners' Free) in 1851. His occupation and residence cannot be positively ascertained. (O)

GRANT, ROBERT (Gilcomston Free). A clock-dial maker living at 24 Frederick Street, he had retired from business by 1851. (G4)

GRAY, GEORGE (Union Free). In 1831 a grocer, tea, and spirit dealer living in his shop at 58 Shiprow. By 1841 he had a house at 26 Union Row; before 1847 he had moved house to 5 Dee Place. (G1–C3)

GRAY, JOHN (Trinity parish, Trinity Free). Commission merchant, Crown Court,

Union Street. He lived in Holburn Street in 1851, but before 1861 had moved to 18 Bonaccord Terrace by which time he appears to have retired from business. Gray was co-opted to Trinity parish session in January 1835. He seceded and became an elder in Trinity Free in 1843. In 1847 he resigned but later withdrew his resignation on the request of the session. He resigned in 1852. (C4)

GRAY, REV. ROBERT (South Free). He would appear to be a 'stickit minister' who became a school teacher at the Public School, Belmont Street. He lived at 41 St Nicholas Street in 1842 and 9 Diamond Street in 1846. By 1850 he was living at Berryden Cottage, and by 1861 at Berryden House—homes of Thomas Gordon. Ordained after the Disruption, he was still serving in 1851. (See THOMAS GORDON.) (F1)

GREIG, JAMES (North parish). Shoemaker, with premises at 85, and house at 83, Queen Street, in 1831. By 1841 he had a house and premises at 89 Queen Street. By 1861 he had a house at 29 Spital in addition to premises at 89 Queen Street. He was ordained sometime before 1847 and was still a member of session in 1851. (G2)

HARPER, ALEXANDER (South parish, Trinity parish). Baker, 47 Green. Harper was an elder of South parish until 1834 and on Trinity session from its inception in 1834 till his death in March 1838. He served on the town council from 1833 to 1838. (G1)

HARPER, JAMES (East parish, Union parish). Commission agent, 19 Union Buildings. He lived at Morningfield. An elder of East Church in 1831, he removed to Union Church in 1834 when first kirk session was formed. He had ceased serving on session by 1842. (C4)

HARVEY, GEORGE T. (Holburn Free). In 1841 he was a clerk (Aberdeen Rope and Sail Co.) living at 123 Skene Street. By 1846 he had a similar job with the Railway Company and lived in Marywell Street. He continued in same job and thereafter lived at Victoria Terrace (1851) and Neptune Cottage, Ruthrieston (1861). (F2)

HAY, ALEXANDER (St Clement's parish, St Clement's Free). Shipowner, 54 Wellington Street. By 1861 he had moved house to 4 Mount Street. Ordained after 1836, he seceded in 1843 and became an elder in St Clement's Free. He was still a member of session in 1851. (D1)

HAY, ALEXANDER (Gilcomston Free). He cannot be positively identified, but one of two men—both G2 category. (G2)

HAY, JOHN (South parish, South Free). Carver and gilder, with premises at 77, and house at 75, Union Street in 1831. By 1841 he was also an optical and philosophical instrument seller, and agent for Thames Plate Glass Co., 2 New Market Street, with workshops in Guestrow. The firm was later appointed to H.M. the Queen. Hay retired to Broomhill Cottage before 1851. Ordained to the South parish in 1836, he seceded in 1843 and became an elder in South Free. He was still a member of session in 1851. (C2-D2)

HENDERSON, JAMES (North parish, North Free). Between 1831 and 1837 he was a builder living at 6 Innes Street; before 1841 a builder and wood merchant at 120 Loch Street and by 1846 he was also an agent for roofing felt. In 1861 he described himself as an architect and agent for Duke of Devonshire's slate quarries. He lived in a house at 24 Belmont Street. An elder of North parish, he seceded in 1843 and became an elder in North Free Church. He was still serving on the session in 1851. (G2-C1)

HENDERSON, WILLIAM (East parish, East Free). A builder with premises at 66 Loch Street and 91 Gallowgate, and later at 72 Loch Street. He lived at 66 Loch Street in 1841, but before 1851 he had moved to 1 Carden Place. By 1861 his son had become a partner in what was now a firm of 'architects and builders'. Henderson was an elder in East parish in 1843 and seceded to become a member of East Free session. He played a leading part in the design and building of standard, low-cost Free churches in the north east and the highlands to the specification of the General Assembly of the Free Church. An elder of East parish from c. 1836, he seceded in 1843 and was still a member of session in 1851. Henderson served on the town council 1849-57 and 1863-9. (C1)

HENDERSON, WILLIAM, M.D. (Bonaccord, Established and Free). Medical practitioner and lecturer in materia medica at Marischal College, 1819-58. He lived at 49 Schoolhill. Born in 1792 Henderson (according to W. Robbie) was 'not entirely dependent on his professional income' and inherited a considerable estate from his father in 1843. Educated at Aberdeen and Edinburgh, he was a linguist and also author of works on biblical studies. He was an elder from 1837 until his death in 1877. (A2)

HENDERSON, WILLIAM (Gilcomston Free). A soapmaker with house and premises at 55 Loch Street. He retired to Raeden House before 1841, but by 1847 he had moved to 28 Skene Terrace. (D2)

HENRY, GEORGE (West parish). Senior partner in Hugh Gordon & Co., ironmongers, blacksmiths, coppersmiths, brass founders, tin smiths, dealers in foreign and British irons, 89 Broad Street. Factory and warehouse, Copper Company's Court, 14 Gallowgate. He continued to live at 1 Gallowgate until the mid 1850s when he moved to Rubislaw Terrace. Henry was born in 1784 and died in 1867. He was educated at Robert Gordon's College and initially learnt the trade of weaving. Ordained between 1836 and 1843, he remained loyal at the Disruption and was still a member of session in 1851. He was lord provost of Aberdeen, 1850-2. (C1)

HILL, ISAAC (Melville Free). A teacher, he had a house and seminary at 19 Queen Street. (F1)

HORN, JAMES (St Clement's parish, St Clement's Free). Ordained after 1836, he seceded in 1843 but had ceased serving on kirk session by 1851. Horn was probably a shipmaster living at 70 Wales Street but cannot be positively identified. (O)

HUNTER, WILLIAM (Trinity Free). Advocate (1840). He lived at 14 Adelphi in 1841 but soon moved to 113 Crown Street. He became junior partner with William Gordon (Gordon & Hunter) before 1851 and lived with Gordon at his house—Raeden. By 1861 he had moved to a house at 36 Albyn Place. Ordained after the Disruption, he resigned from Trinity Free session in 1881. (See WILLIAM GORDON.) (A1)

INGLIS, JAMES (St Clement's parish, St Clement's Free). A baker with premises 32 and house 30 Gallowgate. In 1861 he moved to house and premises in Waverley

Place. An elder in St Clement's parish, he seceded to become elder in St Clement's Free and was still a session member in 1851. (G1)

INGLIS, WILLIAM (St Clement's Free). A baker with premises at 67 and house at 61 Broad Street. He became an elder after 1843 and was still serving on session in 1851. (G1)

IRONSIDE, WILLIAM (South Free). Builder. House 8 Well of Spa. Ordained after the Disruption, he was still on kirk session in 1851. (G2)

JESSIMAN, WILLIAM (Gilcomston Free). He was a house carpenter living at 16 Summer Street in 1836. Before 1841 he had formed a partnership (with a Robert Middleton of Thistle Street) and had moved house to 44 Bonaccord Street. He had retired from business before 1851. (G4)

JONES, RICHARD (Union Free). He cannot be traced. (X)

JOHNSTON, ALEX. (West parish). House of Tullos, Nigg. Ordained after 1836, he remained loyal in 1843 and was still serving on kirk session in 1851. (D2)

JOHNSTON, JAMES (Mariners' Church) in 1843. He seceded and became an elder in Mariners' Free. He was still an elder in 1851. His occupation and residence cannot be positively ascertained. (O)

JOHNSTON, JOHN (Mariners' Church) in 1843. He seceded and became an elder in Mariners' Free where he was still an elder in 1857. He was described as a mason in Free Presbytery minutes and probably lived in Virginia Street. (G2)

JOHNSTON, ROBERT (Greyfriars parish). Timber merchant with premises at 34 Marischal Street and a house at 36 Bonaccord Terrace (1841); premises at York Place and a house at 3 Golden Square (1851). He was ordained elder in 1850. (C1)

JOHNSTON, WILLIAM, jun. (East parish). Tobacco manufacturer (T. Craig & Co., Schoolhill). In 1831 he lived at Denburn Terrace; by 1835 he had moved to Berryden. An elder c. 1831, he had ceased serving on session by 1836. (C1)

KAY, JOHN (Holburn Free). A teacher of English, 62 Loch Street; house 11 Innes Street in 1831; 78 Shiprow, house 54 Quay in 1836 and Strawberrybank in 1841; West Prison, house 20 Chapel Street in 1851. He would appear to have died or left city before 1861. (F1)

KEITH, WILLIAM (Holburn Free). A slater with house and premises in Chapel Street in 1836. By 1846 he had premises at Union Row and a house at 24 Summer Street. By 1861 he was also acting as a slate merchant from same business premises. (G2)

KEITH, WILLIAM (South parish, South Free). Doctor. He moved from Union Place before 1851 to 257 Union Street after becoming surgeon at the Royal Infirmary and lecturer in clinical surgery at the University. Keith was an elder of the South parish from 1833 to 1843. He seceded and became an elder in the Free South Church. He was claimed to have 'the distinction of performing the first operation with the aid of chloroform'. (Gammie, op. cit., p. 206.) He was still serving on the session in 1851. (A2)

KERR, DAVID, M.D. (West parish). Lecturer in surgery to the University and King's

College. He lived at 83 Union Street in 1831, 155 Union Street in 1841, 4 Golden Square in 1851, and 9 Union Place in 1861, by which time he appears to have retired from his university post. He was ordained between 1847 and 1851. (A2)

KNOWLES, WILLIAM (St Clement's parish). Timber merchant, Footdee. He lived at 27 York Place. Knowles was an elder of St Clement's parish from c. 1834 to 1843, but his denominational allegiance is uncertain after that date. (C1)

LAING, JAMES (South parish). Cannot be positively identified. An elder in 1831, he had ceased serving on session by 1836 and is not listed on the 1835 Communion Roll. (O)

LAING, WILLIAM, M.D. (West parish). Doctor, and consulting surgeon at the Royal Infirmary. He lived at 19 Belmont Street in 1831, but before 1841 he had moved to 7 Golden Square. Ordained after 1836, he remained loyal in 1843 and was still a member of session in 1851. (E1)

LAURIE, THOMAS (Trinity parish, Trinity Free). Founder (of J. Abernethy & Co., Ferryhill), Laurie was a member of Trinity parish's first session in 1834 and in 1843 seceded and became an elder in Trinity Free session. He had retired by 1861 and died in 1863. (See JAMES ABERNETHY.) (C1)

LEDINGHAM, JAMES (East parish, East Free). Teacher of English, elocution, writing, geography, Latin, and arithmetic. Lived at Duthie's Court, 35 Guestrow in 1831. He had moved to 12 Correction Wynd before 1841. By 1861 his house was described as 'an academy'. An elder in East parish, he seceded in 1843 to become an elder in East Free. He was still a member of session in 1851. (F1)

LEDINGHAM, ROBERT (South parish). An advocate (1827) of Ledingham & Walker, King Street, he lived at 50 King Street. He was ordained elder c. 1847-51 and served on the town council from 1851 until his death in 1856. (A1)

LEITH, JOHN (South parish). A coppersmith at 18, house at 16, Huxter Row in 1830. He had retired by 1835 to Cooperston Buildings. He was an elder c. 1831 but had ceased serving on the session by 1836. (G2-D2)

LESLIE, ALEXANDER (West parish, Free West). Lived at 35 Bonaccord Terrace between 1841 and 1861 but by the latter date had also an estate at Birkwood, Banchory. Ordained elder of West parish some time after 1836, he seceded at the Disruption and became an elder in Free West. He was still a member of session in 1851. (D2)

LESLIE, ALEXANDER (Union Free). He cannot be positively identified but may have been a brewer living at Virginia Street. (O)

LESLIE, GEORGE (East parish). Shipowner, 11 Quay, he lived at South Crown Street. An elder in 1831, he had ceased serving on session by 1842. (D1)

LESLIE, WILLIAM (East parish). Surgeon. In 1832 lived at 20 Adelphi Court, Union Street. Ten years later he lived in the same area in St Nicholas Street. By 1851 he had moved to a house at 10 Golden Square. Ordained after the Disruption, he was still serving on session in 1851. (E1)

LINDSAY, ROGER (Union Established and Free). Ordained before Disruption, he seceded and became an elder in Union Free. He was still a member of session in

1851. A mealseller, he lived next door to his premises at 82 George Street. He had retired by 1861. (G2)

LITTLEJOHN, WILLIAM (North parish, North Free). Cashier with Aberdeen Town and County Bank. He lived at 32 Dee Street in 1831. Before 1841 he had moved to 91 Union Street—next door to the Town and County Bank. An elder before 1836, he seceded in 1843 and became an elder in North Free session. (B2)

LOW, ALEXANDER (West parish, Free West). In 1831 employed by Milne, Foularton & Co., manufacturers and woollen drapers, 1 Union Buildings, and lived at 49 Gallowgate. By 1841 he had become a partner in firm (Milne, Low and Co.) and lived at 31 Union Place. Ordained in West parish after 1836, he seceded and became an elder in the Free West until his death in 1863. (C1)

LUMSDEN, HARRY (East parish). Member of prominent and influential local family with estates at Belhelvie, Tilwhilly and Balmedie. A merchant at 34 Broad Street with a house at 102 Union Street in 1831—he later appears to have inherited the Auchindoir estate at Lumsden, Aberdeenshire. He also lived at properties in Golden Square and 255 Union Street. He was an elder from 1831 until the Disruption when his allegiance is uncertain. (See WILLIAM LUMSDEN.) (C1)

LUMSDEN, WILLIAM (East parish). Grocer and spirit merchant 58 Union Street. In 1831 Lumsden had a house in Upperkirkgate. By 1841 he had moved to Millburn Cottage, in Dee Village, which had formerly been occupied by Alexander Dingwall Fordyce. He later had an estate at Eastbank, Fonthill. Ordained after the Disruption, he was still serving in 1851. (C3)

LYALL, GEORGE (West parish). (George Lyall & Co.) Silk mercer, 97 with a house at 99 Union Street (1831-61). By 1861 firm had been appointed silk mercers to the Queen. Ordained after 1836, he remained loyal at the Disruption and was still a member of session in 1851. (C2)

MCCOMBIE, JAMES BOYN (South Free). Advocate (1831). In 1831 had premises at 52 Netherkirkgate and lived at Richmondhill. He was a son of Thomas McCombie —owner of an old-established firm of tobacco and snuff manufacturers, McCombie's Court, 51 Netherkirkgate. In 1837 he had moved to house at 4 Golden Square. By 1841 had premises at 103 Union Street and lived at 33 Union Place. Before 1851 was in partnership with Andrew Murray (Murray and McCombie) and lived at 2 Albyn Place. Ordained after the Disruption, he was still serving on kirk session in 1851. He served on the town council, 1842-3. (See ANDREW MURRAY.) (A1)

MCCOMBIE, REV. ROBERT, (North parish, North Free). He lived in Justice Street in 1831, but before 1842 he had moved to Rosehill, Skene Square. A probationer of the same name was purged by the Established Presbytery when he failed to compear. (Est. Presb., 3 October 1843.) Ordained elder of North parish between 1837 and 1842, he seceded but had ceased serving on North Free Church session before 1851. (F1)

MCCONDACH, HARRY (Gilcomston Free). Between 1831 and 1841 changed the spelling of his name from 'McCondoch' (1831) to 'McCondack' (1837), 'McCondach' (1841). A maltster with house and premises in Holburn Street down to 1841, before 1846 he had changed his designation to that of grain dealer. He continued to live at same address. (G1)

MCDONALD, ALEX. (South parish). M.D., later of the Royal Artillery. He lived at Rubislaw Park. McDonald would appear to have been ordained an elder of South parish as early as 1831 and was brought back into service sometime between 1847 and 1851 as in the case of William Paterson of South parish. He died in 1860.
(D2)

MACGILLIVRAY, WILLIAM (Greyfriars parish). Professor of Natural History, Marischal College. He lived at 67 Crown Street and was ordained in 1850.　(A2)

MCHARDY, DAVID (South Free). General blacksmith and bell-hanger. House in Back Wynd. McHardy was one of a large family engaged in same trade but with various premises in the area of Netherkirkgate and Back Wynd. Ordained after Disruption, he was still in kirk session in 1851. He served on the town council 1853-62. (See JOHN MCHARDY.)
(G2)

MCHARDY, JOHN (South parish). General blacksmith and bell-hanger. In 15 Back Wynd. He was ordained between 1847 and 1851 and died in 1865. (See DAVID MCHARDY.)
(G2)

MACHRAY, ALEXANDER (East Free). In 1836 Machray was a teacher at Greyfriars parish school and lived near the school in Mounthooly. Before 1841 he became teacher at John Knox parish school and lived at Kingsland Place. By 1846 he was teacher at East Free school and lived at same address. Before 1851 he became superintendent at the House of Refuge, 45 Guestrow. Ordained after Disruption, he was still serving on kirk session in 1851.
(F1-E2)

MACHRAY, ALEXANDER (Gilcomston Free). A dyer, he had premises at 79 (house 77) Woolmanhill in 1836. Ten years later he had moved house to 93 Woolmanhill. He would appear to have retired from business by 1851.
(G2)

MCKAY, HECTOR (Bonaccord Free). A ropemaker, he was an elder from 1851 to 1860 although he had previously been an elder in the Gaelic Free Church where he was ordained at the age of 22. McKay was an active worker in the Church and was one of 'the men' attached to Dr Kidd at Gilcomston chapel-of-ease where he took a Bible class early on Sabbath mornings to a large attendance. He undertook numerous visits to the sick and dying of all congregations. Born in Sutherland c. 1807, he came to Aberdeen in 1815 on the death of his father. He became a member of Gaelic chapel. He became member of Bonaccord congregation about 1849—the minister Rev. Samuel Grant was a Gaelic-speaking highlander. He was elected elder in 1851 and died in 1860.
(H2)

MACKIE, ALEXANDER (St Clement's parish). Ship agent with an office at Water Lane and living at 37 Whitehouse Street. He was succeeded by his son, Alexander Mackie, jun. before 1841. He was an elder of St Clement's parish c. 1831.　(C4)

MACKIE, ALEXANDER, jun. (St Clement's parish, St Clement's Free). Retired ship agent, Mackie Place. An elder in St Clement's parish from 1831 until 1843, he seceded at the Disruption and became an elder in St Clement's Free session on which he was still serving as senior elder in 1851.
(C4-D2)

MCLAREN, JAMES (Greyfriars parish, Greyfriars Free, Free West). Collector of excise. Office: 112 King Street. He lived at 51 Schoolhill, but had retired by 1851 and was living in 53 Schoolhill. An elder of Greyfriars Free c. 1836, he seceded in 1843 but soon after left Greyfriars Free Church and in 1844 was ordained elder in

Free West. He was still a session member in 1851. A member of large family all of whom left the Establishment. (See JOHN MCLAREN.) (E2)

MCLAREN, JOHN (Greyfriars parish, Greyfriars Free, Free West). In 1837 a flesher in Wales Street market with a house in Albion Street; by 1842 he described himself as a commission agent and had a house in Crown Street. By 1845 he had premises at 25 Gallowgate and a house at 65 Bonaccord Street. Before 1850 he had moved to 7 Dee Place. Ordained elder of Greyfriars parish along with Connon and Philip in 1840 despite protests from members of the congregation regarding the form of election which was by co-option. Protest appears to have been supported by the minister and those dissenting only reluctantly agreed not to take the matter to the Presbytery. (See *Est. Greyf. Sess.*) McLaren seceded in 1843, but left Greyfriars Free in 1844 and was ordained elder of the Free West. (See WILLIAM CONNON, JOHN PHILIP, JAMES MCLAREN and ALEXANDER MORRICE.) (G1-C4)

MCNAUGHTON, GEORGE (West parish). Manufacturer (Gordon, Barron & Co., cotton spinners) with a house at Woodside. He retired from business some time between 1838 and 1842. McNaughton was an elder in West parish *c.* 1831 until the Disruption—thereafter he cannot be traced. (D2)

MACROBIN, JOHN, M.D. (West parish, Free West). In 1837 physician to lunatic asylum and assistant professor in Marischal College. By 1842 he was professor of Medicine. Ordained after 1836, he seceded in 1843 and became elder in Free West but resigned office on 23 November of that year. On 4 June 1844, however, he re-accepted office as his university post now appeared secure. (See *Free West Sess.*) Macrobin lived at East Craibstone Street in 1837, 13 Silver Street in 1842, and Migvie House, 23 North Silver Street 1861. He remained an elder of the Free West until his death in 1879. (A2)

MARQUIS, GEORGE (Trinity Free). Accountant, 147 Union Street. He lived at 134 Crown Street in 1841, 16 Albyn Place in 1845, and 27 Albyn Place in 1861. Ordained after the Disruption, he was an elder until his death in 1875. (B2)

MARSHALL, DAVID (East parish). Painter and glazier, 13 Diamond Street. Ordained after the Disruption, he was still serving on session in 1851. (G2)

MARTIN, ALEX. (East parish, East Free). Clothier, haberdasher, and stay warehouseman, 21 Broad Street and living at Jopp's Court, 31 Gallowgate. He had retired by 1841 and lived at 3 Little Chapel Street. An elder in East parish from 1831 to 1843, he seceded but was no longer a member of East Free session in 1851. (D2)

MARTIN, ALEXANDER (Greyfriars parish). In 1831 Martin was a shipmaster living in Bonaccord Street. By 1841 he had retired from his profession as a ship's captain and was collector of the Merchant Seamen's Fund with an office at 33 Regent Quay. He then lived in Constitution Street. His son was a ship's captain also. Ordained in 1845, he was still a member of session in 1851. (D2)

MAVER, DAVID (Bonaccord Free). A teacher at Bonaccord Juvenile school, he lived in Marywell Street (1847—No. 12; 1851—No. 61; 1861—No. 6). He was ordained elder in 1851. (F1)

MELVILLE, THOMAS (South parish). Thomas Melville & Sons, iron merchants, wholesale ironmongers, plane, lock, and hinge manufacturers, 106 and 108

Gallowgate, he lived at Melville's Court, 106 Gallowgate. A son lived at Gallowgate address; other two sons had houses on the west end at Springbank Terrace and Carden Place. He was ordained between 1847 and 1851. (See WILLIAM MELVILLE.)

MELVILLE, WILLIAM (East parish). Ironmonger (Thomas Melville & Sons). In 1831 W. Melville was a plane manufacturer and ironmonger and lived at 10 Young Street. He gradually shifted nearer the west end. In 1841 he lived at Kingsland Place, Broadford; (1851) 4 Springbank Terrace. Ordained *c.* 1836, he was still an elder in 1851. (See THOMAS MELVILLE.) (C1)

MELVIN, JAMES (West parish). Rector of Grammar School. In 1831 he lived at 209 Gallowgate but had moved to 41 Belmont Street before 1841. He served on the West parish session *c.* 1831 until after 1851. (A3)

MENNIE, JOHN (South parish, Trinity parish). Linen yarn manufacturer, 37 Gallowgate, he lived at 1 Jopp's Lane. Mennie was an elder of the South parish until 1834 when he became an elder on the first Trinity session until his death in March 1839. (C1)

MICHIE, GEORGE (Holburn Free). A slater with house and premises at Barnett's Close throughout period. (G2)

MIDDLETON, JAMES (St Clement's Free). Cannot be positively identified. Ordained after Disruption, he was still serving on session in 1851. (O)

MIDDLETON, JAMES (East parish). Cannot be positively identified. Ordained elder of East parish after 1843 and was still serving in 1851. (O)

MILLER, GEORGE (Greyfriars parish). Tobacconist and cigar merchant, 60 Union Street. He lived at same address. Ordained in 1845, he was still serving in 1851. (G1)

MILNE, THOMAS, sen. (Gilcomston Free). He was a nurseryman and florist; house and premises at Sunnyside. (G2)

MIRRIELEES, WILLIAM (Trinity parish, Trinity Free). Haberdasher, 72 Union Street with a house at 9 Correction Wynd in 1831. By 1837 he appeared to be living in his Union Street premises. He moved to Holburn Street by 1841 and about 1845 he formed a partnership with a Charles Cattanach—Cattanach and Mirrielees, clothiers and furnishing tailors, 126 Union Street. Mirrielees was co-opted on to the Trinity session in 1835, but although he seceded in 1843 he was not listed as serving on Trinity Free session. His resignation as elder was accepted in 1847. (G1-C2)

MITCHELL, DAVID (Free West). Advocate (1837), agent for Manchester Fire and Pelican Life Assurance Companies, 12 Adelphi Court. He lived in Diamond Cottage, Holburn Place, but before 1861 he had moved to 2 Carden Place. He was ordained in June 1844 after receiving the largest number of votes. He was still a member of session in 1851. (A1)

MITCHELL, JAMES (St Clement's parish). Cannot be positively identified. An elder in 1831, he had ceased serving on session before 1836. (O)

MITCHELL, JOHN (East Free). Builder (Mitchell and Ross). Lived in Chapel Street in 1831 but by 1837 he had moved to new house at 4 Little Chapel Street. By 1851 he had formed partnership with John Ross, Summer Street. Ordained after the Disruption, he was still a member of session in 1851. (G2)

MITCHELL, ROBERT (St Clement's parish). Manager of Aberdeen, Leith and Clyde Shipping Company. He lived at 18 St Clement Street (1831), 20 Regent Quay (1841-51). He also had a house at Middleton, Banchory-Devenick. Before 1861 he had retired and was living at Elmbank House, near Kittybrewster Toll. Mitchell was an elder in St Clement's parish from c. 1835 until the Disruption, when he remained loyal to the Establishment. He had ceased serving on the session before 1851. (B2)

MOIR, GEORGE (John Knox Free). One of two men both of whom fall into G2 category. (G2)

MOIR, WILLIAM (Mariners' Free). In 1851. He was a shore-porter living at 18 Shiprow. Before 1861 he had moved to 7 Marischal Street. (G2)

MOLLISON, GEORGE (North parish). May have been a hosier living in Trinity Street in 1831. Mollison was an elder of the North parish c. 1831 but was no longer a member of the session by 1836. His absence from the Post Office Directory from 1835 suggests that he had died or left the city by that date. (G2)

MORRICE, ALEXANDER (Greyfriars parish, Greyfriars Free, North Free). In 1831 an ironmonger with W. McKinnan & Co., ironmongers and ironfounders at Gallowgate and Windy Wynd. By 1841 firm had also become blacksmiths, coppersmiths, tinsmiths, and bone manure manufacturers. By 1851 firm had new premises at 20 Spring Garden. Morrice lived at 9 Princes Street (1831), 15 Princes Street (1841), 36 King Street (1845), 10 Albyn Place (1851)—by which time he called himself an iron founder—and 21 Albyn Place in 1861. Morrice seceded from Greyfriars parish in 1843 but left Greyfriars Free Church before 1851 to become an elder in North Free Church. (See JAMES MCLAREN.) (C1)

MORRISON, WILLIAM (John Knox Free). He cannot be positively identified regarding his occupation and residence. (O)

MORTIMER, ALEXANDER (St Clement's parish, St Clement's Free). Ship bread baker, general commission agent and ship broker, Waterloo Quay, and 1-4 North Gallery and 2-3 South Gallery, New Market. In 1831 he described himself as a 'baker and shipowner'. An elder in 1831, Mortimer seceded at the Disruption and became an elder in St Clement's Free Church. He had ceased serving on session before 1851. (C4)

MURDOCH, WILLIAM, sen. (Gilcomston Free). He was a cabinetmaker living in 15 Denburn Terrace. (G2)

MURRAY, ANDREW (South Free). Advocate (1831). A writer with Alexander Jopp, Jopp's Court, 31 Gallowgate, in 1831, he appears to have set up on his own account by 1841. Before 1851 he was in partnership with J. B. McCombie at 103 Union Street. Murray lived at 2 Long Acre in 1831 but had moved to 44 Skene Terrace before 1841. About 1861 he moved to a house in Belmont Street. Andrew Murray was a communicant in South parish in 1835. He was ordained to South Free after the Disruption and was still a member of session in 1851. (See J. B. MCCOMBIE, JOHN MURRAY, JOSEPH NORRIE, and WILLIAM ALLARDYCE.) (A1)

MURRAY, JOHN (East parish). Tobacconist (of McCombie, Dunn & Co., 79 Green); he lived at 92 George Street. He lived at 7 Rosemount Terrace in 1841. By 1851 he was acting on his own account from premises at 15 Upperkirkgate. He then lived at North Broadford. Murray appears to have been related to Andrew Murray who was in partnership with J. B. McCombie—a son of the tobacco and snuff dealer, McCombie's Court, Netherkirkgate—and connected with the firm McCombie, Dunn & Co. in which John Murray was a partner. (Andrew Murray was indirectly connected to William Allardyce through William Jopp—Murray served legal apprenticeship with Jopp's father.) John Murray was an elder from 1831 to 1843. His allegiance in 1843 is uncertain. Another advocate, James Murray, Schoolhill, a partner of James Garden, may have been related. (See J. B. MCCOMBIE, ANDREW MURRAY, WILLIAM ALLARDYCE, JOSEPH NORRIE, and JAMES GARDEN.)   (C2)

NICOL, GEORGE J., M.D. (West parish). A doctor living at 1 St Nicholas Street in 1841, he had moved to a house at 17 Belmont Street by 1851. He was ordained after 1847 and before 1851.   (E1)

NICOLL, JAMES (East parish). Cannot be positively identified. An elder before 1831, he had ceased serving on session before 1836.   (O)

NISBET, ALEXANDER (South parish, Trinity parish). Mason, 19 Fisher Row (1831), Stonytown (1841). Nisbet was an elder on the South parish and became an elder in the first session of Trinity parish in 1834. He was one of the two elders who did not secede in 1843. (See WILLIAM REID.)   (G2)

NORRIE, JOSEPH (East parish). Tobacco manufacturer (Thomas McCombie & Co., 51 Netherkirkgate). Home: 64 Dee Street. Norrie was an elder in East parish in 1831 until his death about 1835. (See JAMES BOYN MCCOMBIE.)   (C1)

OGG, HENRY (Holburn Free). Distiller (Henry Ogg & Co., Strathdee Distillery, Cooperston). He lived in Holburn Street. He appears to have retired or left city before 1861.   (C1)

OGSTON, FRANCIS, M.D. (West parish). A member of long-established family of soap and tallow manufacturers, he became professor of medical jurisprudence at Marischal College. Ogston lived with his parents at 2 Gallowgate in 1831. By 1841 he had moved to a house at 84 Broad Street and before 1851 he had moved to 68 Adelphi Court. In the same period the Ogstons concerned with tallow manufacturing moved from 2 Gallowgate to an estate at Ardo, Banchory-Devenick. Francis Ogston was ordained between 1847 and 1851.   (A2)

PATERSON, ALEX. (Greyfriars parish). Cannot be positively identified but one of three individuals of same name—all of whom were in G1 category of occupations. Ordained in 1845, he was still member of session in 1851.   (G1)

PATERSON, WILLIAM (South parish). Retired leather merchant and tanner (Paterson & Co., Jack's Brae and Denburn Terrace) he lived at Jessiefield, and 2 Denburn Terrace. Ordained 1799; retired from eldership but recalled immediately after Disruption. Died 1855. Family well known in shoemaking trade.   (D2)

PEARSON, ALEXANDER (Trinity parish, Trinity Free). In 1841 Pearson was manager of G. & W. Davidson, rope and twine manufacturers, Footdee, with offices at 17 Quay. He lived at 20 Virginia Street, but by 1837 he had moved house to Bonaccord Street. Before 1851 he appears to have become a partner in the firm and lived at 63 Dee Street. Pearson was co-opted on to Trinity session in January 1835. He seceded and became an elder in Trinity Free in 1843, and continued to serve until his death in 1860. (C1)

PHILIP, ANDREW (East parish). Cabinetmaker (Andrew and William Philip, cabinetmakers and upholsterers, 111 Union Street), house: 13 Union Row. Before 1841 they had moved to premises in Union Row. Ordained about 1836, Philip was an elder in 1843, but his denominational allegiance is uncertain. (C2)

PHILIP, JOHN (Greyfriars parish, Greyfriars Free). Bookbinder, 46 Queen Street in 1831; by 1837 he had premises at 54 and a house at 50 Queen Street. Philip was ordained elder of Greyfriars parish in 1840 along with John McLaren and William Connon. Certain members of the congregation lodged a protest on the mode of electing the three elders (co-option by existing session). Philip seceded from the Establishment in 1843 but had ceased serving on the Greyfriars Free Session before 1851. His son, John Philip, was the first minister of John Knox chapel-of-ease within Greyfriars parish in 1836. (Gammie, op. cit., p. 32.) (G2)

PIRIE, WILLIAM (Union Established and Free). Formerly of a firm involved in woollen manufacturing, hosiery, and carpet-weaving and which had also engaged in insurance broking and grain importing. He lived at 67 Bonaccord Street. He left the Establishment in 1843 and was still an elder of Union Free in 1851. (D2)

PIRRIE, WILLIAM (Greyfriars parish). Ordained 1850. In 1831 he was a lecturer in anatomy at King's and Marischal Colleges. He lived at Hanover Court, 2 Upperkirkgate. By 1841 he was professor of surgery at Marischal College with a house at 238 Union Street. He was also surgeon to the Royal Infirmary. He moved to 247 Union Street before 1861. (A2)

PITTENDRIGH, ALEXANDER (St Clement's Free). In 1831 Pittendrigh was beadle of the Seamen's Chapel and a funeral waiter. He lived in Sugar House Lane. By 1841 he had become beadle of St Clement's Church and lived at 5 St Clement's Lane. Before 1851 he had set himself up in business as a wright and funeral waiter at same address. By 1861 he had moved house to 8 St Clement's Street. Ordained after Disruption; still serving in 1851. (C2)

RAGG, ROBERT (South parish). Described as a 'paper manufacturer' and 'merchant', he lived at 104 George Street before 1831. His residence cannot be traced thereafter, but he may have lived with his relative, David R. Ragg of the firm Brebner & Ragg. He was 'frequently in London' (Est. South Sess.) and his absences were not only intermittent but lengthy. In the 1835 Communion Roll his name is not included as a communicant, which is unusual for an elder. Ragg became an elder before 1831 and in 1843 was claimed by the Establishment although one suspects that his presence on the session list is largely nominal by that date. His name is not listed after 1847 and as this coincides with the firm of Brebner & Ragg becoming Brebner & Grant (see DAVID R. L. GRANT) he may have died or left the city permanently about that date. (C2)

RAIT, WILLIAM (Bonaccord Free). A teacher at Bonaccord Infant School, Marywell Street. He lived at 12 Marywell Street in 1847, at No. 4 of the same street in 1851. By 1861 he had moved to 2 Prospect Terrace, Ferryhill. Born in Dundee in 1812, his father was a crofter. According to Robbie he was apprenticed to a commercial concern and later had his own business. Converted by revivalists, he met Rev.

Gavin Parker who offered him the job as teacher in 1841. He became an elder in 1851 and retired from the session 1872. He died in 1886. (F1)

RANNIE, THOMAS (South parish). Cannot be positively identified but one of two men both of whom fall into G2 occupational category. An elder *c.* 1831, he had ceased serving on session before 1836. (G2)

REID, JAMES (Gilcomston Established and Free). He was a nurseryman (James Reid & Co., 60 Union Street) and member of large family associated with the occupation. He lived at Belville, Gilcomston. (G2)

REID, JOHN (Gilcomston Free). He cannot be positively identified but probably was a gardener living at Pitmuxton. (O)

REID, ROBERT (West parish). Cannot be positively identified. He was an elder of West parish *c.* 1831 but had ceased serving on session by 1836. (O)

REID, WILLIAM (East parish). Ship and insurance broker (Aberdeen Marine Insurance Company). In 1841 conducted business from house in Crown Street. By 1861 he had premises in Marischal Street at an annual rental of £31.10s. and had moved his house to 1 Springbank Terrace and also acted as agent for Scottish Sea Insurance Co., Dundee, and for the United Kingdom Life Assurance Co., London. Ordained after Disruption, still serving in 1851. (B2)

REID, WILLIAM (North parish). Shipbuilder (Nicol, Reid & Co.), Footdee. He lived at York Street in harbour area throughout period, and in his retirement. He retired from business 1841 when the company changed its name to John Reid & Co. The family had shipowning connections. Reid was an elder in North parish from before 1831 until the Disruption, when he alone remained in the Establishment. He was still serving on session in 1851. His role in the North parish was similar to that of Thomson in Greyfriars parish. (D2)

REID, WILLIAM (Trinity parish, South parish). Teacher, 3 Denburn. Reid was co-opted to Trinity Session in January 1835. He was one of the two elders who did not secede in 1843 from Trinity parish. He was introduced on to South parish session between 1843 and 1847. (See ALEXANDER NISBET.) (F1)

RENNIE, GEORGE (South Free). A printer with premises at 61 Broad Street and a house at 6 Donald's Court, Schoolhill, in 1845. By 1850 he was living in his business premises at 61 Broad Street. Before 1860 he had moved to a house at 15 Skene Terrace. Rennie was ordained elder in 1850. (G2)

RETTIE, MIDDLETON (North parish, North Free). M. Rettie & Sons. House: Rettie's Court, Broad Street. An elder of North parish in 1831, he seceded in 1843 and became an elder in North Free Church and was still serving on session in 1851. (See WILLIAM RETTIE.) (C2)

RETTIE, WILLIAM (East parish, East Free). Partner in Middleton Rettie & Sons, lamp manufacturers, tinsmiths, japanners, and oil merchants, Rettie's Court, Broad Street. Firm had lamp and fancy ornament saloon at 101 Union Street (1831). House: 9 Bonaccord Street (1831), 23 Dee Street (1851). By 1861 the firm had expanded and diversified with additional premises at 28 Diamond Street—'lamp manufacturers and purveyors of oil to her Majesty'. They also dealt in silverware, jewellery and watches at 151 Union Street. An elder of East parish from 1831 to 1843, he seceded and became an elder of East Free and was senior elder in 1851. (See MIDDLETON RETTIE.) (C2)

RIDDEL, JAMES (St Clement's parish). Treasurer to the harbour trustees, living at Harvey's Court, 90 Gallowgate, in 1831; before 1841 he had moved to a house in Waterloo Quay. By 1851 he was accountant and collector of Poors' Assessment (city parish) and lived at 4 North Broadford. Riddel was an elder of St Clement's parish from 1831 to 1843. His denominational allegiance at the Disruption is uncertain. His son, Peter, who was a clerk at the harbour office, became an elder in St Clement's Free Church. (See PETER RIDDEL.) (B2)

RIDDEL, PETER (St Clement's Free). A clerk at the harbour office, he lived at Waterloo Quay in 1841. Before 1851 he had become principal clerk and had moved to a house at 3 St Clement Street. (See JAMES RIDDEL.) (B2)

ROBB, JAMES (East parish, Trinity parish). A wright living at 22 Gerrard Street. He was an elder of East parish from before 1831 and moved to Trinity parish at its inception in 1834. He served on the session until his death in February 1838. Robb was a member of the town council 1833-4. (G2)

ROBERTSON, ALEXANDER (St Clement's Free). Ship's engineer ('Bonnie Dundee'). House: 20 Prince Regent Street. Ordained after Disruption, still serving in 1851. (E3)

ROBERTSON, GEORGE (Greyfriars parish). In 1841 a blacksmith with premises at 207 Gallowgate and a house at 2 Gerrard Street. By 1851 he had opened an ironmongery shop at his Gallowgate premises. He continued to live at same address. His son was later employed as a clerk in firm of Thomson, Catto and Buchanan and lived at Prospect Terrace. Ordained in 1845; still serving in 1851. (See GEORGE THOMSON.) (G2)

ROBERTSON, THOMAS (North parish). Cannot be positively identified, but one of two men both of whom fell into tradesmen group. Served as elder from c. 1831 to c. 1840. (G2)

ROSE, DONALDSON (East parish). In 1831 described as a ship owner and timber merchant, Footdee. By 1841 had formed a company and had moved house to 11 Golden Square. He later bought an estate at Hazlehead. Rose was a director of the Union Bank of Scotland, Aberdeen. Ordained before 1831; he was senior elder by 1851. He served on town council 1833-7. (See WILLIAM ROSE.) (C1)

ROSE, WILLIAM (East Free). A member of the firm of Donaldson Rose. William Rose continued to live in Footdee at 27 York Place until about 1861, when he moved to family house at 11 Golden Square. He was an assessor of the Dean of Guild Court and an ex officio manager of the National Security Savings Bank by 1861. Ordained after Disruption; still serving in 1851. Rose also served on the town council 1855-7. (See DONALDSON ROSE.) (C1)

ROSS, ALEXANDER (St Clement's parish). Clerk with W. Simpson & Co., Footdee, (1841-51) later managing clerk with Thomson, Catto, Buchanan & Co., York Place (1861). (Both firms associated with George Thomson of Greyfriars parish.) In 1841 lived at 28 Wellington Street; by 1861 he had moved to 10 Constitution Street. Ordained after Disruption; still serving in 1851. (See GEORGE THOMSON, GEORGE ROBERTSON.) (F2-B2)

ROSS, JOHN (East parish, East Free). Assistant commissary of ordnance. In 1831 lived at Salter's Court, 39 Lochside, (1837) Reform Street, (1841) 91 King Street, (1845) Skene Square, (1851) 8 South Constitution Street. An elder of East parish 1831-43, he seceded and became a member of East Free session, in which he was still serving in 1851. (E2)

ROY, JAMES, jun. (East parish). Seedsman, nursery-man, florist, and fruiterer (and agent for Caithness pavement stones), 50 Union Street. Various nurseries at North Street and South Ferryhill. In 1831 he had a house at North Street Nursery. 1841: house at South Ferryhill Nursery. Ten years later he lived at Rotunda Lodge, where he retired by 1861. Firm continued in partnership of his son and a Joseph Belcher. Father was a gardener. Ordained after the Disruption, he was still a member of session in 1851. (C2)

RUNCY, CHARLES (St Clement's parish). Had an estate at Millbank which was developed as part of Berryden Road before 1861. He lived at Millbank and (after the development) in Bankmill House, Berryden Road. He had an office at 32 Quay and would appear to be a shipping agent. His son was admitted to Society of Advocates in 1855. Ordained between 1831 and 1835, he remained loyal in 1843 and by 1851 was senior elder of a kirk session of three members. Most of the others would appear to have left about the time of the Newlands case. (D2)

SCOTT, ALEXANDER (Greyfriars Free). Cannot be positively identified, but one of two men both of whom fall into G2 occupational category. Ordained after Disruption; still serving in 1851. (G2)

SIEVEWRIGHT, WILLIAM (North parish, North Free). Grocer and mealseller, Park Street. He would appear to have retired from business by 1851 and to have died before 1861. Ordained between 1837 and 1842, he seceded at the Disruption; became an elder in North Free. He was still a member of session in 1851. (G1-G4)

SIM, GEORGE (St Clement's parish, South parish). Clerk of the Customs and living in East North Street. He had retired by 1850 but continued to live at same address. Ordained in 1817, he was an elder of St Clement's parish c. 1828 until the Disruption when he remained loyal to the Establishment. He became a member of the session in the South parish after 1843, and died in 1852. (E2)

SIMMIE, ROBERT (South parish, South Free). In 1831 he was a reed-maker with premises at 10, house 12, Harriet Street. He had retired to 31 Harriet Street before 1841. Ordained about 1836. He seceded from the South parish session in 1843 and became an elder in South Free Church. (G4)

SIMPSON, ALEXANDER (East parish). A clothier living at 13 Guestrow in 1831. He retired to live at 15 Bonaccord Square before 1841. He was in partnership with John Whyte and had relatives in partnership with the sons of Alexander Cadenhead and John Whyte. (D2)

SIMPSON, JOHN (South parish). Wright, 74 Windmill Brae. Ordained 1844; died 1850 although still listed as elder in *Aberdeen Almanac* in 1851. (G2)

SIMPSON, ROBERT (West parish). Cannot be positively identified. Simpson was an elder c. 1831-6. (O)

SIMPSON, WILLIAM (South parish). Advocate (1813) and procurator fiscal for the county. Office 56 and house 58 Bonaccord Street. He was ordained between 1847 and 1851. (A1)

SLIGHT, ALEXANDER (St Clement's parish, St Clement's Free). Clothier and haberdasher 133, house 126, Union Street. Ordained elder in St Clement's parish after 1836, he seceded in 1843 and became an elder in St Clement's Free. He was no longer a senior member in 1851. (G1)

SMART, WILLIAM (South Free). In 1842 he was a clerk with Farquharson & Co., family grocer, tea, wine and spirit merchants, 131 Union Street, and lived at 2 St Nicholas Lane; by 1850 he had moved to a house in west end at 1 Langstone Place. Ordained after Disruption, he remained a member of session in 1851. (F2–B2)

SMITH, ALEX. (Greyfriars parish, East parish, East Free). Cannot be positively identified. An elder in Greyfriars parish c. 1831 until 1837, he became an elder in the East parish in 1838. He seceded in 1843 but was no longer a member of the East Free session in 1851. (O)

SMITH, FERGUSON (Greyfriars parish). A clerk with James Edmond, 150 Union Street, and a house in Nelson Street in 1851. By 1861 he had become a writer with premises at 23 Adelphi Court and a house at Westfield. He was ordained in 1845; still served on session in 1851. (See JAMES EDMOND.) (F2)

SMITH, GEORGE (South parish). A glazier with premises at 17 and a house at 21 Netherkirkgate. He was an elder c. 1831 but had ceased serving on session by 1836. (G2)

SMITH, JAMES (Greyfriars parish). Cannot be positively identified. An elder c. 1831, he had ceased serving on the session by 1842. (O)

SMITH, JAMES (Holburn Free). Cannot be positively identified, but one of several men all of whom fall into G2 occupational category. (G2)

.SMITH, JOHN (East parish). Architect and superintendent of town's works, 142 King Street. In 1831 lived at 142 King Street. By 1851 he had formed a partnership with his son, William Smith, and had moved to 'Rosebank' in west end. Ordained after Disruption; still serving in 1851. He may have left Greyfriars session before 1836. (See JOHN SMITH.) (E2)

SMITH, JOHN (Greyfriars parish). Cannot be positively identified. An elder c. 1831, he had ceased serving on the session before 1836. He may be the same 'John Smith' who was co-opted on to East parish session after the Disruption. (See ALEX. SMITH and JOHN SMITH.) (O)

SMITH, JOHN (West parish, Free West). In 1851 an auctioneer of Wilson's Court, 84 Broad Street. By 1842 he described himself as a general commission agent with an office at 8 St Nicholas Lane. He lived at 32 Dee Street. Smith was an elder of the West parish from c. 1831 until the Disruption. He seceded and became an elder in the Free West until his death in 1846. (C4)

SMITH, NEIL, jun. (West parish, Free West). Commission merchant with Neil Smith & Sons, 40, house at 39, Loch Street in 1831. Before 1837 was acting on his own behalf at 52 Loch Street and lived at 49 Gallowgate. By 1841 he moved to

65 Bonaccord Street. By 1851 he was acting from premises in Frederick Street and lived at 114 King Street. By 1861 he had premises in Marischal Street (Neil Smith & Co.) and lived at 14 Carden Place. Ordained in West parish after 1836, he seceded in 1843 and continued to serve on Free West session until he resigned in 1867. He served on the town council 1834-7, 1840-3. (C4)

SMITH, ROBERT (Mariners' Free). Serving in 1851. He cannot be positively identified. (O)

SMITH, WALTER (Holburn Free). A wright and cabinetmaker living in Blackfriars Street since c. 1831. He appears to have died or left city by 1861. (G2)

SMITH, WILLIAM (North parish). Cannot be positively identified. He was ordained after 1843 and was still serving in 1851. (O)

SMITH, WILLIAM (East parish). Cannot be positively identified. An elder before 1831, he was still serving on session in 1843 but thereafter his allegiance is unknown. There is no evidence that he was connected with John Smith who was ordained in East parish after 1843, nor with the William Smith who was ordained in the North parish after 1843, nor with William Smith who ceased serving on Greyfriars session before 1836. (O)

SMITH, WILLIAM (North parish). He appears to have become an elder of North parish some time between 1843 and 1847. His partner, John Smith, became an elder in East parish after 1843. (See JOHN SMITH.) (William Smith does not appear to be the general session clerk of the same name, as he is designated as living in Footdee.) (E2)

SMITH, WILLIAM (Bonaccord, both Established and Free). Elder from 1834 to 1883. He cannot be positively identified regarding his occupation although he lived in Summerfield. (O)

SPARK, GEORGE (St Clement's parish). A grocer, ship's chandler, and spirit dealer, 58 Quay, house, 10 Garrock Street. By 1861 he had moved his premises to 8 Garrock Street and occupied a house at 1 St Clement's Street. Spark was ordained following the Disruption but was no longer an elder in 1851 and may have resigned as a result of the Newlands case. (See ALEXANDER DAVIDSON, THOMAS BROWN and ROBERT THOMSON.) (G1)

STEWART, LEWIS (Greyfriars parish). An agent with premises and house at 71 King Street between 1831 and 1837 but before 1842 he had moved to 55 Netherkirkgate. Stewart was an elder of Greyfriars parish c. 1831-43. He is listed as having demitted from Establishment in 1843 but does not appear on Greyfriars Free session by 1851. (G2)

STILL, WILLIAM (East parish). Late coal-broker. House 81 Shiprow. Served as an elder in East parish c. 1831 but was no longer member of session by 1836. (D2)

STOTT, GEORGE (Melville Free). A shoemaker, he lived at his premises at 85 St Andrew Street. (G2)

STRACHAN, JAMES (Mariners' Free). Serving in 1851. He cannot be positively identified. (O)

STRAITH, REV. ALEXANDER (East parish). In 1831 he was a teacher of English with premises at 1 Drum's Lane and a house at Donald's Court, 20 Schoolhill. By 1841 he had also become official keeper of baptismal and other records and was teaching at the Public School in Belmont Street. Straith was an elder from about 1834 and remained loyal to the Establishment. He had ceased serving on session and ceased being keeper of records by 1851. (F1)

STUART, JAMES (St Clement's Free). Cannot be identified. (X)

STUART, WILLIAM (Gaelic Free). Serving in 1851. Cannot be traced. (X)

SUTHERLAND, ANDREW (Trinity parish, Trinity Free). A textile manufacturer living at 1 Black's Buildings in 1831. Sutherland before 1841 had opened additional premises at 2 Black's Buildings and lived next door. By 1851 Sutherland had brought his sons into the business—Sutherland & Sons—and occupied 1, 2, 3 Black's Buildings. The firm also had premises at Canal Road, Causewayend, where worsted spinning, hosiery and girth manufacturing were undertaken. Sutherland continued to live at 2 Black's Buildings, until after 1851. He resigned from Trinity Free session in 1858, having been an elder since 1843. Prior to the Disruption he had served on Trinity parish session since 1835. He would appear to have left town after 1858—although the business was continued by his sons. He served on the town council 1848-50. (C1)

SUTHERLAND, JOHN (West parish). Cannot be positively identified. Sutherland was ordained an elder in the West parish between 1832 and 1835. At the Disruption he remained loyal to the Establishment. He had ceased serving on the session before 1851. (O)

SUTHERLAND, ROBERT (South parish). A glazier and painter, 9 King Street, in 1831; before 1841 he had premises at 29 Union Street. House, Crown Court, 36 Upperkirkgate. An elder c. 1831-6. He died in 1842. (G2)

TAYLOR, ROBERT (West parish). Music seller (Taylor and Brown, 128 Union Street). He lived at 2 East Crown Place. Taylor was an elder in West parish c. 1831 until the Disruption when he remained loyal to the Establishment. He was no longer a member of session by 1851 and appears to have retired or died by that date. (He does not appear to be connected in business to Alex. Brown who seceded but whose occupation is uncertain.) (C2)

THAIN, JAMES (St Clement's parish, St Clement's Free). Master boat-builder (Hall & Sons), he lived at 60 York Street. Thain was an elder in St Clement's parish from about 1834. He seceded at the Disruption, became a member of St Clement's Free session but had ceased serving on session by 1851. (G3)

THAIN, ROBERT (St Clement's Free). Teacher, Mariners' school. House, 62 Virginia Street. Ordained after Disruption; still serving in 1851. (F1)

THOM, ALEXANDER (West parish, Free West). A surveyor of taxes in 1831; he lived in family house in Albyn Place. After the death about 1835 of James Thom (late of Halifax, Nova Scotia) who lived at same address, Alexander set himself up in business with his brother William. (A. & W. Thom, commission merchants, 21 Quay.) He moved house twice in the 1840s—first to Ashley House and then to 50 Union Place. About 1846 he became consul for Belgium—an appointment to which his nephew, William Thom, succeeded after Alexander Thom's death.

Ordained in West parish after 1836, he seceded at the Disruption and served on Free West session until his death in 1856. (See WILLIAM THOM.) (C4)

THOM, WILLIAM (East Free). Commission merchant and general merchant (A. & W. Thom), 21 Quay. He lived 76 Dee Street (1841), Albyn Place (1845) and 50 Union Place (1851). Ordained after Disruption he was still a session member in 1851. (See ALEXANDER THOM.) (C4)

THOMSON, ARTHUR (West parish). In 1831 manager for the Aberdeen Sea Insurance Co., ship and insurance broker, surveyor of shipping and agent for Lloyd's, 25 Marischal Street. He lived in Skene Terrace. By 1841 agent for Bank of Scotland, vice-consul for Russia, Prussia, Netherlands, Sweden, and Norway (also for France by 1851), Bank of Scotland Court, 35 Castle Street. Ordained between 1832 and 1835, he remained loyal in 1843 and was still a session member in 1851. (B2)

THOMSON, GEORGE (Greyfriars parish). The only Greyfriars elder to remain loyal to the Establishment in 1843. He was ordained c. 1831 and was still serving on session in 1851. In 1831 Thomson was a merchant living next door to his premises in Thomson's Court, 22 Quay. By 1851 he had brought his son into the business and firm was described as wine merchants, commission agents and ship brokers. Thomson was also a shipowner. (His son had interests in ship-building—Thomson, Catto, Buchanan & Co.) He continued to live at 22 Quay. He served on town council 1857-60. (See GEORGE ROBERTSON and ALEXANDER ROSS.) (C1)

THOMSON, JOHN (Bonaccord Established and Free). A builder, in 1841 he had premises at 7 Princes Street, and lived at 29 East North Street. Before 1847 he moved house to 31 Frederick Street. He had retired before 1851 and lived at same address but before 1861 he had moved to 16 Thistle Street. He was an elder from 1837 to 1869. (G4)

THOMSON, ROBERT (St Clement's parish). Cannot be positively identified. Thomson became an elder of St Clement's parish after the Disruption but had ceased serving on session before 1851 perhaps as a result of the Newlands Case. (See ALEXANDER DAVIDSON, THOMAS BROWN and GEORGE SPARK.) (O)

TRAIL, JAMES (Bonaccord Free). A wright and cabinet-maker, 9 Rose Street. He lived at 22 Union Row. By 1861 he had premises at No. 6, and a house at No. 8 Rose Street. Ordained in 1851, he resigned in 1861. (G2)

TRAILL, ADAM (John Knox Free). Cannot be traced. (X)

TROUP, ALEXANDER (St Clement's Free). Grain merchant and miller, Aberdeen Lime Company, Blaikie's Quay; house at Sclattie. Ordained after Disruption; still serving in 1851. (C1)

TULLOCH, REV. GEORGE, LL.D. (Free Trinity). Schoolmaster. Academy Street. House: Bellevue, Hardgate. Ordained after Disruption; he was an elder until his death in 1873. (F1)

URQUHART, JOHN (South Free). A druggist, he took part in various associated business enterprises between 1830 and 1850. He was involved in a series of partnerships with members of Fullerton and Gordon families in different business premises in St Nicholas Street and Union Street. By 1840 he was also partner in

J. & R. Urquhart, wholesale tea and coffee dealers and commission agents, 7 (later 30) Schoolhill. This firm became his main interest. He lived at 49 Upperkirkgate in 1830; thereafter he lived in two different houses in Schoolhill. By 1846 he had bought a house called 'Rosemount', and by 1860 he lived in Arthurseat—a mansion in the suburbs. Urquhart was ordained after 1843 and was an active session member in 1851. He served on the town council 1837-40, 1846-9, 1858-64.
(C4)

WALKER, JAMES (Union Free). His occupation and residence cannot be positively identified. (O)

WALKER, JOHN (St Clement's parish, St Clement's Free). Cannot be positively identified, but probably a ship master living at 4 St Clement's Street. Ordained after 1836 in St Clement's parish, he seceded in 1843 but was not a member of session in St Clement's Free in 1851. (O)

WALKER, WILLIAM (West parish). In 1831 a grocer, tea, wine and spirit dealer at 43, house 41, George Street, by 1841 he had moved to new premises at 65 George Street (house 63) and had opened a new shop at 52 Union Street. Before 1851 he closed George Street premises and moved house to 3 Adelphi Court. He continued his Union Street premises where he also acted as a general importer. His sons were brought into the business (Walker & Sons) before 1861. Ordained between 1832 and 1835, he remained loyal to the Establishment in 1843 and was still a session member in 1851. (C3)

WATSON, ALEXANDER (St Clement's parish, St Clement's Free). Ship master ('Scottish Maid'); house 6 Hanover Street. An elder of St Clement's parish in 1831, Watson seceded at the Disruption and became an elder in St Clement's Free Church. He was no longer a member of session in 1851. (E3)

WATSON, GEORGE (Trinity parish, Trinity Free). Shoemaker, 14 Netherkirkgate in 1831 and living in Diamond Street. By 1837 he had moved house to 25 Bonaccord Street and by 1841 to 68 Bonaccord Street. He had retired from business before 1851. Watson was co-opted to Trinity session in 1835. He seceded and became an elder in Trinity Free, until his death in 1863. He served as a town councillor 1848-58. (D2)

WATT, ALEXANDER (East parish, Union parish). An elder in East Church c. 1831, he transferred to Union Church in 1834 when first session was formed. He had ceased serving on kirk session by 1842. He cannot be positively identified regarding occupation. (O)

WEBSTER, ALEX. (South parish). Advocate (1794) of Alex. and John Webster, 42 King Street. Ordained before 1831, he remained loyal in 1843 and was a member of the kirk session until his death in 1855. His son and partner, John Webster, seceded. Alex. Webster served on the town council between 1837-48. (See JOHN WEBSTER.) (A1)

WEBSTER, FRANCIS (North parish). Weaver, 1 Flourmill Lane. An elder c. 1831, he was no longer a member of session by 1836. His absence from the Post Office Directory in 1835 suggests that he had died or left the city by that time. (G2)

WEBSTER, JOHN (South Free). Advocate (1831), of Alex. and John Webster, King Street. He lived at 31 King Street. Ordained after the Disruption, he was still a member of session in 1851. Webster's conduct may have been the subject of enquiry by the kirk session. (See ch. 4, n. 31.) (See ALEXANDER WEBSTER.)   (A1)

WEBSTER, WILLIAM (East parish). Baker and confectioner at 4, house 6, Skene Terrace. In 1832 he lived at 21 Skene Street. He moved house next door to shop before 1841. Ordained after Disruption; still serving in 1851.   (G1)

WHYTE, JOHN (West parish). A woollen draper living at 52 Dee Street, and in partnership with Alexander Simpson (Simpson & Whyte) who retired before 1841. The firm described itself as being 'clothiers to Her Majesty and Prince Albert', 21 Union Buildings. The firm also had associations with Cockburn and Campbell, wine merchants, Edinburgh. John Whyte's son—John Whyte, an advocate—was in partnership with the nephew of Alexander Simpson, an advocate with Yeats and Whyte, 48 King Street. (See ALEXANDER CADENHEAD and ALEXANDER SIMPSON.)   (C2)

WILL, JOHN (East parish, Union parish). He cannot be positively identified. An elder in East Church in 1831, he transferred to Union when it set up a kirk session in 1834. He was no longer a serving member in 1842.   (O)

WILLIAMS, JAMES (South parish, Trinity parish). Cooper, 7 Virginia Street. Williams was an elder South parish and of Trinity parish from its inception in 1834 to his deposition in May 1840 for 'unlawful intercourse with an unmarried woman belonging to the Episcopal Church'.   (G2)

WILLIAMSON, PETER (South parish). In 1831 he was a druggist and lived at 3 Exchequer Row. Before 1841 he had premises at 141 Union Street and a house at No. 143. Williamson was a member of the town council on two occasions between 1837 and 1840 and continuously from 1841 to 1847. He was ordained after 1843 and died in 1859.   (E1)

WILSON, JAMES (Greyfriars parish). Cannot be positively identified but one of two men both of whom were in occupational category D2. Ordained 1845; still serving in 1851.   (D2)

WYLLIE, DAVID (South Free). He would appear to be the son of David Wyllie, the bookseller, but he did not follow his father into the business. In 1837 he lived at family house in 17 Bonaccord Street and was an accountant at the National Bank of Scotland branch. By 1842 he was a cashier with the Union Bank, 53 Castle Street, and lived at 2 Marischal Street. Ordained after Disruption; still serving in 1851.   (B2)

YEATS, GEORGE (South parish, South Free). Silk mercer. In 1831 had premises at 35 Union Street and lived at 28 Union Place. In 1835 at 3 South Crown Street. Before 1841 he had moved to premises at 87 Union Street and had moved house to 149 South Crown Street. His son became an advocate in 1860. Ordained about 1836, George Yeats seceded from South parish session in 1843 and became an elder in South Free Church. He was still serving on kirk session in 1851.   (C2)

Index

Aberdeen: Crown Street area 59, 60, 74, 80, 81, 82, 83, 84, 85, 89, 106, 109, 110, 115, 119[48], 119[51], 130, 170, 177, 185, 210, 225, 226, 227, 228, 229, 233, 234, 237, 239, 241, 242, 245f, 252, 255; Denburn 4, 5, 72, 73, 74, 75, 77, 78, 79, 80, 81, 82, 83, 84, 86, 88, 90, 93, 94, 186, 210; English residents 6; exports 1, 2, 3, 7, 19, 25[83]; harbour 1, 2, 3, 4, 74, 86, 110, 195, 196, 226; Irish 6; population 5f, 37, 51, 93, 140[32], 149; urban development 4f, 74, 226, westward residential migration 4f, 87, 91, 93, 94, 110, 123f, 172; *see also* Aberdeen, industries; Presbyterian society

Aberdeen, industries: comb making 3, 161; engineering and shipbuilding 2, 3, 21, 70, 74, 82f; fishing 1, 3, 51, 86f; granite 3; iron founding 2, 3, 82, 85; meat preserving 3; paper manufacturing 3, 19, 77; rope-making 3, 84; snuff manufacturing 19; textiles 2, 7, 8, 17, 19, 21, 22, 81, 84, 158, 183, 207[148], 252; *see also* banks and bankers; entrepreneurship; finance and finance houses; railway

Aberdeen Almanac 114, 218, 249

Aberdeen Banner 55, 101f, 116

Aberdeen Education Society 151

Aberdeen Fire and Life Assurance Company 21, 80

Aberdeen Herald 20f, 22, 33, 46[29], 56, 57, 58, 93, 117[12], 209; *see also* Adam, James

Aberdeen Journal 73, 228

Aberdeen, Leith and Clyde Shipping Company 244

Aberdeen Market Company 4

Aberdeen Sea Insurance Company 253

Aberdeen-Inverurie canal 25[83]

Aberdeenshire: Aboyne 9f, 24[77]; Alford 9; Birse 24[77]; Braemar 16, 24[77]; Clatt 10; Crathie 16, 24[77]; Culter 19; Daviot 10; Fintray 9,

24[81], 174, 175; Glenmuick 7; Glentanner 9f, 24[77]; Kincardine O'Neil 7; Kinellar 24[68]; Leochell-Cushnie 19, 25[87], 141[57]; Lonmay 16, 24[76]; Lumsden 195; New Deer 10; Old Deer 8, 9; Peterhead 24[71]; Pitsligo 9; Rayne 7, 9, 25[83]; Rhynie 195; Skene 19; Stewartfield 24[81]; Strathdon 7, 9; *see also* rural society

Abernethy & Co. 82, 224, 239

accommodation 36f, 59, 105, 109, 201, 206[135]; *see also* seat rents; sittings

Adam, James 20f, 56, 57, 58, 117[12], 209; *see also Aberdeen Herald*

admission certificates 150; *see also* kirk sessions (quasi-legal functions)

age factor *see Presbyterian society*

agricultural improvements *see* rural society

Aiken, James (district missionary) 81, 184, 224

Albion Street Mission *see* Congregational Church (Albion Street); Wilson, James R.

Allan, Rev. John 57, 221

Anderson, Alexander 21

Anti-Burgher Church 26, 195, 207[149]

Anti-Popery 188, 203[45], 205[115], 211; *see also* Catholic Emancipation Act

Argus Life Assurance Company, London 226

Assembly Rooms 117[22]

Associate Presbytery 26

atheism 57, 182, 183, 201, 204[84]

attendance 34, 35, 36, 37, 39, 40, 42, 43, 44, 47[29], 47[30], 60, 61, 126, 127, 128, 135, 137, 138, 144, 145, 146f, 148, 162, 167, 174, 176, 177, 181, 188, 199, 200, 213ff; *see also* suitable clothing, importance of

Australia 21, 152

Banffshire 6, 222

bankruptcy, cases of *see* kirk sessions

banks and bankers 123; Aberdeen

Index